THE Child IN SOCIETY

SAGE was founded in 1965 by Sara Miller McCune to support the dissemination of usable knowledge by publishing innovative and high-quality research and teaching content. Today, we publish more than 750 journals, including those of more than 300 learned societies, more than 800 new books per year, and a growing range of library products including archives, data, case studies, reports, conference highlights, and video. SAGE remains majority-owned by our founder, and on her passing will become owned by a charitable trust that secures our continued independence.

Los Angeles | London | Washington DC | New Delhi | Singapore

HAZEL R. WRIGHT

THE *Child* IN SOCIETY

Los Angeles | London | New Delhi
Singapore | Washington DC

Los Angeles | London | New Delhi
Singapore | Washington DC

SAGE Publications Ltd
1 Oliver's Yard
55 City Road
London EC1Y 1SP

SAGE Publications Inc.
2455 Teller Road
Thousand Oaks, California 91320

SAGE Publications India Pvt Ltd
B 1/I 1 Mohan Cooperative Industrial Area
Mathura Road
New Delhi 110 044

SAGE Publications Asia-Pacific Pte Ltd
3 Church Street
#10-04 Samsung Hub
Singapore 049483

Editors: Jude Bowen/Amy Jarrold
Associate editor: Miriam Davey
Production editor: Tom Bedford
Copyeditor: Salia Nessa
Proofreader: Caroline Stock
Indexer: Avril Ehrlich
Marketing manager: Dilhara Attygalle
Cover design: Wendy Scott
Typeset by: C&M Digitals (P) Ltd, Chennai, India
Printed and bound in the UK by Henry Ling Ltd.,
at the Dorset Press, Dorchester, DT1 1HD

© Hazel R. Wright 2015

First published 2015. Reprinted 2017

Library of Congress Control Number: 2014937681

British Library Cataloguing in Publication data

A catalogue record for this book is available from
the British Library

MIX
Paper from
responsible sources
FSC
www.fsc.org   FSC™ C013985

ISBN 978-1-4462-6632-8
ISBN 978-1-4462-6633-5 (pbk)

At SAGE we take sustainability seriously. Most of our products are printed in the UK using FSC papers and boards.
When we print overseas we ensure sustainable papers are used as measured by the Egmont grading system.
We undertake an annual audit to monitor our sustainability.

To Alex, Jonathan, Katie, Chris, Joyce and Brian

CONTENTS

LIST OF FIGURES

ABOUT THE AUTHOR

Dr Hazel Wright is a social scientist who has worked in education – in the pre-school, the community, further education and higher education – for many years and is currently course leader for the BA Early Childhood Studies and deputy director of the Doctorate in Education at Anglia Ruskin University.

Originally a historical geographer her current research activities span a range of disciplines, particularly sociology, psychology, education – and through her work on Amartya Sen's capability approach – economics. Thus, she embraced the writing of the current book with a degree of prior knowledge and a great deal of enthusiasm.

Her doctoral study considered the role of education in women's lives. It focused on students' training to work with children and is published by Trentham Books as *Women Studying Childcare: Integrating Lives Through Adult Education*. Current work is extending this project and examining links between women's lives and their narration of their experiences of childhood in addition to exploring changing attitudes to professionalism within the Early Years sector.

ACKNOWLEDGEMENTS

My interest in childhood stems from my roles as child, mother, practitioner and academic, so I thank my mother and father for a rich and stimulating childhood, my three children Alex, Jonathan and Katie for giving me the chance to revisit these experiences from a different perspective, and my husband, Chris, for sharing the ups and downs, and supporting my endeavour. Colleagues motivated me to stay focused and students gave me insight into the subjects I should write about. Jude and Amy, my editors at SAGE, were generous with their advice and encouragement.

Together, you made this book possible. Thank you, all of you!

PREFACE

This book is written from the standpoint of a single academic, who reads widely across the disciplines and strives to create a coherent but nuanced overview of a complex subject when she teaches aspects of childhood studies. Its chapters separate the distinctive disciplinary strands to enable an examination of childhood from a range of perspectives. They document the contribution of foundational theorists in the field while also looking to contemporary additions and extensions to our knowledge. Where possible, they draw on lesser known examples and specialist sources in order to add something new to the early years tapestry without obscuring salient points or diminishing the field in any way.

Of necessity, many subjects are abbreviated or summarised to make an overview possible in one volume. However, the overall aim is to contextualise our knowledge of children and childhood, and that is why the book takes an interdisciplinary approach. The intention is to broaden rather than deepen knowledge, but in striving for the first of these, the book tries to point the reader to sources that will also enable the second. Do use the lists of sources as this book cannot, on its own, cover all aspects and perspectives to the level of a specialist text, but it does bring multiple ideas together to form a single narrative.

CHAPTER 1

INTRODUCING CHILDHOOD

Overview

This chapter starts by asking the questions:

- What is childhood?
- How do we know about childhood?

In answer to these questions, it presents a range of sources – physical, pictorial, numeric and written – that can tell us more about childhood, using classic examples to demonstrate how this has been achieved. Among others, it introduces the work of:

- Philippe Ariès
- Linda Pollock
- Neil Postman
- Barbara Hanawalt
- Harry Hendrick
- Sally Crawford
- William Corsaro.

It then discusses the changing paradigms affecting childhood.

For early years educators, childhood is a topic of central importance but for many of those who first explored the subject it was a means to another end – a way of furthering their knowledge of living things, of animal behaviour, of human cognition, and the adult psyche – in order to develop a better society.

The advantage of this heritage is the breadth of expert knowledge that contributes to the field and ensures that, whatever aspect we choose to explore, we have access to a range of credible theory and research. As a topic, childhood is truly interdisciplinary. As a subject, the child is central to our collective and continuing existence, so it is right that we should take his/her needs seriously and readily support the journey to adulthood. To what extent this is genetically pre-determined or socially constructed has long formed the central nature–nurture debate fundamental to the discipline, and views of childhood have varied considerably through time as circumstances and knowledge bases change. Yet children remain less visible and less powerful than the adult members of any community so it is appropriate here to start by examining how people can, and have, investigated the experiences of childhood.

What is childhood?

Richard Mills claims (2000: 8): 'such is the nature of childhood that its study cannot be confined within one academic discipline'. As he rightly says, it comprises aspects of: 'anthropology, art, computing, education, history, literature, medicine, philosophy, physiology, psychology, psychoanalysis, psychotherapy, sociology, statistics or theology' (ibid: 8) and these are perspectives that are discussed within this book.

The concept of childhood passes unchallenged in everyday speech. Yet there are questions around its definition. Should this be in terms of status, power, age or physical maturity? Should it be defined independently, or in contrast to adulthood? Do we follow tradition and mark adulthood by rites of passage, or rely on legal acts, independent of individual achievement and capability? Morrow (2011), recognising this complexity, views childhood as both legal and relational, but also behavioural in the sense of acting 'childishly' and being 'innocent'. Questions of definition raise parallel issues around boundaries. Can children really become adults overnight or should the change be gradual, acknowledging that children adopt adult abilities and behaviours progressively as they encounter different situations? What marks the ending of childhood? In Western society it is often bounded by the completion of compulsory schooling but in many parts of the world childhood ends with early marriage as this can bring forward the age of majority (Morrow, 2011).

Over time and place, notions of childhood vary considerably, making it, in the words of Wyness (2000) a 'contested' concept. Jenks (1982: 9) describes how, for centuries: 'theorists have systematically endeavoured to constitute a view of the child that is compatible with their particular visions of social life', and seeing childhood as a social practice, explains how in Western society at least, we endeavour to formalise children's social position. Jenks believes that these formal structures then shape and delimit our views of the child.

The child status has its boundaries maintained through the crystalliza-
tion of conventions into institutional forms like families, nurseries, clinics and schools, all agencies specifically designed to process the status
as a uniform entity. (1982: 11)

This is a process that, I think, may be coincidental rather than intentional.
Turmel (2008: 6) supports a more active construction. He sees childhood as
a 'product of a complex movement of cooperation, conflict and resistance
between a broad range of social actors, including children themselves' rather
than an 'inevitable consequence' of public policies and expert guidance, a
view that sees power as more loosely distributed.

How do we know about childhood?

Researchers use a variety of sources to explore the concept of childhood
and its practical manifestations as children. Sometimes there is choice of
material – it depends on geographical and chronological contexts. In some
disciplines, investigatory methods can use primary and secondary sources,
and researchers consult documents, observe and talk to real children, but
for those interested in earlier historical periods, the available resources can
be minimal. Archaeologists, for example, often have to hypothesise from
isolated physical artefacts. Their understandings are gleaned from examining multiple sources that, viewed collectively, enable broader interpretation.
Early documentary evidence is scarce and carefully filed away, but with the
advent of printing, the number of descriptive texts increased exponentially,
making data available to a broader range of researchers, which in turn led to
a greater proliferation of printed material. Visual images, statistical analyses,
observational data and official documents provide additional secondary
records of what it was or is to be a child, and these are often supported by
artefacts that were designed and made to support children's mobility, their
play and learning, and general well-being. However, many of these materials
are hidden amidst general records and collections that focus on the adult
population. Through the centuries, children, like women and the poor, were
largely invisible. Even now, their problems are sometimes concealed within
general household data that studies the family rather than the child.

Using pictorial records

Although his work has been highly criticised, Phillipe Ariès (1962) is generally credited with the origination of a modern interest in children and
childhood. Ariès examined the nature of childhood in medieval times and
considered how it differed from more modern interpretations, setting out

hypotheses that 'have become the benchmark for all subsequent students' (Cunningham, H., 2005: 5).

Ariès was a demographic historian who wanted to understand the modern phenomenon of family better. Recognising the connection between childhood and family, he set out to study childhood to find out more about families. In the introduction to his book, *Centuries of Childhood*, he clearly identifies his fundamental concern (that children were seen as miniature adults) and identifies his main source of data (the detailed study of historic works of art), examining children's clothing, demeanour and activities to see how this came to change.

> In the tenth century, artists were unable to depict a child except as a man on a smaller scale. How did we come from that ignorance of childhood to the centring of the family around the child in the nineteenth century? (Ariès, 1962: 8)

Ariès also investigated extant written records, but like works of art, these too focused on the wealthier members of society. In part, his claim that 'the idea of childhood did not exist' (ibid: 125) is based on the prurience of the French court under Henri IV where adult courtiers revealed a casual attitude to children's sexuality. In making this claim, Ariès was careful not to deny that children were treated with affection, simply, that once they no longer needed the 'constant solicitude' of the mother, they belonged to adult society. He does, however, talk of 'the huge domain of unexpressed feelings' (ibid: 127) and might more accurately have referred to 'unrecorded' rather than unexpressed feelings. Ariès' discussion is intricately linked to his portrayal of schooling for he sees this as an expanding disciplinary space that extended the duration of childhood and divided society into those (mainly male and upper class) who attended school and those (girls and the lower classes) who did not, whether or not they entered the world of work. Making another strong claim, Ariès asserted that:

> The whole complexion of life was changed by the differences in the educational treatment of the middle-class and the lower-class child.
>
> (ibid: 223)

Strong claims often invite further investigation and, to quote Hugh Cunningham (2005: 27), 'Medievalists never seem to tire of proving Ariès to be wrong'. Shahar (1990: 3) has tried to establish that 'childhood was in fact perceived as a distinct stage in the life cycle, that there was a conception of childhood, and that educational theories and norms existed'. She challenges Ariès' hypothesis but does acknowledge that it was the 'historians who followed his lead' (ibid: 2) who claimed that 'parents made no effort to keep their children alive and accepted their death with equanimity' (ibid). In Ariès' text, these ideas were only 'implicit'.

Using personal documents

Linda Pollock (1983) studied parent–child relations and presented significant evidence from primary sources, mainly autobiographies and diaries kept between 1500 and 1900, to refute the notion that medieval parents were emotionally distant from their offspring. Like Shahar, she is arguing against the 'sentiments' approach (Heywood, 2001: 6) of Ariès followers, Lloyd De Mause, Edward Shorter and Lawrence Stone, rather than Ariès himself. Translation of Ariès' French term 'sentiment' as 'idea' rather than 'feelings' stripped it of its original broader sense as an affective concept, leaving his views open to a degree of misinterpretation.

Pollock uses personal documents to build her argument: adults and children's diaries and autobiographies, occasionally letters and wills if they were included within the other sources. She located 144 American and 236 British diaries, 36 autobiographies, and 17 unpublished British manuscripts. So this was an extensive study, enabling her to judge whether her findings were representative, if people censor their own diary entries, and overall, whether such records have importance beyond their individual contexts. After analysis, she concluded that, despite a slant towards the middle classes: 'the majority of diarists were not exceptional, but ordinary people living out their lives in anonymity' (1983: 87). The virtue of these accounts is their intimacy and detail, the way they reveal the actuality of childhood rather than popular attitudes towards it, and the way that children are seen as members of families rather than in isolation.

Both Ariès and Pollock relied on representations of childhood, Ariès favouring pictorial records, Pollock using written accounts to view the lives of children through the memories of their parents. Both approaches used a limited number of individualised sources to make more general points. In Ariès case, the pictures were intended for public viewing, at least within the home, whereas Pollock's sources were written for private purposes. Whether this makes them more or less accurate can be argued indefinitely.

Using contextual knowledge

In a study carried out in 1982, Neil Postman (1994) examined the influence of popular culture on childhood, specifically the effects of new media. Firstly, he argued that the advent of the printed word promoted childhood because it created adults as a literate elite, as the sharing of new ideas became dependent upon the ability to read. The rise of cheaper printed material made information both more and less accessible: 'print closed off the world of everyday affairs with which the young had been so familiar in the Middle Ages' (ibid: 49). Dissemination passed from the oral to the written tradition, supporting higher levels of control at both points of delivery and reception, and enabling a new stability of content. This excluded children (and workers unable to read), supporting Ariès' argument that education marked the path to maturity. As Postman also claims 'childhood became defined by school attendance' (ibid: 41) and a 'level of symbolic achievement' (ibid: 42).

Secondly, Postman explored the role of television and other visual media in eroding those barriers, as they again made material equally accessible to children and adults. He describes television as a 'total disclosure medium' (ibid: Chapter 6) for it 'makes public what has previously been private' (ibid: 83). Unlike the printed book, it is an 'open-admission technology to which there are no physical, economic, cognitive or imaginative restraints' (ibid: 84). Information is even more accessible to children than it was when it was shared orally, for as Postman claims, television 'eliminates' one of the principal differences between children and adults (ibid: 84) and displaces elders as a primary source of knowledge (ibid: 89).

Overall, Postman argued that accessibility to knowledge plays a key role in determining whether and when childhood is bounded. Supported by Tuchman (1978), he claimed that medieval childhoods ended at seven, as at this age the child achieved functional language skills. In a society where information was shared orally, the skills of talking, listening, understanding and remembering were key to full participation within the community. Postman cites historian J.H. Plumb's claim that in earlier times children and adults occupied the same 'world', sharing the same games, toys and stories (Plumb, 1971: 7, in Postman, 1994: 15–16).

Postman argues that the growing sophistication of medieval and later society extended the range of childhood. Children needed to be educated, initially to become literate but also to acquire the practical skills, the mathematical and scientific knowledge and the social awareness necessary for engagement with an increasingly complex world. Postman feared that television was undermining the status of childhood. He decried the way that 'children had virtually disappeared from the media, especially from television' in the 70s and 80s, as they were everywhere 'depicted as miniature adults in the manner of thirteenth- and fourteenth-century paintings' (1994: 122). Postman's views were voiced before the internet and other new technologies (addressed in Chapter 9) further, and more radically, altered children's access to media and communications. Perhaps we should be mindful of his arguments later, when we consider the artificial creation of ranges of children's goods, the television programmes, books and clothes that at least make some attempt to differentiate between adult and children's markets. Does their proliferation purely reflect the commercial imperative for new markets or are parent's supporting this consumerism in a desire to keep their children apart from the adult mainstream?

Postman's views date from 1982 but his arguments can be carried forward into new contexts, as they are not tied to original sources in the way that Ariès' and Pollock's were. Postman was using ideas and concepts to create a view of childhood but not drawing heavily on original research documentation, either written or pictorial.

Using public records

In contrast, Barbara Hanawalt (1993) used archival material already in the public domain. Official documents form a useful historical record but rarely focus uniquely on children or childhood. Hanawalt examined court records in detail to build up a picture of children's lives in medieval London, and used literary sources and advice books to supplement her narratives. She found that the English legal system clearly recognised children as minors and carefully protected the rights of those orphaned at an early age. She also found that court cases often reported background personal information whether the subject was a child or adult. Hanawalt consulted a range of reports, including land registration, common pleas and coroners' rolls, which described incidences of child death (and frequently documented how the children were housed and cared for, and the grief expressed by bereaved parents). She also studied wills and last testaments, which brought together information from all classes of person.

Eminent British social historian, Harry Hendrick, was also interested in the fate of children and wrote an account of child welfare in England (Hendrick, 1994), which was updated in 2011 and is still widely acclaimed. He compiled a survey of sources on childhood that arranges material in 'age-related' chapters, which summarise salient points (Hendrick, 1997).

Combining archaeological evidence with anthropological insight

If we want to study childhood in earlier periods of history, the material becomes scarcer. For ancient civilisations, historians have some recourse to written records, and art in the form of carvings, mosaics and depictions on pottery. Such sources exist for the civilisations of Mesopotamia (Sumer and Akkadia), Egypt and the Indus valley, which were developing between 3000 to 2000 years BCE; and for the important civilisations arising between 2000 to 1000 BCE in China (Shang), South America (Olmec and Chavin) and ancient Greece (Minoa and, later, Mycenae). These civilisations were richly endowed compared to the rural Bronze Age settlements in Western Europe in the period

2000 to 600 BCE. From 1000 BCE empires flourished in Rome (Etruscan) and South America (the Mayan, and later the Aztec and Incan empires), but the majority of Europeans still lived in rural Iron Age settlements.

However, to understand really early cultures – the people of the Stone Age – we rely on limited archaeological evidence, using extrapolation from known events within anthropology to suggest credible interpretations. This period includes the first humans of the Palaeolothic (2.5 million to 20,000 years ago), the hunter-gatherers of the Mesolithic (20,000 to 12,000 years ago) and the early farmers of the Neolithic (12,000 to 5,000 years ago).

Kathryn Kamp (2001: 2) argues that archaeologists tend to neglect childhood, perhaps because it is 'too intangible'. Baxter (2005: 1) supports this view, explaining that even when they are included, children tend to be cast in 'peripheral roles'. Traditionally, children were seen to be unimportant in terms of their contribution to society, their lives unknowable as they left 'few material traces, with the exception of child burials' (ibid: 2). Artefacts are typically classified 'according to the (implicit adult) function for which it is presumed they were made' (Crawford, 2009: 59). However, the rise of feminist approaches in anthropology and sociology in the 1970s triggered a desire to restore the woman and child to the archaeological record, a move captured in Greta Lillehammer's (1989) seminal paper, *A Child is Born: The Child's World in an Archaeological Perspective.*

Views on how to establish children's presence in prehistory were, and are, greatly contested. Initially the focus was on identification of artefacts specifically for children but to decide whether miniature items were toys, tools, learning materials or votive offerings was difficult, reliant on evidence from contemporary cultures or historic ones for which there is a written record. Within bioarchaeology, there were also significant debates around definitions of childhood, as this could be described in terms of biological age (by dating skeletal development), chronological age (by establishing time since birth) or social age (based on socially constructed norms of behaviour and status). Archaeologists tended to establish site-specific categories, making it difficult to compare data from different 'finds' to enable comparison or generalisation. Yet, when bioarchaeology adopts a child-centred focus, stable isotope analysis can provide information about breastfeeding and weaning practices, and diet, while skeletal examination can ascertain patterns of physical activity, pubertal development and general levels of health (Halcrow and Tayles, 2008).

When we recognise that children's relationships with the world are 'fundamentally different from those of adults' (Baxter, 2005: 4) it becomes possible to identify 'patterning' in the distribution of children's artefacts and thereby make visible their presence. As Sally Crawford (2009: 64) explains, children were given and appropriated a range of household items, discarded or borrowed, to embellish their play so a juvenile presence may be apparent in the location of items and 'their unnatural proximity to other objects'. Children play a role in collecting and depositing material, so the co-presence of broken or multiple fragments of bone, bead or pottery may indicate that the items were used for play purposes. Similarly, the discovery of imperfectly crafted items, like pots, identifies the presence of novice potters who could be children, but also the elderly and infirm. However, archaeologists are able to distinguish between the old and young through scientific studies of fingerprint patterns (Kamp et al., 1999). As an example, this process has shown that it was children who made the animal figurines found among utility ware in Northern Arizona's early Sinaguan culture (Kamp, 2001), demonstrating that they were allowed to play with clay while their parents made the pots necessary for domestic survival.

Using interactive methods

A traditional ethnography involves living within a culture to examine the minutiae of people's customs and beliefs. This is a long-term project requiring researchers to become accepted by communities so that their presence does not disrupt normal practices and has tended to focus on complete cultures rather than children in isolation. It involves observing people, talking to them and joining in their activities to gain a sense of their lives. However, Hammersley and Atkinson (1995 [1983]): 1), long-time advocates, state that the term can be interpreted in a 'liberal way, not worrying much about what does and does not count as examples of it'. In contemporary research terms, studies of lesser duration that involve observing or talking to children, possibly examining their pictures and writing too, are said to use ethnographic techniques. William Corsaro (2006: 53) describes his 'prolonged fieldwork' to study peer culture in pre-school settings in the United States and in Italy as ethnographic, referring to the intensity of his involvement and his need to establish a 'reactive method of field entry' (ibid: 54) by simply sitting down in free play areas and waiting for children to approach him. Jane Payler (2007: 240) also refers to her comparative study of four-year-olds in an English school and playgroup setting as ethnographic.

Other researchers use a range of child-friendly strategies to take a participatory stance. Tim Waller (2007) encouraged children to tour their outdoor area, take photographs and make maps and books to create personalised 'learning stories' (Carr, 2001). This was a multi-strand research methodology, one that Clark and Moss (2001) term the 'mosaic approach'.

Observations can be carried out without interrupting the child's normal activity so are a particularly useful way to capture children's natural actions. Talk, or more formally, interview, enables the researcher to check his/her understanding of observed activities or discuss different subjects entirely. It is arguable whether this is a more or a less accurate process for so much depends on contexts and relationships. Participatory methods empower the children to carry out their own research but still require an adult analysis to develop a fuller interpretation. Whichever approach is chosen, studies of contemporary children, apart from one's own family, require researchers to seek ethical approval to ensure that children are not 'hurt' or disadvantaged by taking part in a study that may be of no direct benefit to them. This, a 'relatively new' requirement (Gray, 2012: 65), awarded if the researcher develops a well-designed and presented proposal that details the aims of the research and its potential value for society.

Using statistical data

It is possible to build a picture of distant or contemporary childhoods using statistical data too, even when this was initially collected for a different purpose. Because survey material is usually extensive in coverage, it permits the researchers to make supported claims. It can sometimes be used alongside ethnographic material to enable a degree of generalisation beyond a small-scale study.

Monica Magadi (2010) used data from the 2004–5 *Family Resources Survey* (DWP, 2005) to examine the extent of severe child poverty in the UK. Her study employed regression techniques to establish the risk factors associated with child poverty. This means that possible factors were analysed together to see if they trended in parallel or in opposition and this particular study found the risk of poverty to be positively associated with a number of factors: parental unemployment, poorly educated parents, large family size, minority ethnicity, and disabled adults. Contrary to expectation, the regression found that lone parents often fared better than dual-parent families in similar circumstances and that non-receipt of benefits disproportionately increased the likelihood of child poverty. Thus, the statistical analysis tells us a considerable amount about the economic well-being of children in the UK, creating a predictive capacity to inform new policy initiatives.

Another study, Bayliss and Sly's (2009) report on child well-being in the UK, took a very different approach in its use of statistical data. These researchers were interested in non-aggregated data and examined a broader range of statistical sources to consider factors independently. They were interested in the geographical incidence of well-being so data was plotted onto national and local maps to reveal which areas were problematic. In their conclusion, the authors were able to identify the distribution of specific problems but still able to demonstrate that overall there is a strong north–south divide. Such conclusions would be difficult to substantiate without resorting to large-scale statistical analysis.

Using adult recollection

Biographical research prompts people to remember past events so can investigate childhood through adult memory. Done well this enables the creation of in-depth but idiosyncratic accounts that can be useful in explaining people's current situations and in recording detail that may not be available in published historical accounts. My own work on women studying childcare (Wright, 2011) used psychosocial interview techniques to encourage ex-students to recall their educational experiences to build up a picture of the role of education in their lives.

In New Zealand, Sonja Rosewarne and colleagues (2010) employed collective biographical memory work (CBMW) to jointly explore the concept of transition to inform ways of dealing with children's transitions in early childhood settings. Rather than viewing transition as a rite of passage, this method enabled practitioners to capture the child's perspective, which foregrounded uncertainty, loss, powerlessness and shifting identity. By recalling the emotions associated with transition, the early years educators became aware of the stress that children experience and of the need to 'see' the inadequacy of generic treatment. The researchers found that transitional experiences are cumulatively stressful: this is important as even very young children may have a broad range of prior stressors. Thus, biographical recall can make staff more sensitive to the challenges children face.

Dorothy Moss (2011) used oral history to present a tapestry of childhood memories. She collected together adult accounts that gave a children's perspective on growing up in difficult conditions, during times of warfare, civil unrest and other hardships. Thus she captured the non-ideal childhoods experienced by disadvantaged children from whom we hear very little.

Using literature

Childhood as a concept operates at a level higher than individual childhoods. For this reason Jean and Richard Mills (2000) suggest that its 'timeless essence' can be conveyed through works of literature like the classic fictions of J.M. Barrie (*Peter Pan*), Lewis Carroll (*Alice in Wonderland*), Kenneth Grahame (*Wind in the Willows*), Charles Kingsley (*The Water Babies*), C.S. Lewis (*The Chronicles of Narnia*), A.A. Milne (*Winnie the Pooh*) and J.R.R. Tolkien (*The Hobbit*). Mills and Mills suggest that such stories, unbounded by the confines of reality, offer an archetypal sense of childhood, its 'illusory and elusive nature' (Mills and Mills, 2000: 9), which overrides the differences that individual children experience in their real lives.

This is an interesting argument. Such fiction can transform the prosaic rituals of daily existence, transporting children into imaginary and magical worlds. Successful authors are skilled in narration and description, and able to create exotic worlds that change less than the one in which we live, which are accessible to children through the generations.

Changing views of childhood

These are some of the different ways by which childhood can be made visible. In later chapters we will see how childhood is theorised within specific academic disciplines and how children themselves experience it differently in real world contexts. First, however, it is useful to consider how commonly held views (or paradigms) of childhood develop and to reflect on the power of overarching paradigms.

In the social and academic spheres, paradigms dominant at a particular time or place and time shape the way that people think about childhood as a concept, and how these views are applied to policy and practice, so future chapters will add detail to the brief overview given here. For almost 100 years from the mid-nineteenth to the mid-twentieth centuries, a developmental paradigm arising within psychology was uncontested (Turmel, 2008). In this period, the modernist discourse of progress formed a theoretical framework for more specialist perspectives. This anticipated a stepped linear pathway from the primitive to the advanced and described child development as a series of defined physical stages towards the goal of maturity. In a similar vein it was assumed that traditional societies would pass through stages of industrialisation and urbanisation to achieve higher levels (Western standards) of development. In contrast to psychology, sociologists took an ahistorical perspective. They also focused on families rather than children (Elias, 1987; in Turmel, 2008). In Chapter 6 we will see how a structuralist view (that everyone in society has a particular role to play) was undermined by the more radical propositions of Marxist, feminist, and postcolonial thinkers. In parallel, the social history tradition gave way to more critical perspectives that challenged the invisibility of the poor, the racially oppressed, the woman, and later the child, in the historical account. In turn, post-structural and postmodern thinking, further questioning the validity of universal dominant discourses, led to a greater awareness of the variety of childhood experiences, encouraging researchers to consider more fully the contexts and conditions in which real childhoods are lived.

From the 1970s onwards, postmodern perspectives undermined belief in a universal childhood. The 1990s saw the emergence of a growing interest in children and a 'new' sociology of childhood that recognised the diversity of childhood experiences (James and Prout, 1997). Growing media coverage informed the public of the differing ways that people live around the world and the disparity in the ways that children are treated in different societies. Yet global organisations sought to promote the commonalities of childhood, aiming to establish international policies that protect children everywhere. The United Nations Convention on the Rights of the Child (UNCRC) (1989) is a powerful 'instrument' with 'institutional power' which uses international law to frame 'global childhood ideals' (Boyden, in James and Prout, 1997: 216).

Thus, childhood is dominated by two opposing discourses – one of diversity and one of commonality – that are difficult to resolve. It is readily apparent that universalist approaches underplay significant differences between childhoods but, conversely, relativist perspectives risk undermining efforts to empower children through a collective voice.

Contemporary interest, fuelled by an increasingly globalised society and the connectivity forged by the world wide web, is focused on children's rights. In the global north (the developed societies of America and Eurasia, plus Australia) the concern is to give children more control over their own lives, taking the discourse to one of independence and autonomy within safeguarded home and school environments. In the global south (the less developed nations in continental Africa and large parts of Asia) the aim is to provide essentials like clean water and sanitation, shelter, health care and education (SOWC, 2012). Both sets of aims can be subsumed within a more general plea for well-being that is increasingly used at national and international levels to maintain a shared focus on improving children's lives.

Summary

This chapter has explored the ways we view childhood and the ways we can examine childhoods other than our own. It has discussed well-known studies of children past and present and other work that broadens our range of knowledge, using these examples to begin to answer the questions posed at the start of the chapter: What is childhood? How do we know about childhood? It provides material that suggests how the concept can be further investigated and understood. In so doing it has set the scene for the varying treatments that follow in later chapters, each of which focuses around one or more academic fields.

Points for reflection

- Consider the range of sources outlined in Chapter 1. Which do you think have the most potential to build up a realistic picture of childhood in a bygone age? Why?
- Do the commonalities between children override the differences? Which characteristics are essential to differentiate between a child and an adult?
- How would you design an original study of childhood? How and where could you access physical evidence and documentary sources?

Further reading

Kehily, M.J. (2009) *An Introduction to Childhood Studies,* 2nd edn. Maidenhead: McGraw-Hill.
Qvortrup, J., Corsaro, W.A. and Honig, M-S. (2009) *The Palgrave Handbook of Childhood Studies.* Basingstoke: Palgrave Macmillan.

General texts with chapters on most issues central to childhood. Dip into these to understand the contexts.

Websites

www.20thcenturylondon.org.uk/children
London Museums Hub with historical overviews of children's lives and possessions.

www.unicef.org
Major international site offering overviews, data and resources.

http://developingchild.harvard.edu
Downloadable research studies on child development.

Documentary

Baxter, S. (2011) *Too Much, Too Young: Children of the Middle Ages.* First shown on BBC Four on 24 August.
This BBC documentary examines some of the sources that historians use and offers a visual and aural introduction to the study of childhood.

To gain *free* access to selected SAGE journal articles related to key topics in this chapter, visit: www.sagepub.co.uk/hazelrwright.

CHAPTER 2

GEOGRAPHICAL AND ANTHROPOLOGICAL PERSPECTIVES

Overview

This chapter briefly describes the world's common geological heritage and the shared genetic inheritance of its people, demonstrating that diversity is an evolutionary process rather than a foundational characteristic. It introduces the concept of eco-cultural niche and explains how lifestyles are adapted to specific geophysical conditions.

It refutes the universality of the Westernised view of childhood and offers case studies of alternative childhoods to illustrate that differences are significant, describing:

- Kipsigis tribespeople of rural East Africa
- urban survivors of India, Africa and Latin America
- socialised children of the Israeli kibbutzim
- variations in welfare systems in Europe.

Broadening the scope, it reflects on how migration initiates cultural change. Narrowing the scope, it considers the importance of geography at local levels as children move around their immediate locality.

The characteristics that enable us to link specific peoples to different geographical locations are evolutionary phenomena (a result of long-term generational change) rather than fundamental ones. For the human species, and its children, commonalities are greater than differences. We all live on the same planet, possessing similar needs and skills, and a shared genetic inheritance. Indeed, humankind originated from a single site – all humans are literally 'out of Africa'. Furthermore, the Earth was once covered by a single landmass – *Pangaea* (Greek for all lands) – so countries, too, share a common geological heritage.

Initial divergence

Scientists – matching fossil and coal distributions, coastline shapes and rock strata patterns – have established that around 200 million years ago the single land form began to split into a northern block (Laurasia) and a southern landmass (Gondwanaland), comprising most of Antarctica, South America, Africa, India and Australia. The 'splitting' process created a series of tectonic plates that enabled sections of the world's surface to move very slowly in different directions. By a process of continental drift (see Figure 2.1)

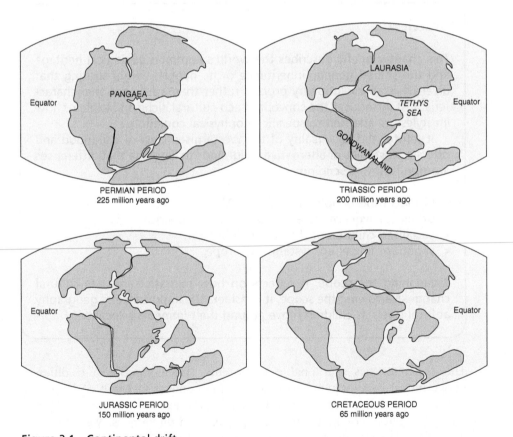

PERMIAN PERIOD
225 million years ago

TRIASSIC PERIOD
200 million years ago

JURASSIC PERIOD
150 million years ago

CRETACEOUS PERIOD
65 million years ago

Figure 2.1   Continental drift

(Based on US Geological Survey, 2013)

(US Geological Survey, 2013), the sections of dry land have slowly shifted into the current land positions, forming the seven continents that we recognise today: Antarctica, Asia, Australia, Africa, Europe, North America, and South America (see Figure 2.2) (US Geological Survey, 2013).

Fossil and archaeological evidence shows that c.150,000 years ago the first recognisable human beings occupied part of central Eastern Africa, which is present day Ethiopia. Initial population movements were confined to Africa but about 60,000 years ago humans began to migrate out of Africa, populating the world in a series of waves. Combined genetic and archaeological research has revealed that the maternal lineages of all human beings trace back to a common ancestor, 'mitochondrial Eve'. Late twentieth century developments in deoxyribonucleic acid (DNA) testing enabled scientists to trace genetic links between early and present day humans that prove this common ancestry. In *The Seven Daughters of Eve*, researcher, Bryan Sykes (2001), explains how in 1991 a frozen body newly exposed on a German mountain slope was carbon-dated and found to be between 5,000 and 5,350 years old. Laboratory comparison with donated DNA samples showed that this 'iceman' was an ancestor of a Dorset woman, Marie Moseley, for her DNA was a perfect match. Further research led Sykes' team to conclude that almost all modern Europeans have an unbroken genetic link with one of only seven remote female ancestors – the daughters of mitochondrial Eve.

Researchers have tested (and are testing) the contemporary world population to establish 'haplogroups' – those who share similar characteristics as a result of natural mutation of the genes. Haplogroups are labelled by letter, and then by number to identify subsequent adaptations, and this material has been used to chart the successive patterns of human migration across the globe. It shows that the founding group moved out of Africa and into the

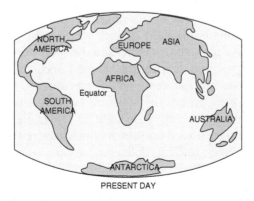

PRESENT DAY

Figure 2.2   The world today

(Based on US Geological Survey, 2013)

Middle East, then Asia and Australia. Thereafter, distinctive groups moved into Europe and East Asia, with an Asian route into the American continent, probably towards the end of the Ice Age while there was still a land bridge across the Bering Straits joining Asia to present day Alaska. These groups are tracked across time and place on websites listed at the end of this chapter.

Thus, before we begin to consider the diversity of childhood character-istics and experience, we should remember that all human beings have a shared genetic inheritance.

Eco-cultural niches

The characteristics that differentiate races and ethnic groups have devel-oped over generations of selective reproduction among people who live together. However, it is not only inherited genetic material that explains the differences between societies. Groups adopt norms of social behaviour and communication that determine how they function, and their lifestyles are also greatly influenced by geographical features. The type of terrain, the proximity of seas and rivers, hills and forests, and the climate, all pro-foundly affect the ways that communities develop in different areas of the globe. For example, in the Amazonian rainforests the humid conditions and luxurious vegetation encouraged tribes to adopt a 'slash and burn' culture, clearing temporary sites in which to plant subsistence crops, but slowly damaging their environment as population numbers grew, lifestyle became more sedentary, and the forest had insufficient time to recover between bouts of cultivation (Lokja et al., 2011). In these communities children would live in nuclear families, helping their parents to tend the fields, har-vest the crops and carry out other subsistence tasks.

Life was similarly itinerant in the Sahel region south of the African Sahara desert but here transience arose from *lack* of rain and vegetation. Pastoral nomads of the Fulani tribe had always migrated to find grazing for their cattle during the dry season, as frequent periods of drought could not support a sedentary lifestyle. As populations increased the men were forced to lead the animals to further pastures, leaving the women and children to a domestic existence: basket-weaving, gathering wild foodstuffs and tending subsistence crops near to the rivers where the soil was better quality. After the severe drought of 1973 and a secondary drought in 1984, men in more wealthy families began to migrate to the cities to find seasonal work to boost the family income: butchery, trading, delivering goods; sometimes merely beg-ging (Hampshire, 2002). The less affluent (and therefore less able to travel) sought local work in mines, or contracts to care for other people's animals. Thus, the women and children frequently lived independently of their men-folk, the children working alongside the women until the males became old enough to join the herders. Traditionally, Fulani men could have more than one wife and family group and this shared familial status further encouraged the women to bond together to care collectively for the children.

In comparison, in temperate Britain the grassland was good. Traditionally, farmers could graze their cattle on a single farmstead handed down from generation to generation along with an associated workforce. So children experienced a settled existence, enjoying a 'private' existence within their immediate family and community. However, even in a small country like Britain, the landscape significantly influenced lifestyle (Pryor, 2011). In the northern uplands, farms were often isolated, causing the family to depend entirely on each other for support and company, whereas in the south and west of England, farms were often close to a nucleated village with services and amenities, giving children access to friends and other family groupings on a daily basis. As Britain industrialised, the north–south contrast became more apparent (see Chapter 3). Heavy industry concentrated in the northern highland areas where fast-flowing rivers provided an early power source for textile and other manufacturing industries prior to the invention of steam power that led to the establishment of major industrial conurbations, as in Lancashire and Yorkshire. Contrast this to the quasi-rural lifestyle in the eastern market towns of Suffolk where wool was a staple market commodity and village life centred around the guildhall or market cross.

These 'snapshots' of different lifestyles are generalisations but, nevertheless, demonstrate the geographical variation between and within nations, and how diversity supports the development and continuation of social differences. In anthropological terms populations can be described as occupying a particular eco-cultural 'niche' (Super and Harkness, 1982) as they adapt to the physical and consequent social practices a region can support. Customs and traditions are passed from generation to generation: in Vygotskian terms, society perpetuates sociocultural identity (Daniels, 2001).

Anthropologists have long been interested in the study of different peoples and their findings are increasingly of interest within mainstream childcare. Postmodern thinking (see Chapter 6) also challenges the notion of universal childhood, leading to recognition that this often describes a narrowly Westernised perspective centred on the nuclear family, the mother as key carer and the child as dependent until the late teenage years. To countermand the notion of a universal childhood, it is useful to look at alternative patterns, as in the three case studies that follow:

- the Kipsigis, a traditional rural community in Eastern Africa
- city children in India, Africa and Latin America
- the kibbutzim of Israel, a unique attempt to collectivise the upbringing of children in a country striving to occupy new lands.

Diverse childhoods

Rural childhoods: the Kipsigis of Kenya

The Kipsigis, one of many indigenous African peoples, have attracted repeated anthropological attention following an early study by Peristiany (1939). Native to the highlands of western Kenya (East Africa), the Kipsigis were originally a semi-nomadic people who, like the Fulani of the Sahel, lived by cattle herding, growing simple subsistence crops as they moved from pasture to pasture. Traditionally, marriages were polygamous with men marrying up to 12 wives but making each one a 'bridal wealth' endowment of cattle and cash. This tradition ensured the women and her children a degree of economic independence even though they had no rights of inheritance to parental property, as this was shared equally between the male heirs (Borgerhoff Mulder, 2000).

The arrival of European settlers around 1900 created a demand for grain and this led to families abandoning their subsistence plots in favour of wholesale commercial cultivation of maize (Sørensen, 1992). This practice eroded women's ability to grow food for family consumption apart from the cash crops traditionally farmed for sale, making women and children more dependent on the vagaries of the marketplace. European colonisation also introduced Westernised concepts of land ownership and inheritance, usually through the male heads of household, and a reduction in the number of wives each man married. Increasingly the Kipsigis adopted more sedentary lifestyles and, when Kenya achieved independence in 1963, villagers were granted their land under a settlement scheme set up by the government.

When, in the 1970s, Super and Harkness (1982) carried out a three-year anthropological study of a Kipsigis village (a *kokwet*), the traditional culture was already undergoing Westernisation, but slowly. The study focused on a village of 54 homesteads, ranged along a three-mile ridge close to the Mau forest and not far from the tea plantations of Kericho. Homes, round houses built with mud walls and straw roofs, were clustered in small groups at the edges of the village and each family had individual ownership of some 18 acres on which to grow food and cash crops. Family units commonly comprised a man, two wives and their children, but the community shared major tasks, like harvesting. Kipsigis society was still practicing initiation rites for both male and female adolescents (circumcision and clitoridectomy) to mark the transition into adulthood, but these customs were slowly declining due to the teaching of Christian missionaries. By the 1970s, children attended a few years of schooling so the community was beginning to embrace outside influences (ibid). However, children were still essential contributors (Harkness and Super, 1985), watching over the cattle from as young as three, weeding and running errands from about five or six, and regularly caring for younger siblings by eight to ten. Their lives were focused around their homestead and up to the age of six children usually interacted with just a small number of siblings and neighbours, playing in mixed gender groups. On average, the Kipsigis child regularly mixed with six to seven people, a highly social existence compared to the one to two figure for an American child pre-day care. Mothers kept babies and very young children close by, taking them around the community on visits until about six, when they were deemed to have sufficient commonsense to need less supervision. Babies were usually in close physical contact until three or four months of age, carried on the hip around the house or strapped to the back of the mother for longer journeys or while the mother worked on the land. At four months, older siblings often cared for the baby but usually in sight of the mother.

Research in the mid-1980s in the Kericho village of Mossop (Sørensen, 1992) described a further shift towards traditional Western practices – monogamy, privatisation of land and working practices, and gendered division of labour. Women were increasingly responsible for the home and men were involved in the commercial world, having exclusive control of the family budget and earning a wage in order to pay for goods like fertiliser, school fees and clothes. Children lived in a male-dominated society. They generally started school between four and six and were often the second generation to receive an education. Sørensen's co-researcher, Von Bulow, claimed that 'a successful man is defined as someone who is independent, has his own land, his own cattle and makes enough money to provide for his family, educate his children and build a modern concrete house' (Von Bulow, 1992: 536). This suggests that while still helping out around the home, children's lives were more restricted than previously with a greater definition between indoor and outside activities.

Another study carried out between 1982 and 1991 (Borgerhoff Mulder, 2000) showed the Kipsigis cultural practices to be challenged by overpopulation. Over the generations, male family members had inherited increasingly smaller plots of land and variable rainfall, pest and disease (possibly due to higher densities of occupation) reduced agricultural yields. Young men were finding it increasingly difficult to attract wives as they had less 'bridal wealth', so were leaving the homesteads to seek work elsewhere, disrupting familial allegiances. In 2001, Harkness and Super described a society where men and women occupied separate spheres. The men cared for the cattle and socialised together. The women took care of the household and subsistence, planting vegetables and weeding the staple crops. Small groups of women, *morik,* worked together cooperatively, supporting each other through illness or childbirth, and socialising together apart from the menfolk. Thus children were again brought up in a largely female environment where men were absent for a great deal of the time.

Together, these studies show how cultural traditions in Kenya were influenced by and then moved away from European patterns. However, despite these changes, the Kipsigis childhood is still very different from the Western European norm and the rural lifestyle continues, if changed. In contrast, in many areas of the world, the growing Western demand for cheaply produced goods has led to rapid industrialisation and consequent urbanisation. Factories require a localised labour force so families leave their rural farming communities to live in the towns. This seriously disrupts family and community bonds, divorcing young families from their support networks, the grandparents and village elders who traditionally ruled the community, providing established homesteads from which to seek work and an additional layer of 'caring' for the young. The struggle to survive in urban areas without this support leaves many parents unable to house, feed and clothe their offspring. As a result, many of those children establish an independent existence on the city streets.

Urban childhoods in rapidly developing countries: India, Africa and Latin America

From a Westernised perspective, which portrays the child as 'dependent' and in need of nurture, children who fend for themselves are seen as victims. For the wealthy they represent a risk, a threat to property (as many steal to survive) and to health (as many live in insanitary conditions, contracting and spreading disease). Possible solutions are widely discussed but little done to change the underlying conditions that perpetuate their lifestyle, the poverty and chaos that overwhelms the urban infrastructure. In 1979, the United Nations year of the child, the term 'street children' replaced the more general descriptions of runaway, homeless or abandoned children. The term was first used by Henry Mayhew in 1851 in his contemporary study of *London Labour and the London Poor* (completed in 1861) but is now largely applied to less developed countries, an adoption that reminds us that childhood is defined historically as well as geographically.

Until the 1980s, the term 'street children' was the favoured label for those children who lived apart from their families, forging an existence on city streets but anthropologist, Catherine Panter-Brick (2002) explains that the term is now highly contested and criticised for several reasons: it disguises the varied characteristics of different groups of children and their circumstances; it pays no attention to the ways that the children move on and off the street; and draws attention away from the significant number of children who live in poverty within their own families. Some critics consider the term to be disrespectful towards those children who prefer independent living to a life in poverty within a family that is struggling to survive. Nevertheless charities often distinguish the homeless from the working child who returns home to sleep and maybe eat, using the terms endorsed by The United Nations Children's Fund (UNICEF) in the late 1980s: children 'of' and 'on' the street. Children 'of' the street are 'street-living'. Children 'on' the street (street-working children) retain a sense of belonging and may sometimes attend school, working to supplement the family income in their spare time or when parents or older siblings are ill or away. In reality, however, many children move between the two categories over time, some continually adjust their lifestyle and some spend time in institutions – in refuges, orphanages and reformatories. Others live in 'street-families', family units with nowhere to call home (Thomas de Benitez, 2011).

The UNCRC (1989) marked another transition in the discourse around childhood – a shift from children with 'needs' to children with 'rights'. The UNCRC enshrined children's legal right to 'protection, provision and participation', a voice in the decisions that affect them. However, whether this includes the right to determine their own lifestyles is often clouded by discussions of competence. The age at which children are sufficiently mature to make decisions that deviate from the normative expectations of society is difficult if not impossible to determine. The 45 articles of the UNCRC grant children rights to survive, live safely, belong and develop, but also, perhaps more controversially, protection from unwanted media interest and charitable intervention. Children are seen as citizens with an entitlement to the resources they need to develop their adult potential yet street children cannot claim these resources as they lack the registration documents, birth certificates and permanent addresses that are normatively used to allocate access to education, health care and welfare services. Most developing countries lack the funds and infrastructure needed to meet the terms of the convention so becoming a signatory indicates a predisposition to act rather than action itself. The semblance of compliance can mask a failure to act as 'many states pay no more than lip service to the Convention' (Archard, 2004: 59).

More recently the discourse of 'needs' has moved to one of 'risk', but in practice, children's needs remain unmet. Many remain threatened by drug abuse, gang violence, school abandonment and lack of parental guidance (Hutz and Koller 1999: 61, in Panter-Brick, 2002: 159). However, studies that specifically compare street dwellers with other children from impoverished backgrounds find no evidence that the former are worse off than the latter. Indeed Panter-Brick (2002) claims that some street children have higher incomes and better diets than home-based children who are dependent on the care of parents that may not be forthcoming. She also presents some evidence that children who live with stress adapt to it and thereby avoid the physical reactions suffered by others whose lives are less frequently stressful (ibid: 161–2). Street children develop resilience. Together, these views challenge the Westernised ideal of the dependent child nurtured within a nuclear family. The children do, however, often live cooperatively.

Mizen and Ofosu-Kusi (2010) describe how friendship groups look out for each other in Accra. Children share food and work, laugh and play games together. Naterer and Godina (2011) describe how street children in the Ukraine form groups with codes of reciprocity and obligation to provide physical and emotional support and compensate for the lack of family.

Information about street children is rudimentary as these children exist outside official systems. Save the Children disseminate an article from Outlook India (Nayar, 2011) which states that India has the largest number of street children in the world, with Delhi and Kolkata being home to most of these children. It reports a survey in August 2010 – *Surviving the Streets* – carried out jointly with the Indian Institute for Human Development, that calculated that 51,000 children under 18 lived on the streets of Delhi. Eighty per cent of youngsters were male and 70 per cent of them fended for themselves despite having living relatives within the city. It found that about half the children were illiterate and that over three-quarters earned a living – as ragpickers searching the communal waste dumps for reusable material (20 per cent), or as street vendors (15 per cent) or workers in roadside repair shops or stalls (12 per cent). Others (15 per cent) beg for alms, sometimes performing acrobatics to draw attention to themselves, often supporting their younger siblings while they work. Smaller numbers work in *dhabas* (roadside cafes) or factories but their number is hard to calculate as access is restricted and the children themselves rarely leave the workface. As fewer than 20 per cent possess either identity cards or birth certificates they are hard to track and ineligible for any government schemes that might provide support. Average earnings are low, 2,240 rupees (£25) per month, and it is estimated that about 57 per cent hand half of this money over to other people; to their families or relatives to support them, or to gang leaders or the police to ensure their own survival. It is calculated that half of these children are abused verbally, physically or sexually, sometimes by the police themselves, yet many of the children have no desire to return home, enjoying the independence, excitement and companionability of street life despite extreme poverty and often hunger. Street children were less commonly a feature of African countries until the AIDS and HIV epidemics decimated many families, forcing the children to care for themselves. As in Delhi, street children are more typically males, gangs of boys who live by a mix of begging, stealing, extortion and legitimate but casual work, finding their recreation in camaraderie but also in sexual and substance abuse: drugs, alcohol and glue-sniffing. Street children in Harare, Zimbabwe are typically older teenagers working as casual porters, vendors and car minders in high-density suburbs, resorting to other means when times are bad. Bourdillon (1994: 524) describes the Mutibumba (literally, those who sleep under the trees) of Harare as 'generally aggressive' but sometimes with a sense of 'community obligation'. He also explains how many live by 'charasirira', a slang word that roughly means 'making people lose things' (ibid: 522). Some youths live in temporary groupings under the patronage of an older youth or 'monya' who both exploits and protects his followers. In a slightly more regular arrangement, refugee children escaping national wars in neighbouring countries, are often 'housed' by patrons in exchange for long hours touting sweets and cigarettes on the streets. Only five per cent of girls live on the streets. Most are 'taken in by relatives' to do domestic work: cleaning, cooking, and childcare or by 'aunties' to act as prostitutes (ibid: 519).

Generally politicians see street children as deviant – rejecting the ties of extended family – and a symbol of poor governance. In times when this matters – for state visits or international events – street children are rounded up and moved elsewhere. Children are shot by gangs or even by police, in the guise of law enforcement. The massacre of eight individuals outside the Brazilian cathedral of Candelabria in 1993 (Veash, 2000) was widely publicised and condemned but represents only a tiny proportion of the children so killed. Scanlon and colleagues (1998) describe a pioneering study of street children in Brazil that recorded 457 murders between March and August 1989 mostly by vigilante 'death squads' who worked in unofficial alliance with security firms and police to 'eliminate' the problem. Scanlon reports an Amnesty International claim that 90 per cent of such killings are unpunished. Children are thus ill-served by law enforcement officers who should protect them and consequently many view other services as potentially threatening, too. Law and order problems are manifest in countries undergoing rapid urbanisation and drug-related crime is a growing problem in many parts of the world. This affects street children but also those who live with parents too, as in Juarez City, Mexico.

Journalist Ed Vulliamy (Vulliamy, 2011) described Ciudad Juarez in the state of Chihuahua on the Mexican side of the border with the USA, as the 'most murderous city in the world'. Over a 20-year period, it developed a 'maquila' industry, a network of foreign-owned factories making goods for immediate tax-free export to America. Ciudad Juarez is wracked by drug cartels, violent gangs and corrupt police officers, and in 2010 an estimated 3,100 people were killed in drug-related incidents (The Associated Press, 2011). Friedman-Rudovsky, writing for the Bernard van Leer Foundation newsletter *Early Childhood Matters* (2010, November), describes the problems in Juarez in detail. He explains how the maquila employs 90 per cent of the city's workforce. The factories make everything from clothes to electronic goods but working conditions are poor and wages pegged. The 2010 wage buys only a quarter of the goods it bought in 1975, a form of exploitation that forces families to find two incomes to survive and to work long shifts. Fifty per cent of the city's population are migrants and without family support to provide childcare, so many parents regularly leave children as young as three or four to fend for themselves. Thirty per cent of the population are under

14 years of age, compounding this problem. Despite the rapid industrialisation there have been no policies aimed at improving housing or health care. Although the population is twice the size, its childcare provision is half that of the state capital.

Criminal activity is rife in Juarez. In the two days prior to Friedman-Rudovsky's report, the city witnessed 37 murders and numerous kidnappings, and it is commonplace to see dead bodies in the streets – outside schools, churches, parks – traumatising young children who used to frequent these places but increasingly are kept indoors. A few lucky children attend a community day centre, arriving to sleep at 6am and staying until their parents can collect them much later in the day but, despite persistent campaigning, the city remains seriously under-resourced. Even the day centre – a valuable initiative – has a depressing association. It was established after two young children were killed in a landslide that engulfed their home. They had been left home alone and locked in for their own safety so were unable to escape, demonstrating that even when parents care 'about' and 'for' their children they are not always able to protect them if their society is corrupt and/or impoverished.

Regulated childhoods: the kibbutzim of Israel

In contrast to Ciudad Juarez, the Israeli kibbutzim exemplifies state intervention in, even appropriation of, responsibility for childcare. For a time, children's lives were regulated by the community. Biological parents handed them over to state carers almost from birth.

Contemporary Israeli kibbutzim are socially and economically autonomous communities of about 400 to 900 people who elect to share a cooperative lifestyle (Aviezer et al., 1994). The first kibbutz was established in 1909 and by 1921 there were about 800 members living in nine settlements (Neuman, 1991), a figure increasing to 77,150 people residing in 224 settlements by the 1960s, partly due to the establishment of the Israeli state in 1948. After the First World War, the waves of first generation settlers who arrived in Israel were highly committed to group ideals (Shepher, 1969). These early pioneers rejected the patriarchal structures common within Eastern Europe, and strove to create new societies based on Socialist and Zionist principles. Men and women were to enjoy equal rights and responsibilities so children were to be cared for collectively by the kibbutz as a whole (Aviezer et al., 1994).

Children were housed in central brick buildings where they were cared for by trained staff, *metaplot* (metapelet, in singular) in structured regimes where cleanliness, timekeeping and socialisation to cooperative endeavour were seen to be vitally important. This made sense in isolated communities with limited medical facilities, limited infrastructural support and where the adult settlers lived in tents, and were subject to food rationing and attack by the indigenous population. Women were expected to develop and defend the community alongside their male partners, and the children's houses made this possible. Children lived and slept in dormitories in the communal houses, and were clothed from a central store. Adult couples had private sleeping quarters but their meals, laundry and clothing were all centrally organised, too. Men were expected to share the nurturing role of parents but neither parent was to try to influence their child's social development as this was the responsibility of the trained professional. It was thought that exclusion from the family home during the night would also free the children from incidental contact with the 'primal scene' and from adult conflicts, protecting them from the Oedipal influences then being propounded by Freud. Thus, practices in the kibbutzim were heavily influenced by the key beliefs of the time. However, not all kibbutzim were so organised. Four of the older kibbutzim continued an earlier practice whereby children slept in the family home.

After the Second World War, under the Israeli state, legal frameworks replaced the voluntary nature of kibbutzim, undermining personal commitment to communal practices. Efforts were made to raise the standard of living and this refocused attention on the family home. As second generation settlers reached marriageable age, they became more family-oriented. Women found, too, that despite equal educational status and freedom from childcare they were still largely employed in traditional female arenas, as they lacked the strength to work alongside men in the fields (Vallier, 1962: 240). European refugees who sought safety rather than ideological change often challenged the communal practices. They chose to make tea in their own homes, store their children's clothes in the family home and sought more prolonged contact with their children, precipitating a change of policy. Between 1951 and 1963 nine kibbutzim changed their children's housing system so that children slept at home (Shepher, 1969).

As society became more aware of children's emotional needs the residential homes were scaled down. More carers were introduced and dormitories replaced with bedrooms for two or three children with each child allocated a 'corner' of their own to house their personal possessions. The dining room, rooms for play and recreation, and classrooms were better equipped and parents allowed greater contact with their children. In the 1960s mothers were allowed to visit daily, and by the 1970s, new-born babies stayed at home with the parents for the duration of the mother's maternity leave (Aviezer et al., 1994). The 1980s were a period of transition but by the 1990s only three of the country's 260 kibbutzim still maintained collective sleeping arrangements. Now, in most communities, babies stay with their mothers for the first three months and she oversees their transition to the children's house between three to six months, working part-time during this period. Between 6 to 12 months the *metapelet* gradually takes over the care of the child who is in full-time day care in a group of 10 to 12 children by the end of this period.

At about 18 months the child joins the larger toddler group and has a change of carer but an adult–child ratio of 1:3 is maintained until the child transfers to the nursery class at three years where the ratio becomes 1:4. Thus the patterns of caring more closely resemble the day care patterns prevalent in modern Western societies except that the children probably experience more consistent substitute care as employment patterns are more stable within the Israeli community and there is a greater sense of collective responsibility.

Research has shown that children brought up collectively developed independence and self-reliance and showed no impairment in their ability to form attachments or cope with separation and change. There is some evidence, however, that such children were less responsive to strangers (Levy-Shiff, 1983). Collectivised care appears to develop collaboration and cooperation, perhaps from necessity (Shapira and Madsen, 1969) but fails to promote the ability to problem solve, perhaps because the learning process is more clinical, devoid of maternal warmth (Levy-Shiff, 1983). Children brought up in a collectivised regime were unwilling to perpetuate the system when they became parents themselves, suggesting that, overall, they found it lacking.

Hierarchies of scale

European geographies

Even when countries are aligned politically and economically, as is the trend within the European Union (EU), social differences remain and these will influence the way that children experience childhood. Esping-Anderson (1990) subdivided Europe by type into Social Democrat, Liberal and Conservative models, terms that described their attitude to social welfare. In the second millennium the picture is more complex, encouraging analysts to base their discussion around the five categories proposed by Aiginger and Guger (2005).

- Scandinavian model (Denmark, Finland, Netherlands, Sweden, Norway)
- Continental model (Germany, France, Italy, Belgium, Austria)
- Anglo-Saxon model (Ireland, UK, but also USA, Canada, Australia, New Zealand and other countries)
- Mediterranean model (Greece, Portugal, Spain)
- Catching-Up model (Czech Republic, Hungary, but also more recent members like Latvia, Estonia, Romania, Bulgaria).

This categorisation better reflects traditional cultural distinctions but, in so doing, risks perpetuating these divisions. The Scandinavian model equates to the social democrat model and high standards of public services are seen in the excellent pre-school provision that these countries enjoy – benefits that are present but less universal within the Continental model (that more nearly approximates the Conservative model). The Anglo-Saxon countries emphasise individualised responsibility, attempting to scale payment to match a family's ability to pay. Perhaps a Liberal model, this tends to divide children according to advantage despite attempts to bridge the gap through state subsidy. Benefits for poorer citizens are more limited within the Mediterranean model and children's needs met by the immediate family and community. Thus many poorer children are home-based, educated in local village schools. They often take time out to help at harvest and other busy times, perpetuating the common patterns of times past. Provision for children in the Catch-Up states rather depends upon their pre-existing arrangements and previous political persuasion. Change is required as the rigid state structures of the socialist regimes meet the variable arrangements of the modern market economy. Significant numbers of these newly European citizens are taking advantage of their new mobility to see what opportunities are available. Statistics from the Migration Observatory at the University of Oxford (Vargas-Silva, 2012) show that internal migration accounted for 35 per cent of the total migration within the EU in 2010 with significant numbers leaving eastern Europe, from Poland, Romania and Portugal and countries like Germany, Spain and France having large influxes of new European citizens. For any individual country it is possible to calculate the 'net' migration patterns and statistics. In the UK, there has been significant immigration from Poland but also a significant emigration to Spain. However, these figures represent only a small part of overall inter-European migration patterns (for an overview, see the Migration Observatory's website – listed at the end of this chapter).

Global geographies

During 2012 European population expanded by approximately 1.7 million people and an additional 1.7 million migrated between EU member states (Eurostat, 2014). International statistics for 2006 show some 1.8 million people immigrated into Europe, mainly into Spain, Germany and the UK, compared to around 1.2 million moving within Europe. Roughly equal numbers of people immigrated from Africa, Asia, America and from non-EU Europe, mostly from medium to highly developed nations. Approximately half were under the age of 29, thereby playing a role in redressing concerns about ageing populations (Herm, 2008; European Commission, 2011). Thus, we can see that countries are continually subject to new influences and change, and these will be reflected in the lifestyles of young children who will come into contact with new and different languages, foods, customs and traditions – sometimes experiencing a broad array of distinctive opportunities, sometimes a merging and mixing of differing ways of living.

Contemporary research suggests that 'transnational' children cope well with displacement and describe a sense of belonging to both old and new communities through the people they associate with each location. In a study of British-born Bangladeshi children, Mand (2010) found that although their parents and grandparents talked about Bangladesh as 'home' and the UK as 'away from home' the children saw themselves as having two homes: one bounded by the everyday activities of immediate family, school and homework; and one that was freer and more exciting, if rather hot. The degree of attachment to the new location may depend on the reasons for moving away. In Bak and Von Brömssen's (2010) study of a Swedish suburb, the refugee children that they interviewed described a sense of belonging to both their 'home' and their 'homeland' but the term 'home' described Sweden. Despite this sense of belonging to their new communities, they nevertheless saw themselves as 'other', collectively forming an immigrant subgroup among their Swedish peers, despite their differing ethnicities.

On a global scale, geographical diversity is mediated by long-term historical developments (see Chapter 4). Distinctive patterns of childhood are modified through new cultural associations – notably through the exploration and migration consequent upon the European colonisation of the Americas, Indies and African nations in the eighteenth and nineteenth centuries; through refugee movements following natural disasters, wars and periods of civil unrest; and more recently through the development of transnational industrial and retail chains and the impact of global communications. Normatively, it is the pressure to adopt Westernised standards that threatens indigenous lifestyles, as directly imported equipment and ideas are rarely sustainable in less-developed contexts.

Local geographies

At more local levels, there is a growing interest in the geographies of childhood with researchers consulting children about their likes and dislikes and involving them in the planning of their own recreational space, echoing Montessori's introduction of child-sized furniture into her *casa dei bambini* in the early twentieth century that was designed to enable the child to 'command his movements' (Montessori, 1965 [1912]: 84). Currently, researchers are seeking the children's perspectives on the world around them, seeking to provide opportunities for exploration and problem solving in the artificial environments of the day nursery, primary school, and public park (see Holloway and Valentine, 2000; Valentine, 2001; Holt, 2011, below). Rasmussen (2004) explains how children's lives are increasingly prescribed by an 'institutionalized triangle' of home, school and recreational facility. Children's activities in urban areas are restricted to areas designed by adults as 'places for children'. Presenting an overview of children's use of playground space, Factor (2004: 145) shows that children inventively adapt and appropriate materials and spaces to suit their imaginative purposes, rather than using what is offered to them in predictable ways. This endorses Moore's view that we need a better understanding of children's use of space before we write policies for play and invest in new facilities. We need to know 'what parts of the environment children actually use, and why' (Moore, 1986: xvi).

Summary

Chapter 2 has demonstrated how expressions of human diversity mask fundamental similarities and discussed how, over the centuries, humans have adapted to fill specific eco-cultural niches. It has also tried to counteract the tendency to see the Western view of childhood as dominant, offering case studies from non-Western cultures to demonstrate the variety of children's experiences. If you look around you, there will be families who can offer you a wealth of information about different cultures, countries and practices to develop your ideas further to the benefit of your entire community.

The chapter reminded us that diversity can be recognised at a range of levels. On the one hand we see differences with global and temporal significance. On the other, and particularly when we are considering children's lives, the local and specific can be paramount. For a young child unused to grass or sand, the edge of the picnic mat can constitute an inviolable geographical boundary. Children's perspectives develop from physical and social stimuli that adults may not even notice unless they pay careful attention. They see the world through a different lens.

Points for reflection

- Think back to your own childhood and briefly outline the geographical features of your local area. How did these shape your experiences as a child?
- For the UK, or another country with which you are familiar, consider how urban and rural childhoods differ.
- Choose a country with which you are unfamiliar and use the internet to find out about childhood in that locality. If you cannot find articles specifically about childhood, you may need to build up your own picture from information about the geography and culture of the country you have chosen.

Further reading

Oppenheimer, S. (2004) *Out of Eden: The Peopling of the World.* London: Constable and Robinson.
An alternative to Sykes (2001) account of the discovery of our shared genetic inheritance.

Scanlon, T., Scanlon, F. and Lamarao, M.L.N. (1993) 'Working with street children', *Development in Practice*, 3(1): 16–26.
A good overview to read with the key referenced articles: Panter-Brick (2002) and Scanlon et al. (1998).

Holloway, S. and Valentine, G. (2000) *Children's Geographies: Playing, Living, Learning.* Abingdon: Routledge.
Holt, L. (2011) *Geographies of Children, Youth and Families: An International Perspective.* Abingdon: Routledge.
Valentine, G. (2001) *Social Geographies: Space and Society.* Harlow: Prentice Hall.
These three books provide international and localised perspectives on the geographies of childhood.

Lancy, D.F. (2008) *The Anthropology of Childhood: Cherubs, Chattels, Changelings.* Cambridge: Cambridge University Press.
Montgomery, H. (2009) *An Introduction to Childhood: Anthropological Perspectives on Children's Lives.* Chichester: Wiley-Blackwell.
Morrison, H. (2012) *The Global History of Childhood: A Reader.* Abingdon: Routledge.
These three books provide expert overviews of the broader global and anthropological contexts.

Websites

www.rootsforreal.com/migrations_en.php
Maps the stages of human migration.

https://genographic.nationalgeographic.com
Explains genetic tracing and maps migration routes.

http://epp.eurostat.ec.europa.eu/portal/page/portal/statistics/themes
Up-to-date data for Europe.

www.migrationobservatory.ox.ac.uk
Up-to-date information on migration trends.

www.usgs.gov
US Geological Survey offers an extensive range of resources and world maps.

www.cia.gov/library/publications/the-world-factbook/index.html
Up-to-date global data.

To gain *free* access to selected SAGE journal articles related to key topics in this chapter, visit: www.sagepub.co.uk/hazelrwright.

CHAPTER 3

HISTORICAL PERSPECTIVES

Overview

This chapter sketches a broadly chronological treatment of distinctive events affecting children and the historical contexts in which children have lived. It draws upon documentary evidence and contemporary, sometimes autobiographical, accounts to create a 'feel' for real childhoods.

The chapter chooses themes within three key time frames:

- *early times*: Greek and Roman civilisations; the Early (fifth to fifteenth century) and late Middle Ages (fifteenth century onwards)
- *changing times*: colonisation of the New World; Industrial Revolution; Victorian society
- *recent times*: twentieth century (emigrants and evacuees); the post-war welfare state.

The emphasis is Anglocentric, referring to Scotland, Ireland and Wales, and Britain's role in international affairs, when relevant. This chapter leaves discussion of contemporary childhoods to Chapter 9.

Little is known about children and childhood before historical records began. Surviving artefacts and archaeological remains offer a glimpse of children's lives and sometimes in early records there is incidental mention of individual children, but there is rarely sufficient information for us to fully understand what it meant to be a child in a particular society. Interpreting the historical evidence when it does exist is a specialist task so this chapter draws on respected secondary sources and expert overviews, and limits the discussion to those early cultures that directly underpin Western society rather than attempting to embrace narratives from further afield. It outlines key events that changed society and cumulatively influenced the nature of childhood but not immediately the lives of individual children. This is a limited vision and we should be mindful of the powerful societies that existed elsewhere – the Mayan and Inca traditions, Mesopotamian and Egyptian cultures, and the Indian, Chinese and other Oriental dynasties.

Early times

Greek and Roman civilisations

Greek society was prized for its democratic organisation, evident from around 600 BCE to 322 BCE. By 400 BCE, the time of Aristotle, Greece was a collection of some 1,500 separate cities (*poleis*) bordering the Mediterranean Sea, each with its individual culture. For example, Athens was renowned for its culture; Sparta for its martial arts.

Infant mortality was common so babies were not named immediately. There were two ceremonies to welcome wanted babies into the household: one took place between five and seven days after birth and one at ten days old. Physical perfection was important and unwanted babies (often female) were exposed to die. Athenian babies were tightly swaddled to straighten their limbs but Spartan infants were left unbound (Golden, 1990).

Gendered distinction underpinned Greek society. Houses included male and female quarters and children under seven lived with their mothers, enabling strong sibling bonds. Children contributed to household tasks, helping to prepare food, running errands, and in the case of girls, caring for younger children (ibid).

In Athens, play was encouraged and there is archaeological evidence that the children possessed a range of universal children's toys – rattles, dolls, balls, tops, yo-yos, stilts, hoops, board games, as well as miniature clay household wares. Documentary and visual evidence suggests, too, that children played hopscotch, hide-and-seek, blind man's buff, marbles (often with walnuts), a ball game approximating to hockey, circle games to songs and rhymes, in addition to taking part in organised sports, wrestling, running, jumping, discus and javelin (Andreu-Cabrera et al., 2010). Girls stayed with their mothers until puberty, marking adulthood by offering their childhood possessions to the goddess, Artemis, at 15 when they were entitled to marry. Occasionally they took part in festivals and other rituals but on marriage they were passed to the control of the husband, and a largely domestic existence. Boys socialised with the men after infancy, rarely married before 30, and were encouraged to learn a trade. Wealthier boys went to school first, learning grammar, athletics, music and sometimes drawing skills (Golden, 1990) from the age of seven onwards. In contrast, all Spartan children were bred to be strong. Boys and girls were underfed and sent out to play barefoot in minimal clothing to learn to withstand hunger and cold (Hartley, 1934). Children of both sexes practised the martial arts and took part in competitive sports, achieving citizen status only if physically fit. Boys passed into the care of the state magistrates at seven, entered training barracks at 12 (Rawson, 2003), and joined men's clubs (*Syssitia*) at 16 (Hartley, 1934).

Between 133 and 33 BCE, Rome evolved from democracy to empire, dominating Mediterranean society, and Greece from 146 BCE. Roman society centred on the family with mother, father and child forming a strong and affectionate triad at the heart of an extended household. Roman law protected the rights of all minors whether legitimate, illegitimate or slave, appointing a guardian to stand in lieu of a deceased father. Infant mortality rates were high and siblings commonly widely spaced so parents often fostered, adopted or housed orphan children, treating them almost as additional offspring. Rome was a very sociable city with little distinction between public and private spaces. Women managed the household, and women and children took part in social events. In poorer areas, children and adults socialised on the streets but the wealthy freely entertained in their villas, encouraging a 'mingling' of slaves, family and members of the community. Children also took part in the many rituals, festivals and contests that marked the Roman calendar (Rawson, 2003).

Roman families delayed closely bonding with babies until survival was assured. Parents could choose whether to raise or expose a baby and the wealthy employed wet nurses to suckle infants. Babies that survived a year gained entitlements but public mourning only began at three, reaching full rites at ten, yet betrothal was possible at seven and marriage at 12. Female children were important to Roman parents, the wealthy either educated girls alongside their brothers or tutored them in the home. Slaves accompanied children to school, carrying their satchels and overseeing their studies, suggesting that many slaves became educated, at least alongside their charges. Following Greek practices, a liberal education based on grammar, music and literature was taught orally (ibid, 2003). Good manners were paramount and punishment (flogging and ritual humiliation) could be severe. School started early but children also had time to celebrate birthdays, attend public entertainments and to play at home with toys, games and with their numerous pets – lap dogs, snakes, many types of bird, hares, weasels, and sometimes Barbary apes and monkeys (Lazenby, 1949).

Predictably, the lives of children of the working classes were harder. On entering puberty children might be apprenticed, learning to become builders, coppersmiths, nail-makers, weavers or even to play a musical instrument or to scribe using shorthand. The children of slaves might also be encouraged to learn useful skills, but in the countryside, many were confined to working on the land (Laurence, 2005). However, Roman society showed a sensitivity to child development, making most decisions conditional on a child being ready to take on a more adult role (Rawson, 2003).

Roman settlement of Britain took place between 55 and 43 CE continuing until 425 CE. During this period, Britain underwent extensive modernisation. Roads, baths, villas and towns were built with local labour at local expense, largely to benefit the occupying troops who lived alongside the indigenous population, overlaying Roman culture on existing practices and sometimes taking British wives. The military and bureaucratic forces relied upon local people to rule the land on their behalf, promising power and protection to those who proved loyal servants (Wallace-Hadrill, 2011). Thus, the wealthier and more influential Britons would have observed and taken up Roman practices towards children, while those in outlying districts maintained their own traditions.

The early Middle Ages (fifth to fifteenth century)

The Anglo-Saxons and Viking period (fifth century to the 1066 Norman conquest) was known as the 'Dark Ages' for two reasons: societal decline after the Roman withdrawal; and scarcity of material evidence. After 1066, under the Normans, Plantagenets and the Houses of York and Lancaster, both society and record keeping advanced significantly.

Documentary and archaeological evidence (particularly the survival to adulthood of children with deformities) demonstrates that children were nurtured in Anglo-Saxon England, their rights protected by legislation (Crawford, 1999). Young children were swaddled and breastfed and a rise in mortality rates around three or four years is associated with weaning to solid food (bringing dysentery and malnutrition) and mobility (unsupervised play was common up to eight years old). Early Saxon families lived in isolated farmsteads and several nuclear families lived alongside each other, farming the land. At around eight, older children were customarily sent to live in another household, a practice that enabled them to learn new skills and gain the patronage of additional adults, important in a society where average life expectancy was as low as 30. Girls learned weaving and domestic skills. In the homes of the wealthier thanes, male children learned to ride and to handle weapons. Some children entered monasteries, receiving shelter and a basic education, but not necessarily making a commitment to a lifelong vocation. Adulthood began around 10 or 12 (ibid) but there is evidence that marriage and childbearing were often delayed until later when pregnancy was safer for the woman. Under Christianity (sixth century onwards) bigamy was discouraged and the rights and responsibilities of family members more clearly stated.

Between the tenth and thirteenth centuries, England underwent an agrarian revolution. Forests were cleared, cultivation techniques improved and lifestyles became more settled. European population doubled in this period (from around 22.6 to 54.4 million) and an alternative non-agrarian lifestyle became possible, leading to the growth of market towns (Heywood, 2001: 21). England developed an important wool trade. In the countryside Lords, granted lands by the King, built stone manor houses and took on domestic servants, offering an alternative livelihood to farming. However, this prosperity was interrupted when the Black Death (the plague) swept across Europe with major English epidemics in 1348–49 and 1360–62 (Orme, 2001b: 107). The first epidemic wiped out 50 per cent of the population, the second epidemic was particularly 'a pestilence of children' (Downer, 1972: 222-23; in Orme 2001b: 107), perhaps as they were too young to have gained any immunity from the earlier plague.

Disputes between urban artisans and rural landowners over the apprenticeship system imply that the shortage of youngsters led to their becoming more valued. Seven-year apprenticeships had become common in the towns. Pauper children, lacking parental support, often entered an agreement at around seven, but children with a family able to nurture them signed indentures around 12 year of age (Heywood, 2001). However, landowners sought to keep labourers within the feudal agricultural system. Despite the Peasants Revolt in 1388, landowners procured the limitation of apprenticeship to those with property rights in 1406, thereby continuing to control the livelihoods of the rural poor (Orme, 2001b).

Medieval historian, Barbara Hanawalt (1977: 3), drew attention to an important source of data on family life and childhood for the fourteenth and fifteenth centuries. Coroners' records, despite their focus on untimely deaths, are crowded with incidental comments about society. The coroners' 'rolls' revealed children under four to be most at risk as they were unable to care for themselves. The number of accidents involving animals suggests that both small children and domestic animals were left unsupervised. Burning was the most common cause of death. Children left in cots by the hearth were killed or injured when hens or pigs scattered glowing embers or knocked their cots over. Outdoors children fell into fires, wells, ponds and ditches, sometimes playing with other children, sometimes knocked over by domestic animals. From the age of eight, children were still living at home but were learning adult roles, as injuries mainly related to the misuse of tools and cooking equipment. The coroners' rolls identify 12 as the legal age of responsibility.

These records offer incidental insights into lifestyle. They reveal that, generally, peasant families lived in 'wattle and daub' houses but by the end of the fourteenth century houses were more substantial, featuring internal ovens and wells and protected by surrounding walls and ditches. Women and men shared some tasks but in both urban and rural areas men did the heavy and dangerous work, women the rest. The Bedfordshire rolls refer to 25 families and show that nuclear and extended families were equally common and family size was generally small – probably as a result of high infant mortality rates. As now, urban areas were more mobile and socially mixed: the London and Oxford rolls included references to concubines and transitional family relationships.

Such insights are confirmed and embellished by other records. Gordon's (1991) account of miracles attributable to saints and martyrs between 1170 and 1500 describes common accidents and their contexts but also the prayers and cures that restored children to health. Gordon reports some 358 recoveries from drownings, contusions, lacerations, choking and other incidents in graphic detail. Here, too, animals caused mayhem. In one account, a pig pushed a boy into a harbour nearly causing him to drown (ibid: 159).

Orme's research (Orme, 2001a) into medieval childhoods shows that, over the ages, toys and games varied, mainly in their degree of sophistication. The activities he reports would be instantly recognisable to the contemporary parent but, as in ancient Greece and Rome, weaponry and war play had a more serious intent.

The late Middle Ages

From the late fifteenth through to the sixteenth and seventeenth centuries (the time of the Tudors, Stuarts and the first Hanoverians, Georges I, II, III) there is a significant increase in documentation, but generalised histories rarely address childhood directly. In Europe, the period 1650 to 1800 marked a dramatic 'rebirth' of classical art, literature and architecture – the *Renaissance* – made possible by growing affluence and contact with other cultures. The late Middle Ages is characterised by merchant traders exploring the 'foreign' seas, and nationally, by the development of an infrastructure to support the new economy – the ports and cities, banks and financial institutions needed to enable the British Isles to change from a feudal structure with its wealth in land and property to a commercial nation with the facility to store wealth and use it to generate new profits. Henry VIII's repeal of the Usury Laws in 1546 enabled money-lenders to charge interest and this played a vital role in creating a trading nation, as did the creation of the Bank of England in 1694 (BBHS, 2010).

The English Reformation, the conversion from a Catholic to a Protestant society, was part of this new commercialism achieved through the Act of Supremacy of 1534. Political independence led to the dissolution of the monasteries in 1536, and while this benefited the King financially, it negatively affected local communities, for the 'open' religious orders had traditionally cared for the sick and poor, including the children, and provided a rudimentary education for the local male population. Slowly, the state took on these powers, providing alms-houses for the 'deserving poor' (those genuinely unable to work) through the Elizabethan Poor Laws of 1598 and 1601 (Walsh et al.,

2000: 119). England's population more than doubled to five million between 1500 and 1651. The poor stayed poor but those born into the gentry would have enjoyed better accommodation, food and clothes (Black, 2012).

Nominal Protestantism satisfied neither Presbyterian Scots nor Catholic Irish so England faced unrest within the British Isles as well as fighting the Catholic French and Spanish states, and later the Dutch Protestants. Henry VIII's multiple marriages left several offspring but no dominant male heir. This presented further opportunities for challenges to the Crown, culminating in the 'English Revolution' and the beheading of Charles I in 1625. During the Interregnum, a Puritan 'protectorate' headed by Oliver Cromwell ruled England but monarchy was restored in 1660. Wales united with England in 1536, Scotland not until 1707 despite James VI of Scotland being James I of England for a time (1603–25). Britain only truly became Protestant when the Glorious Revolution of 1688 put William of Orange on the throne and ended the Jacobite rebellions (Kearney, 2012).

Together these religious, political and economic changes marked the end of feudal society. The people of England were freed from the land but needed to find new ways to earn a living: in trade, in transportation, in coal and lead mining, and salt panning. By 1665, a quarter of the English population was urban, and by 1700, between 500,000 and 600,000 lived in London (Black, 2012). For children, this presented both new opportunities and new threats as traditional expectations were overturned. The period 1650 to 1800, marked by dramatic changes in science, philosophy and politics, is commonly known as the 'Age of Enlightenment' or 'Reason'.

Changing times

Colonisation of the New World

In addition to fighting to control Europe, the coastal nations – Portuguese, Spanish, French, Dutch and English – increasingly focused on the wider world. Marco Polo's journey to Cathay in the thirteenth century triggered interest in Chinese and Islamic goods, and European kings commissioned seamen to search for new routes to the East, incidentally discovering 'newfoundland' in the Americas. In 1487 Bartolomeu Dias explored the Indian Ocean, in 1488 Vasco da Gama reached India. Portuguese and Spanish explorers conquered South America in the 1500s, while the French, English, Dutch and Spanish claimed lands on the North American continent (Lucas, 1991).

Portuguese seamen began shipping slaves from Northern Mauritania in the 1440s and the shipping of Africans to the Americas was officially sanctioned in 1516 (Walvin, 2007). By 1562 English traders were legitimately involved, shortly followed by the Dutch and French. The British Royal African

Company was granted a charter in 1672. In the late eighteenth century, at the peak of the slave trade, Europeans transported some 80,000 Africans to the New World each year (Hochschild, 2005). Slave traders rounded up native Africans and incarcerated them in dungeon fortresses on the African coast (see websites listed at the end of the chapter). They were stripped, inspected, branded and imprisoned for 10 to 15 days awaiting calm seas. Families were divided by gender, children imprisoned separately or with the female slaves. Wearing only a loin cloth, male slaves were shackled at the neck and feet and packed into the hulls of large ships for transportation, fed once a day on water and half a bowl of uncooked corn flower or millet, possibly beans (Walvin, 2007). The transatlantic journey took between one and two months. Only occasionally, in fine weather, were small groups allowed on deck to exercise as sailors feared uprisings. Women and children, possibly fared better, sometimes remaining unchained as perceived to be less of a threat but this left them at risk of other abuses. Conditions in the holds were insanitary, messing out infrequent and the 'necessary tubs' overflowing. The severely ill vomited and defecated where they lay on wooden shelves that served as bunks. One contemporary account (Newton, 1788; cited in Walvin, 2007) estimated that about a quarter of slaves died in transit and many others died within a year of arrival. In the 1800s, English Quaker reformers sought abolition. The transatlantic slave trade was abolished in 1807 but not before many generations of black children had grown up to be forced labourers on New World plantations. Young adults were most commonly sold so children often lost their parents at a young age, depending for survival on 'informal kin' (Schermerhorn, 2009). As they reached maturity, they were sold, in turn, into a life of hard labour, further fragmenting the generational family. Slavery itself was not finally outlawed in Britain until 1838 and as late as 1888 in Brazil (Walvin, 2007).

The populating of Australia by Europeans took a rather different form. From an Anglocentric perspective it is often presented as a 'story of journeys and arrivals' (Macintyre, 2009: 3). The country was first discovered around 1601. By 1770, when James Cook claimed the east coast on behalf of the English government, some 54 European ships had visited Australia to trade with the indigenous people. Governor Philip was sent to Botany Bay to found the first British (Australian) colony in 1788. Australia, like Africa, was treated as a British resource, a penal colony between 1788 and 1823, a repository for British emigrants for more than a century.

At its height in the 1850s, the British Empire comprised Canada, most of Australasia, India, significant southern and coastal states in Africa, and important island groups, particularly in the Caribbean and Philippines. Colonial government was imposed on native people, overriding their beliefs and customs, taking over their lands and often dictating how they lived and worked. Yet, often the colonisers lacked the capital to develop countries and contemporary historians believe that the effects of the British Empire were exaggerated. Some governors were despotic, some ruled paternalistically, but other places were 'so little touched by the system that they could barely have been aware that they were colonies at all' (Porter, 2012: 23). Colonisers sought to exploit raw materials and local labour and often this resulted in hardship: enforced migration and urbanisation; the dislocation of families; and religious conversion, perhaps alongside the provision of a rudimentary education.

Colonial practices enforced inequality and later generations challenged the view that colonisation was a legitimate civilising process. Some children grew up accustomed to servitude but others were motivated to seek redress, through political or more aggressive means. The term 'postcolonialism' is an academic label that loosely describes a set of critical approaches that use 'empirical detail' and 'theoretical precision' to unsettle accepted interpretations of historical and cultural processes, seeking an end to human exploitation and patterns stemming from European domination of the globe (Schwarz and Ray, 2005: 5).

The Industrial Revolution (1760–1830)

Around 1760 technological advances enabled mechanisation of British manufacturing, particularly the textile industry. Water-powered machinery encouraged a concentration of production in mills in the upland areas of northern England and Scotland. Boulton and Watts' modification of the steam engine (enabling it to run continuously) made possible the factory system, producing goods for the domestic, colonial and other European markets. Factories needed workers and many owners sought to employ children, as they were small and nimble and could pass beneath and between machines to clean or oil parts, repair breakages or tidy up waste. Easily dominated by adults, children were routinely harshly disciplined and forced to work long hours – often 15 or 16 a day – for very little pay (Black, 2012). Cold water was thrown at children who fell asleep, boys who fell behind were whipped and girls who chatted to lads had their heads shaved (Armley Mills, 2012). Sue Wilkes (2011) offers an extensive account of children's employment in the industrial age that includes reformer Richard Oastler's denunciation of 'Yorkshire Slavery' in the Leeds Mercury of 16 October 1830 and sets local labour patterns within a national political framework.

The growth of cities caused unemployment in rural areas. For example, in Bradford alone, over 17,000 looms had displaced thousands of rural hand-loom weavers by 1850 (Black, 2012: 204). The Enclosure Acts of 1801, 1836 and 1845, the artificial inflation of grain prices due to the 1815 and 1846 Corn Laws, and restrictions on imports, exacerbated problems. Hunger and injustice forced families to move to the towns to protest and demand electoral reform. This led to a gradual extension of the workingman's right to vote but no attempt was made to enfranchise women (Cunningham, 2006).

Victorian society (1837–1901)

By Victorian times, the divide between rich and poor was marked. Between 1801 and 1901 Britain's population rose from 11 to 37 million, and by 1850, half of these were urban dwellers. Wrigley and Schofield (1981, in Cunningham, 2006: 161) claim that for every 1,000 adults over 25 there were 1,120 children under 14 by 1826. As a consequence society became very conscious of children, their needs and contribution. Children of the upper and middle classes lived 'protected' lives cared for by nannies and governesses but poorer children were heavily exploited (Cunningham, 2006: 140). Many worked long hours in factories, others swept chimneys or ran errands. When all else failed they became pickpockets and scavengers. Apart from a brief period in the early 1830s when progressive parents tried to dress girls and boys alike in long white trousers and knee-length dresses, Victorian society was also clearly divided on gender lines with boys from wealthy families sent away to school at seven and girls kept safe within the family, sequestered from newspapers and political debate but learning to paint, sing, sew and play the piano in preparation for marriage (Arnot et al., 1999).

As cities grew, living conditions deteriorated and disease spread. A cholera outbreak in 1830 probably killed 31,000 in Britain (Morgan, 2010: 499) and led to the temporary creation of Boards of Health and a Poor Law Amendment Act (1834) that created a national policy for poor relief – the local workhouses, sometimes described as 'prisons for the poor'. An 'inquiry' into sanitary conditions in 1842 showed need for reform, and in 1854 Medical Officers of Health were appointed to oversee schemes for drainage, water and slum clearance. Reformers, Ashley-Cooper (later Lord Shaftesbury) and Michael Sadler, campaigned for children's rights. The 'Ten-Hour Movement', sought to reduce the working day for children under 16 and in 1831 a 12-hour limit for those under 18 was achieved. The 1833 Factory Act applied this limit to both cotton and woollen industries and established an (inadequate) enforcement inspectorate. It also set the minimum age for work at nine years of age and introduced an element of compulsory schooling. In 1844 a further Factories Act limited work hours for children under 13 to 6.5 hours, but imposed an additional three hours of schooling that left little time to play. Work hours for women and 13- to 18-year-olds were set at 12 hours and in 1867 these limits were applied to other factories employing more than 50 people. Acts in 1878, 1891, and 1895 made further improvements, and after 1891, children under 11 could no longer work in factories (Parliament.UK, 2014).

Legislation was also passed to protect children who worked in mines, controlling the air vents or pulling the coal carts in underground tunnels in the dark, often nearly naked to withstand the heat and humidity. The Mines and Collieries Bill (1842) prohibited all underground work for women and girls, and for boys under 10; a restriction raised to 12 in 1860. In 1834 the Chimney Sweeps Act outlawed the apprenticing of any child under 10 and this was raised to 16 in 1840. Thus, parliament slowly started to reform society in the nineteenth century (Parliament.UK, 2014). However, conditions in cities remained poor and this 'social murder' is described in detail in Engel's (1993 [1845]: 38) account of Victorian Manchester in 1842 to 1844, which he held to be 'true of all great towns'.

Writing *London Labour and the London Poor* in 1861, Henry Mayhew describes how children 'have been flung into the streets through neglect, through viciousness, or as outcasts from utter destitution' (Mayhew, 1861: 468). He describes small groups of boys as 'anybody's children' (ibid: 470) vending fruit and nuts even as they distract themselves by playing marbles and gambling with halfpennies. Mayhew lists a broad array of goods (natural or manufactured) that children can peddle, pointing out that boys can also work (as mud-larks, water-jacks, tumblers and street musicians, errand boys, porters and shoe-blacks) while girls can only sell goods or 'fall into a course of prostitution' (ibid: 469). Street children are clothed in rags 'worn by the children as long as they will hold, or can be tied or pinned together' (ibid: 476). Not surprisingly, the children lack morality, showing 'a willingness to cheat, or take advantage, which is hardly disguised' (ibid: 478). Mayhew describes how street children live on boiled or batter 'pudding', 'baked tatur' and occasionally whelks, eels and oysters bought from street vendors, whereas poor children living in the family survive on tea, bread and maybe butter, and perhaps bacon or stewed mutton on a Sunday (ibid: 476).

Mayhew estimates that street children in London alone numbered 'some thousands' (ibid: 479) and claims that 'steps ought most unquestionably to be taken to palliate the evils and miseries I have pointed out, even if a positive remedy be indeed impossible'. Much of the work, however, was left to individual campaigners. The Society for the Suppression of Juvenile Vagrancy (later the Children's Friend Society) was set up in 1808, and in 1818 a shoemaker, John Pounds, began teaching poor children in 'ragged schools'. In 1870, Thomas Barnardo opened his first children's home (Barnardo's, 2012), and in 1881 Edward Rudolf founded the 'Waifs and Strays Society', a Church of England venture that still functions as The Children's Society. Lord Shaftesbury lent support, helping, in 1884, to establish both the Ragged Schools Union and the London (now National) Society for the Prevention of Cruelty to Children (NSPCC). The NSPCC successfully campaigned for the 1889 Children's Charter that allowed state intervention when domestic abuse was suspected (NSPCC, 2012). From 1894, the Salvation Army, too, established homes for girls and boys in Britain and its overseas dominions (Cunningham, 2006).

Recent times

The twentieth century

Sending 'troublesome' children abroad was a little publicised, negative consequence of Empire. From the seventeenth century, teenage offenders were
sent to work in the American colonies. Between 1868 and 1925 around
80,000 children were sent to Canada to work on the land or enter domestic
service (Cunningham, 2006: 166; Parr, 1980), and to Australia in the 1830s
and 1840s. To organisers, the step from 'rescuing' children from the streets,
to setting up children's homes, then farm colonies, then colonies overseas
was logical. For the emigrating children, the outcomes were less satisfactory,
their treatment 'invisible' until the late 1980s when individuals seeking to
find their British family attracted the attention of Nottingham social worker,
Margaret Humphrey's, who later co-founded the Child Migrants Trust. The
children's often harrowing stories are now well-publicised. Bean and Melville (1989) published a book and documentary, *Lost Children of the Empire,*
and Humphreys herself offers a chronological account later filmed as
Oranges and Sunshine (1994). More recently (2010), a joint venture between
the Australian National Maritime Museum and National Museums Liverpool
created an online resource, *On Their Own: Britain's Child Migrants* (see the
websites listed at the end of the chapter), which directly reports the children's experiences. Many were injured, others abused, most misled, but this
is less evident in a later account, *New Lives for Old*, emanating from the
National Archives (Kershaw and Sacks, 2008).

Some 150,000 children placed in 'care' were sent to Commonwealth countries between 1920 and 1967. Children from 3 to 14 were shipped abroad in
groups of about 300, without passports or birth certificates and often wrongly
informed that they were orphans (Child Migrants Trust, 2012). On the museums' website, one of the children, L.P. Welsh, describes how children were
measured for clothes, inoculated and told that in Australia they would be able
to ride horses to school and chase kangaroos. The children were kitted out in
smart 'school' uniforms (blazers, ties and leather shoes) and their departure was
celebrated with dockside tea parties attended by public officials, even royalty.
On arrival, the story was somewhat different. The uniforms were exchanged
for khaki work outfits and children left without shoes or underwear. From the
age of seven, they were put to work as labourers on farms and in a construction industry that lacked basic safety measures. In the 'schools', children were
poorly fed. They ate from metal plates and mugs like convicts, and often their
porridge and mutton crawled with weevils and maggots. The website reports
that when a British mother, a Mrs Bayliff, suggested that her four boys return
home her letters were intercepted, leaving her children to assume that she had
forgotten about them – an action that belies any suggestion of child-centred

motives. Generally, as adults, the immigrants focus on the positive aspects of their new lives but there are many comments that reveal the distress caused by statelessness.

Only in the twenty-first century did the British government acknowledge these events. The Prime Minister made a public apology in 2010 (BBC News, 24 February). Yet the British Broadcasting Corporation (BBC) had denounced these practices as 'Britain's most shameful secret' in 1999 (BBC News, 19 May).

Within Britain, many children suffered hardship, too. In 1900 their legal status was still that of a 'little' adult: they were allowed to smoke and drink and could still be sent to an adult prison (Humphries et al., 1988), a situation ameliorated by the 1908 Children Act, which sought to make parents responsible for their children and to treat juveniles separately from adults (Hendrick, 1994). In 1900, many lived in terraced houses in towns and cities with few facilities. In *The Classic Slum*, Roberts (1971) describes life in Salford prior to the First World War as 'pathetically modest' with families buying their clothes by weekly instalment, and 'scrimping' and 'saving' to achieve a modicum of comfort and avoid shame. A scrap of carpet or oil-cloth was essential to make the home look lived in, net curtains were highly visible so must be in good repair. Private items, bed linen and underclothes, had to be fit to hang outside to dry after washing. Respectability and cleanliness were so important that families unable to afford 'Sunday best' stayed indoors on the Sabbath. Yet cleanliness was costly: to have a cast-iron bath in 1910 merited an additional shilling on the weekly rent, a luxury when most used a basin and ewer, and the 'privy' (toilet) was outside. Schooling was compulsory until 12 but grossly inadequate. Roberts (ibid) describes four classrooms for 450 children, one without desks even though writing was taught in it. Lighting was from open gas jets, children regularly scavenged the rubbish pit, and privies were left door-less to discourage 'certain practices'.

In contrast, an account of a provincial middle-class home describes the family attending church regularly, keeping a cook and housemaid, employing people to do the washing and gardening, and a governess for the son before he went to school. This family took an annual seaside holiday, had the leisure to read the classics, and a carefully regulated social life, playing golf and tennis, and belonging to clubs for this purpose. The lady of the house would pay and receive calls on 'at home' days. The child was brought up to have exemplary manners and was allowed to invite children for tea if they came from 'a home like ours' (Life of Geoffrey Bradley, in Thompson, 1981).

The First World War disrupted these patterns and an estimated 360,000 children were left fatherless. For his book, *The Quick and The Dead,* Van Emden interviewed adults who lost parents during the First World War. A few of the accounts are summarised below, and clearly reveal the consequent hardships.

- Clare Middleton explains how the school granted permission for her to stay home until her youngest sister went to school so that her mother could work to keep the family, and how she took cleaning jobs, scrubbing floors and stairs for two shillings a time, the washing soda burning into her skin.
- George Musgrave describes wearing his father's cut-down trousers to school and his feelings of intense isolation as he tried to conceal his poverty from his peers.
- Charles Chilton describes living with his grandmother from the age of seven when his mother died, sharing the back kitchen with two uncles, eight people in a four-room house. When Ministry officials called periodically to check on his welfare, the family pretended he slept in one of the bedrooms for fear of losing his father's pension (Van Emden, 2011).

During the Great Depression between the wars, many children lived in serious poverty as parents were unemployed. Medical treatment was costly and although penicillin was invented in 1929 it was not commercially available. Michael and Janet Wood draw attention to the hazards of urban life and the limited resources available to support families on their website (Wood and Wood, 1995). They describe the life of a relative, Victor Holmes, growing up in Manchester, capturing the isolation of illness for the lower-class child when hospital visiting hours were rigid, working hours long and public transport expensive or non-existent.

The Second World War meant that many more children prematurely lost their fathers, and during the Blitz, their homes and other family members, too. The government announced plans in July 1939 to evacuate some three million school children from London, ports and industrial conurbations. Children under the age of five could be evacuated if accompanied by their mothers or 'some other responsible person' (Lord Privy Seal's Office, 1939). The scheme was voluntary and thousands were evacuated to rural areas but returned home when bombing did not start immediately (Starns, 2012). This created major problems for the Ministries of Education and Health as teachers had been evacuated with pupils and school buildings requisitioned for civil defence training, and resources were inadequate to immunise children when diphtheria broke out in 1941. Many children received only limited home schooling, spending their time helping with the war effort alongside elder siblings who were legitimately in cadet schemes. However, children who stayed with their families suffered less long-term emotional, mental and physical damage than those who were evacuated. They were healthier, despite limited diets, and avoided contracting tuberculosis, a common problem for evacuated children unaccustomed to drinking unpasteurised cows' milk (ibid).

For some children, evacuation was not an option. Southern cities, Bristol and Plymouth, had made no plans as the government had not anticipated the rapid German invasion of France. To avoid heavy bombing, the inhabitants trudged into the surrounding countryside to 'camp out' at night. A Bristol resident, aged six when war broke out, describes how his family stayed in the city but he always slept fully clothed 'because you never knew when the bombs might come' (ibid: 118). He lived on a diet of mainly bread, dripping and dried egg but was never ill even though he had to repair holes in his shoes with cardboard. He claims that he was rarely frightened as he was always with his mother or grandmother and they stayed calm whatever happened. Despite the bombs, his childhood story resounds with 'normal' childhood experiences: playing in the street with yo-yos, marbles, conkers and jacks; playing rounders with an old tennis racket; going to the cinema or train spotting. Spending his sweet coupons, he was entertained by the 'little mice running round amongst the sweets in the shop window' (Starns, 2012: 118).

Concerns for younger children focused around the rapid expansion of unregulated nurseries. Yet, disregarding this, a Member of Parliament suggested that 50 children could be allocated to every 40 places to compensate for casualties and sickness. In five months in 1942, functioning London nurseries increased from 25 to 129 (schemes approved from 42 to 71 more) (HoC, 1942). Mostly established to serve specific factories, the Civil Defence or National Fire Service, they were largely collective babysitting services, grouping children together regardless of age and managed by untrained staff. Despite the labour shortage, there was no compulsion for mothers of children under five years of age to work. On the contrary, the Ministry of Health strongly advocated that mothers of children under two years of age should be full-time carers. However, many women wanted to contribute to the war effort, and for some, work was a financial necessity (Starns, 2012).

The post-war welfare state

Aiming to tackle want, disease, ignorance, squalor and idleness, the radical Beveridge Report (1942) proposed a National Health Service, Family Allowances and a National Insurance scheme. The 1944 Butler Education Act set out to reform educational systems, too (see Chapter 8). By 1944, children enjoyed free school meals and milk, and babies free fruit juice. Some nursery provision existed to care for children under five, and widespread vaccination and health education programmes had controlled many contagious diseases. However, the brutalisation of the war experience accounted for widespread homelessness, for more than 100,000 cases of cruelty a year and to more than 2,000 children living in local authority homes. Campaigners found that children were still living in poverty and the Curtis and Clyde committees of enquiry into child abuse confirmed that those in institutions were often subject to neglect and cruelty. To combat this, the 1948 Children Act centralised child welfare under the Home Office, making it responsible for authorising membership of childcare committees, setting standards for training of children's officers, and introducing a system of fostering designed to minimise the number of local authority children's homes (Starns, 2012).

Post-war austerity continued well into the 1950s and, seeking stability and reparation, society focused on the nuclear family and demands for a family wage so that mothers could return to their earlier domestic roles. This is a world of slowly growing affluence, and author Michelle Hanson (2012) offers a good description of a comfortable 1950s suburban childhood. She lived in a house with a garden with pets and was allowed to roam the neighbourhood, making dens and devising imaginative games while mother stayed at home to clean and cook wholesome family meals. She describes a local community where cars were scarce and children able to visit the local shops, cinemas, library and lido on their own, and where black and white television was available for only a few hours a day. In towns, children's play was confined to 'back alleys' and wasteland but children shared a similar freedom to roam.

Through the 1960s and 1970s, affluence increased. Victorian 'slums' were cleared and people rehoused on estates and in tower blocks with 'all mod cons', bathrooms, indoor toilets, and increasingly a range of gadgets that made housework simpler and quicker. The 1960s heralded the beginnings of a distinctive teenage culture based around modern fashion trends, popular music, and television programmes like *Thank Your Lucky Stars* and *Top of the Pops*. This was the time of the 'twist', The Beatles, The Rolling Stones and Dave Clark Five. Cultural changes were not confined to childhood. Parents too embraced new trends, compensating for the lack of material goods and trouble-free childhoods during the war years. As affluence increased and cars became common, children were slowly confined to the parks and playgrounds, leading to territorial disputes as access to open space declined, and the beginnings of rival 'gangs' (Feeney, 2010). To some extent the expansion of the toy market compensated for the reduction in the freedom to roam (Tait, 2011). Expensive toys encouraged solitary or paired play within the home where children could be kept clean and safe, and centrally heated homes converted bedrooms into potential private play spaces. Thus, the solitary sedentary individual gradually displaced the active sociable child (see Chapter 9).

Summary

This chapter traced some of the significant events and practices that have shaped society and the lives of children. It has described childhood in ancient Greece and Rome, in medieval times, during the Industrial Revolution, from the First and Second World Wars to the recent past. The reliance on obscure and specialist sources demonstrates the invisibility of children in times past. Few general textbooks or academic articles about specific historical periods consider childhood or children in detail: most focus more generally on political or social events. Communities and families are mentioned, and increasingly feminist historians seek to restore the gender balance by unearthing accounts that focus on women.

Although we know that the experience of childhood will alter as the historical context changes and other factors will intervene, as yet there is little information about children in the past. Perhaps, contemporary research will replicate the feminist work on women and unearth more information about the lives of children, but it is also possible that the records reflect a contemporary lack of interest in the child as a separate category. If so, there may be little original documentation waiting to be found.

Points for reflection

- Consider what you know about childhood in early times. Would you rather have lived in Greek, Roman or Anglo-Saxon society? Why?
- Reflect on the accounts of 'shocking' childhoods in this chapter: during slavery; in Mayhew's London; by those shipped to Australia; during wartime. Consider why society continually treats children so badly.
- Persuade an elderly friend or relative to talk about his/her childhood. How does this differ from your own? What does this tell you about change within a lifetime?

Further reading

Midwinter, E. (2012) *Britain's Story: An Overview of British History.* London: Third Age Press.
This is an informative summary (60 pages) by an eminent social historian, well worth reading.

Andreu-Cabrera, E., Cepero, M., Rojas, F.J. and Chinchilla-Mira, J.J. (2010) 'Play and childhood in ancient Greece', *Journal of Human Sport and Exercise*, 5(3): 339–47.
Gordon, E.C. (1991) 'Accidents among medieval children as seen from the miracles of six English saints and martyrs', *Medical History*, 35: 145–63.
Hanawalt, B. (1977) 'Childrearing among the lower classes of late medieval England', *The Journal of Interdisciplinary History*, 8(1): 1–22.

Orme, N. (2001) 'Child's play in medieval England', *History Today*, 51(10): 49.
Offer succinct accounts of specific childhoods.

Crawford, S. (1999) *Childhood in Anglo-Saxon England.* Stroud: Sutton Publishing.
Offers an overview of childhood in Anglo-Saxon England.

Golden, M. (1990) *Children and Childhood in Classical Athens.* Baltimore, MD: John Hopkins Press.
Offers an overview of childhood in Ancient Greece.

Rawson, B. (2003) *Children and Childhood in Roman Italy*, Oxford: Oxford University Press.
Offers an overview of childhood in Ancient Rome.

Hanawalt, B. (1993) *Growing Up in Medieval London.* Oxford: Oxford University Press.
Shahar, S. (1990) *Childhood in the Middle Ages.* London: Routledge.
Both of these are key specialist texts on medieval childhoods.

Cunningham, H. (2006) *The Invention of Childhood.* London: BBC Books.
Heywood, C. (2001) *A History of Childhood.* Cambridge: Polity Press.
Both texts give an historical overview of childhood.

Frost, G.S. (2008) *Victorian Childhoods*, Westport, CT: Praeger.
Nelson, C. (2007) *Family Ties in Victorian England.* Westport, CT: Praeger.
Give useful additional overviews of the nineteenth century.

Websites

http://webworld.unesco.org/goree
A virtual tour of the slave fort in Senegal, Africa.

www.dur.ac.uk/4schools/slavery2/timeline.htm
An excellent site on slavery hosted by Durham University: Special Collections-4schools.

http://onlinebooks.library.upenn.edu/webbin/book/lookupid?key=olbp23257
Replicates Mayhew's London of 1861.

(Continued)

(Continued)

www.worldthroughthelens.com/victor.php
Janet and Michael Wood's story of their uncle's life between the wars.

http://otoweb.cloudapp.net
On Their Own: Britain's Child Migrants – online exhibition jointly arranged by Australian and Liverpool museums.

To gain *free* access to selected SAGE journal articles related to key topics in this chapter, visit: www.sagepub.co.uk/hazelrwright.

CHAPTER 4

SPIRITUAL AND PHILOSOPHICAL PERSPECTIVES

Overview

This chapter considers the differing views of children held within religious and cultural traditions, and how these collective viewpoints influence upbringing and education. The philosophers' narratives address whether the newborn child is innately asocial or innocent; and how to socialise children to become both mindful citizens and fully developed individuals.

The chapter considers the spiritual perspectives of:

- Hinduism and Buddhism – the Vedic faiths
- Judaism, Christianity and Islam – the Abrahamic faiths
- Bahá'ism and secularism – alternative beliefs.

Key philosophical viewpoints include: Comenius, Locke, Rousseau, Pestalozzi, Froebel, Dewey, the McMillan sisters, Steiner, Montessori and Isaacs.

Philosophers are ordered chronologically by birth date but their periods of core activity, influence or popularity will vary. Froebel, for instance, died well before the kindergarten movement took hold in Europe and America.

For human society to continue, each generation must give birth to the next so it is not surprising that children and their upbringing has occupied the thoughts of spiritual leaders worldwide. Beliefs about how best to raise children depend on the starting point, so whether children are naturally 'wild' or 'evil', 'innocent' or 'pure' has exercised many brilliant minds and differently informed the customs of different social groups, both synchronically and sequentially.

If the newborn is viewed as innocent, this implies a need for careful nurture; if wayward, this is seen to justify chastisement. In contemporary society we would ask which comes first – a belief in the child's wrongdoing or the desire to have power over the child. We would also question whether punishment encourages good behaviour or the opposite. In earlier times, it was a case of 'driving out the devil' from children seen as possessed and, unfortunately, this phrase is still occasionally heard in contemporary societies.

Religious perspectives

Sources relevant to childhood are limited as, historically, religious leaders were adult males. This makes it difficult to gather accurate insights into what it meant to be a child within a particular faith (Bunge and Browning, 2009). For this reason, the academic account is supplemented by contemporary internet sources that advise parents on bringing up their children.

To different degrees, all the key religions view children as a blessing, with an essential role to play in perpetuating the faith. As a consequence, most articulate their expectations of parental and communal obligations to children (ibid). Early religions crystallised over a period of time, so a strictly chronological treatment can be misleading. Instead, I have adapted Breuilly et al.'s (1997) distinction between the Vedic faiths (Hinduism, Buddhism and Jainism) that believe in cyclical existence and re-incarnation; the Abrahamic faiths (Judaism, Christianity and Islam) whose prophets recall people to live to God's plan; and other major traditions that have evolved their own beliefs and practices. The Christian, Muslim and Hindu faiths account for the greater number of followers (respectively, more than 33 per cent, 22 per cent and 13 per cent) (CIA, 2013) and this relative status is reflected in the treatment here, as is the Anglocentric significance of Christianity.

The Vedic faiths
Hinduism

The Hindu religion began to take shape around 2,000 years ago (Agarwal, 2006) but was only so named from around the tenth century (Patton, 2009). Hinduism was a religion in which early sacrifice was gradually replaced by internalised sacrificial thought, a form of inner meditation (ibid). It focuses on the worship of one 'supreme being' who appears in various forms as a child god or goddess and is worshipped through a series of icons, symbols and elaborate prayers and ceremonies, articulated in two epic texts, the Ramayana and the Mahabharata, and the four vedas (Agarwal, 2006). A belief in reincarnation is fundamental and children viewed as gifts from the gods, but also the consequences of parents' previous karma (Jayaram, 2012b). Life is seen to commence at conception so the future mother is encouraged to engage with sacred texts and hymns during pregnancy and numerous rituals (*samskaras*) are performed during childhood to awaken a child's latent spirituality (Agarwal, 2006). Hindu families are close and child–parent relationships considered to be warm, intimate and enduring (Jayaram, 2012b). Most homes have a private shrine and children are expected to take part in family prayers, pilgrimages and a wealth of religious festivals (Agarwal, 2006).

Hindu society traditionally favoured the male child. It was males who could inherit property and perform funeral rites for parents (Jayaram, 2012b) so the birth of a son guaranteed a good ritual death (Patton, 2009). In traditional Hindu society, polygamy was permitted to continue the family lineage, so under Hindu law, provision was made for children born out of wedlock, in inter-caste and polygamous marriages (Jayaram, 2012b). For males, a period of study in the home of his Guru, led up to the Upanayana ritual that marked adulthood. For higher-caste male children this could take place as early as eight, even five (Agarwal, 2006), but for others, as late as 16 (Patton, 2009). In contrast, girl children came of age with puberty and marriage, and were thereafter expected to care for husband and home. Only if she had waited for three years after puberty could a girl find her own husband, and if she did this, she could not take personal wealth into her new relationship. Male inheritance was also circumscribed, by caste and parental marriage status, but all males were expected to protect the vulnerable (ibid). In contemporary Hindu society, relationships are still stratified, with age and masculinity taking precedence. Children are expected to subordinate their own desires to the good of the family and community, but girls now have the chance of a better education and professional work outside the home, and consequently, can delay marriage (ibid).

Buddhism

Buddhism developed gradually from the fifth century BCE (Nakagawa, 2006) and says very little about the state of childhood. Nor does it practice many rituals for children (Cole, 2009). Indeed, Jayaram (2012a) questions whether Buddhism is a religion or a philosophy for its main messages focus on living wisely. Buddhism is about being centred in the present and 'presentism' is encouraged through serenity and well-being.

Buddha emphasised emancipation through individual effort and this is equally possible for men and women for Buddhism rejects the Hindu caste structure and its male supremacy. Marriage is a secular activity, not a sacrament, and carries reciprocal rights and obligations. Both partners can dissolve a marriage where these are not respected, and often a woman can reclaim her dowry and half the property of the couple. Widows are not expected to endure hardship or social isolation, instead they are traditionally free to remarry. However, the messages are mixed. Men are responsible for administering joint properties and can practice polygamy so enjoy an inherent superiority. Indeed, being a woman is a sign of bad karma in a previous life (Dewaraja, 1994).

Children are treated with respect and encouraged to recognise the consequences of their own actions from an early age. They should learn the Buddhist way of life through living it. Children remain with their families for the first seven years but can then become novice monks if parents consent to this. As novices, each child attends a monk or nun who in turn educates them in a reciprocal and caring relationship. Children are raised according to the 'four immeasurable minds' of loving-kindness, compassion, sympathetic joy, and equanimity, and can be fully ordained when they reach 20 years of age (Nakagawa, 2006).

The Abrahamic faiths
Judaism

Jewish religion is based on the teachings of the Old Testament, and the *Mishnah* and *Talmud* (together, the Oral Law) set clear standards for everyday life. To marry and procreate is a central dictate of the Jewish faith (Baumgarten, 2009) so children are cherished. Historically, Jews have mostly lived alongside other cultures, so a wide range of rituals were developed to initiate children into the Jewish community: male circumcision at birth, naming ceremonies, and distinctive standards for food, dress, education and behaviour. The father confirms paternity by taking part in the circumcision ceremony, but primary caregivers were mothers, and many families had servants and wet nurses, too. A mother's life traditionally took precedence over that of an unborn baby so Caesarean section was allowed only when the mother would die anyway. If babies or young children died, this was often seen as a punishment, the child dying to atone for the parents' sins (ibid). At birth, the child is at risk from 'evil inclination' so parents have a duty to instil the values that will enable the making of positive life choices. As minors, children must respect their parents and boys are to engage with religious practices as soon as they are able to understand them, girls too in more recent times (Shire, 2006). Traditionally, at 13, boys entered a stage of 'moral inclination' and at the *bar mitzvah* ceremony undertook to learn and live as an adult. A *bat mitzvah* ceremony now exists for female children (Baumgarten, 2009). However, nowadays, 13 is seen as too soon to end formal learning so the period has been extended and capped by a later confirmation ceremony (Shire, 2006).

Early marriage was commonplace in the past, particularly among the prosperous, and grooms moved into the bride's family for a period of three years to study the Torah, a practice named *Kest*. Thus, each generation was guided by the elders in the community, through a process that created a continuing respect for familial authority. Parents are advised, in turn, by rabbis and teachers, and urged to love their children but not to let this show so that children learn to obey and respect (Salmon-Mack, n.d.).

Christianity

Christianity began as a movement within Judaism (Bunge and Browning, 2009). It follows the teachings of Jesus, a Jew born 2,000 years ago, whose life and principles form the basis of a New Testament (written in Greek), extending the Bible, which was based on the Hebrew Old Testament. Christianity is still divided on the basic issues of children's nature, the ethical position of the adults who care for them and the practices appropriate for children (Bunge and Wall, 2009). Within the Anglo-Catholic tradition, the child was viewed as born, if not evil, then in need of redemption, hence the rite of baptism at an early age to wash away the original sin (Spierling, 2008). In biblical terms, Adam and Eve fell from grace when they gave in to temptation and partook of the sacred apple, thereby consigning their offspring to a state of guilt. In early medieval times, baptism was often immediately followed by confirmation as bishops visited infrequently, but by the fourth century, these rites were more commonly separated, with parish priests required to carry out baptism. However, it remained lawful to confirm the newly baptised immediately and records show that this often happened.

Orme (2001b: 215) claims that by the twelfth century the Church placed an emphasis on 'understanding' so children were treated differently from adults. Communion and confession became adult practices and children excluded until they were deemed to have reached the age of discretion, around 12 for girls, 14 for boys whose later maturation was universally accepted. Similarly, children intended to enter the Church were discouraged from making a firm commitment until they were old enough to understand what this entailed: a staged process delayed ordination and mandatory vows of celibacy until the age of 17. Early entry into monastic life was also discouraged, but there is evidence that younger children were enticed or abducted into friaries without parental consent (ibid: 226). Other religious institutions compromised, taking on young men as clerks and providing them with education, board and lodgings in hostels outside the monastery walls on condition that they assisted the monks in church.

From the eleventh century, the English clergy encouraged parents to provide a religious upbringing, teaching children prayers and the catechism. By the late thirteenth century, wealthy families possessed children's primers, incorporating the alphabet and short religious pieces. Whether poorer families were equally devout is hard to ascertain but evidence that, post-reformation, people were unsure whether to teach prayers in Latin or English, implies a continuing oral tradition of teaching (ibid: 207–8).

In England, the state became Protestant in the 1530s though rural inhabitants continued their existing practices, perhaps fearful of the Protestant teachings that put them in direct contact with the 'word of God' (Morgan, 2010). Evangelical Puritanism was not universally popular but was significant in the sixteenth and seventeenth century when many Puritans set off to build new lives in the Americas. Others minded their own affairs until Archbishop Laud's experiments with 'popery' led to the deposition of Charles I. For many, civil war and revolution were preferable to a return to papal domination.

Puritanism was an extreme version of Protestantism that gave significant power to male heads of households to bring children up to be sober, hard working and deeply religious individuals. Parents, as God's custodians, were tasked with teaching their children to pray and to read at a young age to enable access to the Bible (I wonder if this explains England's fixation on early literacy?). For Puritans, baptism indicated a dedication to the faith rather than exemption from original sin. The Church exhorted parents to 'break children's will' and bring them to the word of God. They had a duty to feed children but were to remain emotionally detached in order to better correct their misdeeds, and often sent them to live with strangers to prevent indulgence (Moran and Vinovskis, 1985). A Puritan childhood was a severe one anywhere and geographical isolation would have exacerbated hardship in America. Female obedience was paramount and suffering in childbirth viewed as fitting maternal sacrifice. Women and children were expected to submit to male dominance however cruel or scandalous, as husbands and fathers were God's representatives on Earth. Puritan women were expected to succour their children by breastfeeding yet also act as their 'conscience' (Saxton, 1994). Communities were mutually responsible for their joint morality and, like adults, children were encouraged to publicly denounce each other's sins, creating a society where trust and friendship could only be minimally present.

Christianity shaped society within Britain and played a key role in Britain's colonial activities, and in the rescue of children in need. We have seen in earlier chapters that childrearing practices have sometimes been abusive rather than nurturative. Bunge (2006) acknowledges that within the Christian church, despite many instances of concern for children, the underpinning theological discourse on childhood is 'simplistic and ambivalent', and this has led to 'serious consequences' for actual children, even sexual abuse (ibid: 54).

Islam

Muslims view Islam as the original religion. God (Allah) sent prophets like Moses, Abraham (Ibrahim in Arabic) and Jesus to show how humans should live but his messages were corrupted until the arrival of Muhammed in the seventh century CE. The sacred text, the Qur'an, records the word of God so it is always read and studied in the original Arabic, and Muslims expected to follow its teachings precisely. The Hadith records stories and sayings that relate to Muhammed, and these are used as guidance on subjects not found in the Qur'an. Together the Qur'an and Hadith form the basis of Islamic law (*Fiqh*, the consolidation of *Shari'ah*), defining idolatry (and any representational art) and blasphemy (*shirk*) as significant sins. Islam is underpinned by five pillars: the declaration of faith, prayer, fasting, giving of alms (defined through a welfare tax), and pilgrimage (Breuilly et al., 1997).

Islam teaches that children are precious gifts from God and born without sin (Yildirim, 2006). Thus, the principal purpose of marriage is to procreate and Islam had a clearly developed concept of childhood from early times with specific rules governing inheritance, childrearing, medical treatment and the education of children (Giladi, 2009). Male and females are born equal and so any inequality has a cultural rather than a scriptural origin (Yildirim, 2006). Children are to develop spirituality from observing practices within their family and community who are held accountable for their safety and protection. To develop the habits of regular prayer, self-control and self-criticism, children may accompany adults on visits to the mosque, but before the age of seven, it is enough for children to mimic rather than participate in adult behaviours (ibid).

Children need an appropriate environment, bad influences create a 'black spot on the heart', which can cause problems in later life (ibid: 74). Muhammed teaches parents to play with children but education is also important from an early age (ibid). Developing maturity is marked by a series of ceremonies (Giladi, 2009). Traditionally, children became adult around nine or ten years, 15 if immature, but schooling delayed early entry into the labour force (ibid). Islamic law allows child marriage but even in early times consummation was not allowed before puberty (ibid). The Islamic state has a responsibility to oversee the rights of children, individually and collectively, and to check that international agreements are in line with *Shari'ah* (Al-Azhar University, 2005).

Other major beliefs

This discussion of the world's main religions essentially simplifies reality. Between and within these religions lie a significant number of different faiths, sects, cults and smaller-scale religious groupings. Christianity alone embraces Anglicans, Baptists, Congregationalists, Episcopalians, Evangelists, Methodists, Presbyterians, Quakers and Jehovah's Witnesses. Islam divides into Shiite and Sunni. Buddhism has different traditions, Theravada and Mahayana, which itself has distinctive branches in Vajrayana, Pure Land and Zen Buddhism. Significant numbers follow the Sikh religion, which is very family-orientated with children accepted at birth without any need for purification or acceptance ceremonies. Chinese (Taoism, Confucianism), Japanese (Shintoism), Persian (Zoroastrianism) and African traditional religious practices continue to thrive and new religions develop (for example Rastafarianism in the 1930s; Hare Krishna in the 1960s). Within religions, orthodox believers adhere to traditional practices; fundamentalists live by a literal interpretation of their holy scripts; reformers modify their practices in line with changes in society, further duplicating the range of belief systems in existence. One of the fastest growing and relatively new faiths – Bahá'i – seeks world unification, accepting the validity of all religions. Bahá'i originated in the 1860s and teaches that God intervenes at intervals, sending messengers into the world to reveal more of himself (Breuilly et al., 1997). Bahá'i accepts the divine nature of successive prophets in the belief that it is human beings who describe God differently rather than God who changes.

Other people, about a quarter of the world's population (CIA, 2013), take a secular, or non-religious, stance. Atheists deny the existence of God(s), Agnostics express uncertainty, Humanists affirm individual agency, claiming both the right and the responsibility to shape their own existence (International Humanist and Ethical Union, 2009).

Philosophical perspectives

A philosophical perspective of childhood is constructed from the 'chain' of philosophers who developed each other's views and practices to create the early years tradition that characterises contemporary English and European practices.

As European society became more enlightened, the wisdom of chastising children and forcing them to learn came into question. Earlier (Christian) beliefs that children were naturally evil gave way to views of innocence, raising debates about methods of child rearing. How can natural goodness be cultivated? How can children be brought up to contribute to a better society? How can cooperation *and* autonomy be instilled? How can the line between excessive control and overindulgence be trodden? These are questions still debated today, which clearly exercised the minds of philosophers like Locke and Rousseau and the progressive educators that followed them. Yet, predating them all, Comenius seemed instinctively aware of the needs of young children.

Jan Amos Comenius (1592–1670)

Comenius is a worthy father for early years education for his view of children is a benign one. In *The Great Didactic* (1896 [1631]) he planned a universal educational system but of note here are his beliefs that children up to the age of six should be educated within the family in a 'mother-school'. Comenius set out a curriculum that introduced the 'elements', 'basis', 'seeds' and 'rudiments' of most core subjects in 21 clearly numbered and reasoned goals. He recognised that children differ, and some children 'develope much sooner than others' (ibid: 416), so planned a handbook to support mothers, an *Informatory of the Mother-School*. However in his *Sketch of the Mother-School* (Chapter 28) he stated that 'all detail must be left to the prudence of the parent' (ibid: 416). Comenius favoured child-centred approaches to learning, recommending a picture book to 'accustom the little ones to the idea that pleasure is to be derived from books' (ibid: 417) while they learn to read. They are also to use their senses to learn the basic concepts of life, and the labels for the features of their own bodies and their immediate environment to begin to understand the natural sciences.

John Locke (1632–1704)

Born into a Puritan family, Locke rejected the prevailing view that children were born evil and should be forcefully punished. He was 'essentially on the child's side' (Garforth, 1964: 11), believing that parents should be authoritative and manage their children's behaviour through 'esteem' and 'disgrace' rather than physical punishment. Locke claimed that children learned through experience (which could be nurtured), describing the child's mind as a 'white paper void of all characters' (Locke, *Essay*, 2.1.2; in Aldrich, 1994: 9), a phrase often recast as a *tabula rasa* or blank slate.

Aldrich (1994) describes how Locke attended (but never really enjoyed) public school, gained an Oxford scholarship, graduated, and thereafter held a series of academic posts. More interested in radical ideas than the classical curriculum, he pursued a private interest in medical literature, leaving Oxford in 1667 to take up the first of several posts of tutor/medical advisor in important households. Locke grasped the need to exercise both mind and body, advocating simple nourishing food, loose comfortable clothing (not swaddling), and plenty of open air activity. Locke was a member of the Royal Society, founded on the 'new' empirical approaches to science. He applied empirical ideas to children's learning, advocating close observation to inform personalised education, as a child will 'learn three times as much when he is in tune' (Locke, *Thoughts*, s.74: in Aldrich, 1994: 7).

Locke's *An Essay Concerning Human Understanding* (1690) and *Some Thoughts Concerning Education* (1693) set out his views on curriculum and teaching methods, and these publications were influential throughout the world, particularly in America and France. In *Thoughts,* he explained that children should learn to read as soon as possible but by playing with letters and enjoying storybooks with pictures. He challenged the common practice of learning to read from the Bible, recognising that this might create an aversion to reading and learning. Instead, essential religious education should be oral – with prayers and commandments learned by heart. Languages, too, should be taught orally: French should be introduced as soon as a child could speak, then Latin as it would be needed for many careers and a university education. Writing, however, was introduced formally by copying letters, and drawing taught as a more advanced skill as it involved an understanding of perspective and replication of real images. Older children were to balance book and active learning, and be given the opportunity to travel abroad to broaden the mind while still impressionable. Overall, a child's learning should focus on that 'which will be of most and frequentest use to him in the world' (Locke, *Thoughts;*, in Garforth, 1964: 117). These are radical views, deserving of the accolade 'the most significant educationist in English history' (Aldrich, 1994).

Jean-Jacques Rousseau (1712–78)

Rousseau's ideas are harder to summarise. His works reflect the uncertainty of the times in which he lived, when the old social order was widely challenged (Soëtard, 1994a). The strength of his discourses lies in their ambivalence, for Rousseau raises conundrums, leaving his readers to find resolution. His major educational work, *Émile* (1889 [1762]), is a fictionalised account of the upbringing of a young male, outlining how an educator can encourage self-reliance and selfhood without subordinating the child's will to that of the adult. The educator appears to give the child unfettered freedom but actually manages the child's experience to create a satisfactory outcome, causing the child to make the choices he needs to make without coercion or visible enforcement. Thus upbringing is stage-managed so that the child handles the conflict between desire (natural behaviour) and law (acceptable behaviour) to become an autonomous and self-regulating individual.

Rousseau's child is sometimes portrayed as innately good, a Romantic view in contrast to earlier claims that the child was the fruit of 'original sin', but the reality is more complex as the child is constantly curbing his own selfish desires for the good of others. Rousseau's treatment of Sophie, Émile's ideal partner, is questionable, however. He discards his egalitarian principles, stating that 'woman was made specially to please man' (Archer, 1928: 218) and should be educated to fulfil a domestic role. Freedom from constraint is not for girls.

Émile raises a number of polarities that exercise Western thinkers – freedom and necessity, heart and head, the individual and the state, knowledge and experience – and subsequent educators have been drawn to resolve these paradoxes, often through practical experiment and with questionable success.

Soëtard (1994a) describes how Pestalozzi tried to emulate Émile's upbringing with his own child, creating an over-anxious individual who never knew when his parent would be benevolent or harsh. Progressive educators like A.S. Neill (founder of Summerhill School) (1998 [1960]) and Carl Rogers (1994 [1969]) experimented with non-directivity. Pestalozzi (Soëtard, 1994a) and later Steiner (Ullrich, 1994), developed the triple axes of heart, head and hand with some success; Dewey was drawn to activity methods of learning; and others grappled with individual innate abilities, from a bio-psychological (Montessori) or psychological (Piaget) perspective. The breadth of Rousseau's ideas keeps them alive within educational discourse.

Johann Heinrich Pestalozzi (1746–1827)

Following Rousseau's lead, Pestalozzi sought a practical reconciliation of the tension between education for individual development and for the good of society. He set up a community in Neuhof whereby children could learn as they worked, acquiring a basic education alongside an ability to spin and weave cotton goods. They were to develop their 'own personality' within a 'free and responsible society', and finance their own learning rather than be under an obligation to others (Soëtard, 1994b). However, the project went bankrupt. Rather than give up, Pestalozzi turned to theory. In *How Gertrude Teaches Her Children* (1801), he set out a psychology of instruction that aligned with the 'laws' of human nature. Pestalozzi's philosophy was based around six principles: to protect a child's personality; to protect natural development; to love and nurture children; to start with concrete observation; then introduce words and action; then repeat this activity meaningfully (Kilpatrick, 1951).

In 1805, Pestalozzi opened a school at Yverdon to give children a place for reflection apart from the domains of family and society. This was a space for individual growth, an environment where the sensitive educator balancing the needs of head, heart and hands within every activity could guide the child towards personal fulfilment and civic responsibility. Thus, through education, he found a 'solution to Rousseau's paradox, which held that it was impossible to educate natural man and the citizen simultaneously' (Soëtard, 1994b: 4). His method was successful because it was based on spiritual values rather than resources or techniques, on a holistic understanding of the nature of children in a social and physical environment conducive to action. It influenced a number of other educators interested in this conundrum, among them Froebel and Steiner.

Friedrich Froebel (1782–1852)

A lonely child, Froebel developed a love of nature and powers of observation, contemplation and self-education; all within a Christian family culture. He was influenced by Pestalozzi's ideas and, becoming a children's tutor for a time, visited the school at Yverdon. Froebel was interested in bringing people's inner and outer lives together. As a student of crystallography, he had learned how shapes are made up of different combinations of points, lines and planes. As an educator, he adapted this knowledge of form and content to encourage children to study the structural forms associated with objects (Brosterman, 1997).

Froebel translated his ideas about 'unity' into practice in his private school at Keilhau (1817–1831), striving 'to establish a single root for education and science' within a theory of 'caring tuition' that is governed by the 'law of objects' (Heiland, 1993: 7). His ideas, set out in his work *On the Education of Man* (1826), are fundamentally cognitive as he is more concerned to develop human insight than physical mastery, although the latter is not over-looked. Froebel was essentially a theoretician but his grandiose plans for a state education system were too democratic for the German homeland. In Switzerland, as Head of the Burgdorf orphanage school, he did manage to establish a teacher training programme.

Ironically, it was from 1836 onwards when Froebel gave up his plans for formal schooling and turned his attention to family learning through play that he formulated the ideas that underpinned the kindergarten movement. Froebel established a 'factory' in Thuringia to make and sell his archetypal 'gifts', elementary self-teaching materials, to encourage children to explore the characteristics of objects. The series of gifts and, later, occupations, fostered an understanding of unity through separation and synthesis. The child was encouraged to take apart and rebuild 3-d models, 2-d shapes, linear and single-point items and to create 'living' shapes (features of the natural world), 'beautiful' shapes (with aesthetic potential) and 'cognitive' shapes (mathematical groupings). In his kindergarten at Bad Liebenstein, Froebel educated children, (and indirectly, parents) and teachers in his play-based pedagogy, developing a programme that included rhymes and songs, movement games and garden care in addition to the 'gifts' and 'occupations'.

Prussia banned kindergartens in 1851, and Froebel died a year later not aware that the kindergarten movement would later achieve international acclaim. The kindergarten was a highly innovative development – neither care nor formal teaching establishment but a teaching centre for three- to six-year-olds with educational procedures founded on play (Heiland, 1993: 12), the true precursor of modern early years settings.

John Dewey (1859–1952)

American, John Dewey, was another educator influenced by Rousseau's paradoxes. His underpinning interest was in the unification of theory and practice and his philosophy of education was developed over a lengthy period from around 1890 to his death, aged 93. Influenced by the pragmatist, William James, Dewey theorised that knowledge is created by testing thought through action. This viewpoint, in linking theory and practice, challenges Cartesian dualism, the separation of mind and body (Westbrook, 1993).

Dewey took a post as lecturer of philosophy at the University of Chicago in 1894 (staying until 1904 when he moved to Columbia), and insisted on the formation of a 'laboratory school' where he could test his theories. For Dewey, philosophy was merely speculation unless it was translated into actions that changed people's lives. His publications demonstrate his keen interest in educational reform, particularly *The School and Society* (1899), *How We Think* (1910), *Democracy and Education* (1916) and *Experience and Education* (1938).

Dewey believed that both children and adults learn through solving problems that they encounter. Their success enables them to build a knowledge base to use in new situations. Thus children learn from birth and do not arrive in school unformed, waiting for teachers to transmit new knowledge. Dewey thought children had four 'native impulses' 'to communicate, to construct, to inquire and to express in finer form' (1899: 30, in Westbrook, 1993: 3), and the teacher's job was to shape these interests towards profitable goals. Thus, Dewey's philosophy is neither a traditional curriculum nor a romantic child-centred one, but a compromise, leaving him open to criticism from both traditionalists and reformers. Indeed, Dewey saw the distinction as another dualism to be avoided. Dewey is often aligned with progressive educators (and criticised for this) but his pedagogy is actually teacher led. For Dewey, teachers need to understand both the worlds of the adult and child in order to present the curriculum in terms of the children's interests. Like Rousseau, he called for skilled but subtle intervention, believing that through self-realisation the child would contribute to his community.

Dewey put his views on democracy into practice in the laboratory school hoping to demonstrate that education can transform rather than reproduce society. Each year group was given an 'occupation', a cooperative practical task through which they would acquire literacy, numeracy and cultural understanding as they needed it. For example: the under-fives were set to learn life tasks – cooking, sewing, carpentry; the ten-year-olds to study colonial history by constructing a replica of a room in an early American house; the older children decided to build themselves a clubhouse in which to hold debates. Dewey's experiment was cut short when the University of Chicago interfered in the school management. Moving to the University of Columbia, he eschewed practical experimentation and focused on supporting educational reform abroad, writing and debate.

Rachel (1859–1917) and Margaret (1860–1931) McMillan

Both McMillan sisters were important English pioneers – social campaigners determined to improve the lives of the poor. Margaret, who had trained as a governess and an actress, was a successful orator who believed that providing working-class children with a good physical start in life would aid political reform. Settling in Bradford in 1893, she was elected to the School Board in 1894 as an Independent Labour Party representative, becoming involved in home visiting and school inspections.

The 1902 Education Act abolished school boards, vesting power in the municipal and county councils to which only men could be elected, so Margaret moved south to join her sister in Kent. In 1903, she undertook to manage a group of Deptford schools and became a member of the Workers' Educational Association, and in 1904, she was elected to the Froebel Society's executive committee.

The sisters persuaded an American millionaire to support the opening of a school clinic in Bow and Margaret began a campaign for the medical inspection of school children. In 1910, they opened a second clinic in Deptford and a camp school to provide deprived children with the opportunity to wash and sleep in clean clothing. In 1911, they established an open-air nursery school and training centre in Deptford that soon catered for 30 children aged 18 months to seven years. This attracted significant publicity and led to Margaret becoming President of the Nursery School Association in 1923, and to opening the Rachel McMillan Training College in 1930 (Steedman, 2004).

Rudolf Steiner (1861–1925)

Steiner schools are summed up by Ullrich (1994: 10) as 'a beneficial practice on the foundation of dubious theory' for the schools adopt child-centred practices that create successful, well-balanced individuals, but the underpinning philosophical concepts could be termed 'neo-mythical'. Steiner opened his first school in 1919 in Stuttgart for employees of the Waldorf-Astoria factory, and in 1992, there were 582 schools worldwide, mostly established by groups of parents. The schools are housed in buildings designed to 'perfect' proportions with regard to acoustics, colour schemes, lighting and furnishing. They offer a syllabus, based on 'moralizing narratives' (Ullrich, 1994: 7), traditional historical tales that encourage children to find self-expression in a range of writings, paintings and role play activities. Classes form micro-communities, headed by a teacher who leads from the front but in a gentle and unassuming manner, and it is probably this characteristic that allows a successful practical experience to transcend the unusual ideological beliefs. The classroom has a homely feel and children use natural materials in their play, and take part in everyday household tasks and seasonal celebrations. Great attention is paid to the children's physical and spiritual well-being, and their daily activities follow a natural rhythm that affords a relaxed approach to learning. There is a keen focus on nature, music, art, acting and storytelling.

Yet, Steiner's philosophical beliefs – based on theosophy and anthroposophy – are complex and confusing, as he tries to combine multiple philosophical traditions. Ullrich (1994) describes how Steiner believed that behind the visible world there is a hidden world of thought that man can access through intensive meditation. In addition to the stages of sleeping and waking exists an 'intuitive stage of precise and clear vision' (ibid: 3) that reconciles scientific, religious and aesthetic viewpoints. Man should aspire to this stage if he wants to be at one with the universe. Steiner believed in reincarnation and karma, and saw Jesus as a joint reincarnation of the spirits of Buddha and Zarathustra, a cosmic sun being. He viewed the newborn (reborn) as a primeval being unable to express himself and felt that education should help the child to become the person he is disposed to be. He saw the child as having a distinctive temperament – a melancholic, phlegmatic, choleric or sanguine humour – and reasoned that educators must help the child to rebalance this bias.

Seeking unity, Steiner viewed man as a microcosm of the world. He recognised the logic of evolution but linked this to a cosmic pathway, believing that man had passed through the stages of Saturn (mineral), Sun (plant) and Moon (animal) to become human. This led to a view of child development as the successive incidence of vegetative, animal and intellectual cosmic forces, usually in seven-year cycles. Thus, in the first seven years, the child becomes a complete organism, developing his inner senses to become ready for school. From 7 to 14, hidden spiritual forces – drives, passions and feelings – are transformed into judgement and conceptual thinking. By 21, hidden 'ego' forces surface to create a distinctive mature personality. In these phases children learn through imitation, imagination and reason, and at each stage, spiritual and physical development encompasses head, heart and hands to occupy the entire body. Thus the educator must help the child grow and change, and support his spiritual awakening and psychic healing, so that the child can become a balanced individual, the person he was born to be. Not surprisingly, acceptance of Steiner's pedagogies is highly polarised. Despite the positive outcomes, many are concerned about the 'occult neo-mythology of education' on which they are based (Ullrich, 1994: 10).

Maria Montessori (1870–1952)

Montessori, another European pioneer, was the first woman to qualify as a doctor in Italy. She applied her clinical precision to the education of young children, institutionalised because they were physically handicapped and assumed to be 'mentally retarded' (Röhrs, 1994: 2) too. Becoming involved in the modernisation of a 'slum' district, she established a Children's House

(*Casa Dei Bambini*) to support children in learning about the world and how to plan their own lives.

Montessori was heavily influenced by Rousseau, agreeing that many aspects of development be left to nature. However, she also believed that this devel opment was best not left to chance: children should be helped to acquire the skills of comparison and abstraction. She devised a series of exercises and tasks to ensure that this happened, linking theory to practice to 'develop a system of scientific pedagogy' (Montessori, 1965 [1912]: 28). Montessori saw the need to observe children closely, as the educator should start with the interests and experiences of each child, and try to awaken in children a sense of self-discipline and responsibility for their own learning. Combining her medical and educational knowledge, she identified 'sensitive phases' when children were predisposed to learn specific skills and explained how the careful educator could exploit these interests appropriately. This was not a belief in linear development but in a series of successive 'births' (Röhrs, 1994).

Like Steiner, Montessori placed great importance on the physical environment. In the children's houses the furniture was child-sized and the architecture and colour schemes were carefully planned to promote children's learning. She aimed to inculcate concentration through real tasks that required patience, precision and repetition, favouring the education of the senses (Cunningham, 2000). She also encouraged children to develop the ability to be still and to meditate to internalise learning. Montessori wanted children to be content with their own achievements rather than 'disturbed' by the attainment of others so she planned individual tasks that enabled self-assessment, seeing independent activity as a worthy goal for life but also as 'the one factor that stimulates and produces development' (Montessori, 1988 [1949]: 7).

Susan Isaacs (1885–1948)

Isaacs was an English pioneer who trained as a nursery teacher and undertook a degree in philosophy and a masters in psychology. She had also lectured in a teacher training college and qualified as a psychoanalyst before choosing to work with children. Isaacs' time in nursery education was short. From 1924 to 1927 she ran an experimental nursery school, the Malting House, in Cambridge. However, the impact of her work is significant for early years workers. Isaacs (1963 [1932]) was interested in developing the rounded child who would contribute fully to society. She understood how 'the habit of playing with others, and the actual experiences of social give-and-take, [were] laying the foundations of more disinterested social purpose' (Isaacs, 1932: 105).

The Malting House offered a rich and well-resourced environment that children could freely access. Pets, musical instruments, science materials, modelling materials, paints, bricks, see-saws and other equipment were available inside and out, and the children allowed to choose their occupations with very little restraint. For instance, the rule 'only one child on the roof at a time' invited children to explore and climb rather than preventing it. There was little intervention to curb children's interests and verbal expression, and Isaacs and her team documented their play as it really was, complete with aggression, sexual, anal and urethral interest, and questioning (Drummond, 2000). It is this documentation, published in her key works, *Intellectual Growth in Children* (1930) and *Social Development in Young Children* (1933), which led to Isaacs' award of a doctorate from the University of Manchester. In turn, the doctorate led to a part-time teaching position at the London Institute of Education where she influenced successive cohorts of teachers. She also had a profound influence on the early years profession in her post as Ursula Wise, agony aunt for *Nursery World,* a popular UK magazine aimed at early years professionals.

In her book *The Children We Teach* (1963 [1932]), Isaacs sets out her philosophy for education very clearly. She believes that it is the children's activities that lead to their development so the teacher's role is to provide opportunities; that children's activities should be practical; and that physical activity should be supported through talking. It is by describing what they are doing and reasoning aloud that the children structure their intellectual growth and enable their social development.

Summary

This chapter summarised key religious and philosophical views about children. It mixed academic ideas with material written by religious communities to support their members in bringing up children, as it is important for people who work with children and families to understand how different religious communities view childhood.

The section on early years philosophers draws on specialist accounts created for the United Nations Educational, Scientific and Cultural Organization (UNESCO). These were written for an international audience and take a broader view to that of many standard textbooks. The focus is on the pioneers' views about children rather than their own biographies, but often aspects of their personal lives support a fuller explanation. Philosophical views rarely develop in isolation, so it may be useful to link them to developments in psychology (Chapter 5) and the political and policy frameworks (Chapter 7) shaping the lives of children, their care and rights.

Together, these early educational pioneers significantly contributed to the shaping of current educational practices and frameworks, but these are still evolving. Philosophies with more modern origins – Reggio Emilia, High/Scope, *Te Whariki* and the Forest School movement – are discussed in Chapter 8.

Points for reflection

🖑 Consider the ways that different religions treat children. What does this tell us about their views of childhood?

🖑 Reflect on the various philosophical perspectives. Which can *you* best relate to?

🖑 Recall (or visit) a real early years setting. Identify how/where current practice is based on earlier philosophical approaches.

Further reading

Nutbrown, C., Clough, P. and Selbie, P. (2014) *Early Childhood Education: History, Philosophy and Experience,* 2nd edn. London: Sage.
Offers brief biographies for the main early childhood pioneers. Imaginary conversations with key philosophers bring their views to life.

Giardiello, P. (2013) *Pioneers in Early Childhood Education: The Roots and Legacies of Rachel and Margaret McMillan, Maria Montessori and Susan Isaacs.* London: Routledge.
General information on these theorists and their theories.

Miller, L. and Pound, L. (2011) *Theories and Approaches to Learning in the Early Years.* London: Sage.
Includes chapters on Froebel, Montessori and Steiner.

Bruce, T. (2012) *Early Childhood Practice: Froebel Today.* London: Sage.
Feez, S. (2010) *Montessori and Early Childhood.* London: Sage.
Isaacs, B. (2012) *Understanding the Montessori Approach.* London: Routledge.
Nicol, J. and Taplin, J. (2012) *Understanding the Steiner Waldorf Approach.* London: Routledge.
Parker-Rees, R. (2011) *Meeting the Child in Steiner Kindergartens.* London: Routledge.
Support the application of different philosophical approaches.

Brown, D.S. and Bunge, M. (2009) *Children and Childhood in World Religions.* New Brunswick: Rutgers University Press.
Cunningham, H. (2005) *Children and Childhood in Western Society Since 1500.* Harlow: Pearson Education.

Yust, K.M., Johnson, A.N., Sasso, S.E. and Roehlkepartain, E.C. (2006) *Nurturing Child and Adolescent Spirituality: Perspectives from the World's Religious Traditions.* Lanham, Md: Rowman and Littlefield. *Offer detailed coverage of children and their place within religious practices.*

Websites

www.ibe.unesco.org/en/services/online-materials/publications/ thinkers-on-education.html

In 1993/1994 UNESCO commissioned world experts to contribute a chapter on key educationists to Prospects, *the quarterly journal of comparative education. These are now freely available online and include articles on Comenius, Dewey, Froebel, Locke, Montessori, Pestalozzi and Steiner.*

To gain *free* access to selected SAGE journal articles related to key topics in this chapter, visit: www.sagepub.co.uk/hazelrwright.

CHAPTER 5

PSYCHOLOGICAL AND BIOLOGICAL PERSPECTIVES

Overview

This chapter sets the nature–nurture debate in context. It provides the scientific framework for an understanding of recent genetic and neuro-logical advances, enabling greater understanding of the combined importance of the physical basis for personal characteristics and the role of upbringing.

The chapter sets child development in a historical context before looking at:

- the child study movement
- psychoanalysis – the work of Freud, Erikson and Klein
- behaviourism – classical and operant conditioning, social learning theory
- cognitivism – the work of Piaget, Vygotsky, Bruner and Rogoff
- attachment – the work of Bowlby, Rutter and Winnicott
- ecological approach – the work of Bronfenbrenner
- family types – permissive, authoritarian, authoritative and neglectful
- biological perspectives – genetics and cognitive neuroscience.

It is appropriate to consider biological and psychological aspects of child-hood together to move away from earlier approaches that made an artificial distinction between the mind and body. This division was termed 'Cartesian dualism' after its originator, Descartes (1596–1650). It is perpetuated through Galton's (1875) labelling as the nature–nurture debate, becoming a framework that pervades child development, and many other aspects of Western philosophical and political thought.

The period of the Enlightenment (see Chapter 3), 1650 onwards, was increasingly dominated by a belief in rational understanding and scientific explanation, as opposed to more traditional beliefs founded on religion and superstition. 'Modern' society was underpinned by a belief in continual progress towards improvements in the human condition (Wagner, 2008) based on scientific understanding of the forces that maintain life. Child development, as it underpins human development, was a vital element in the 'enlightened' desire to understand, cultivate and control the world we live in.

This 'modern' age was the age of the great explorations: Scott and Shackleton in Antarctica; Livingstone, Burton and Speke in Africa; Burke, Wills and King in Australia; Von Humboldt and Bonpland in South America. Herschel was studying the stars and planets; Lamarck, classifying flowers and shells and developing his theory of 'transmutation'; Lyell was studying rocks and fossils developing the principles of geology; and Hooker and Bentham were identifying the different species of plants. Later, in 1859, influenced by scientists such as these, Charles Darwin was to develop his theory of evolution, published as *The Origin of the Species* (see Victorian Web, 2014). Darwin was also author of the first 'recognised' child study. His *Biographical Sketch of an Infant* (1877) is based on notes made in 1840 (Burman, 1994: 10).

Arising from this broader interest in understanding 'living things', localised research focused on children, their maturation and their educational achievements. Early interest centred around 'ability', with developments in statistical analysis keeping pace with the desire to measure this accurately. Bain's (1859) work on aptitude tests and Galton's (1875) work on normal distributions, percentile norms, and correlation greatly facilitated comparison (De Landsheere, 1988) and Fisher's (1864) *Scalebook* provided graded exemplar to enable the objective measurement of achievement (Romberg, 1992).

The late nineteenth century was a period of political turmoil. When army recruits were found to lack strength and stamina, as happened in England with the Boer Wars of 1880–1881, 1899–1902, this focused national interest on healthy development. Coincidentally, compulsory schooling made children accessible in large numbers to those who would measure, question and observe them. So the study of group behaviours became the concern of psychology, and those interested in the individual pursued a psychoanalytical pathway. Later, as observers sought to modify behaviours, these trends gave way to behaviourist and psychotherapeutic interventions. Later still, the distinction between development and learning gave rise to the notion of the active learner, the cognitive child who is able to act independently on his environment.

The child study movement

Formal child study began in America. In 1888, G. Stanley Hall founded the Child Study Association of America that encouraged parents, teachers and academic researchers to form study clubs to collect data on children's development. His student, the statistician Gesell, set up a 'psycho-clinic' at Yale to study the 'normal' behaviour of white middle-class children, and in 1893 the National Education Association established a Department of Child Study. Universities in Iowa and Detroit also established departments and by the 1920s it was possible to study child development as an undergraduate. Specialist magazines and journals developed to support this new and growing discipline (Huntsinger, 2007). In England, earlier interest at the turn of the century led to the establishment of a Child Study Society in 1907 (Lowe, 2009).

Meanwhile in Europe, 'pedotechnical' offices were opened in Germany, France, Belgium and Switzerland. In 1904, Claparède founded an experimental psychology laboratory at the University of Geneva, followed in 1912 by the J.J. Rousseau Institute, where the cognitivist, Jean Piaget, carried out his seminal work on child development (De Landsheere, 1988).

Russia, too, pursued 'child science', seeking to prevent biological 'degeneration' and protect the future of the state. At first, activity was led by independent professionals, but after 1917 the post-Tsarist State intervened, encouraging academics to explore psychoanalytical (Spielrein and Rosenthal), behaviourist (Pavlov), and educational (Vygotsky) perspectives to develop an integrated discipline. 'Paedology' was to underpin radical social reform but by the late 1920s Stalin's communist party was critical of these approaches. In 1931 the educational system was reformed along traditional lines. Paedology was denounced as 'reactionary pseudoscience' and the associated testing criticised as classist and racist. Significant work by researchers like Vygotsky was suppressed until the 1960s, only becoming generally available in the period of perestroika (restructuring) in the late 1980s, and after the collapse of communism in the early 1990s (Byford, 2012).

Psychological perspectives

This brief international overview draws attention to a number of psychological traditions that contributed to our current understanding of child development – psychoanalysis, behaviourism and cognitivism. Together these perspectives underpin the way Western society understands human thought, actions and learning, and their adaption and adoption in different times and places partly explains shifts of paradigm, changes in the way children (and older humans, too) are viewed. These different traditions and their main proponents will now be discussed in turn, in approximate chronological order, as will attachment theory and the ecological approach as they make a vital contribution to our understanding of young children's social and emotional development.

Psychoanalysis
Sigmund Freud (1856–1939)

Freud, the 'Father' of psychoanalysis, was medically trained. Trying to cure 'hysterical' patients using hypnosis and suggestion, he became aware that earlier, often sexualised, experiences culminate in 'powerful psychic processes' that force the person to act in certain ways without consciously deciding their course of action (Jolibert, 1993). In *The Interpretation of Dreams* (1899) Freud espoused the theory that the 'fulfilment of a hidden wish is the essence of a dream' (Jones, 1961: 301). Freud was predominately interested in the problems faced by adults but saw the 'trials and tribulations of childhood as the source of the adult's distresses and disturbances' (Jolibert, 1993: 3). For Freud, the child's development is not a process of biological maturation but of repression as the child learns to control spontaneous urges by internalising acceptable responses.

Freud proposed that human minds embrace three core mental states. The unconscious *id,* present from birth, seeks instant gratification. Driven by the *libido* force, the child pursues the 'pleasure principle'. By about five, the *ego* develops, and this enables modification of instinctual desires, as the child becomes aware of social expectations and capable of making conscious decisions. The *superego* represents the internalisation of parental demands and social rules. Through the mechanisms of conscience and guilt, behaviour is self-regulated. Thus, Freud sees childhood as a struggle to balance the 'pleasure' and the 'reality' principle, a view that is far removed from that of childhood innocence and a gently unfolding personality (Schaffer, 1996: 17).

Freud divided childhood into five key stages: oral (birth to one); anal (one to three); phallic (three to six); latent (six to puberty); and genital (post-pubertal). He believed that a child needed to cope with the demands of each period to avoid associated problems or *fixations* in later life. However, he also recognised that humans are essentially versatile and develop coping mechanisms to avoid problems. They *repress* difficult memories and *regress* to earlier stages of behaviour under stress. Through *identification* children adopt adult standards rather than risk disapproval (Schaffer, 1996). Controversially, Freud formulated the *Oedipus* (male) and *Elektra* (female) complexes within the phallic stage whereby children rival their parent of the same sex for the attention of the parent of the opposite sex, before settling into a gender identity in parallel (Birch, 1997).

Freud's theories have been highly influential and many of his specialist terms are adopted in common parlance in society. Critics complain that his views were reductionist (interpreting human activity in terms of biological needs and responses) (Schaffer, 1996; Flanagan, 1996). The irreversibility of early experience is also challenged: 'that we remain victims of our past is no longer credible' (Clarke and Clarke, 1976, in Schaffer, 1996: 19; Gittins, 1998). There are concerns that Freud's theories derive from individual case studies so could be describing the exceptional rather than the norm (Birch, 1997). Additionally, Freud's betrayal of women patients' confidences is heavily criticised by feminist thinkers, particularly as he first believed and then discredited tales of abuse, terming them fantasies (Gittins, 1998). However, Freud's work on the concept of the unconscious, on the importance of dreams and the centrality of sexuality 'even if they need qualifying' are of lasting importance (ibid: 15), and overall his beliefs served as a useful counterweight to the behaviourist views that were developing from 1910 onwards (Burman, 1994). His ideas significantly influenced the work of later psychologists, directly, and through his daughter Anna Freud who, for instance, greatly influenced Erik Erikson (Hopkins, 1995).

Anna Freud, worked closely with her father and practised children's psychoanalysis in Vienna in 1923, where she further explored the nature of defence mechanisms, publishing *The Ego and the Mechanisms of Defense* in 1936 (Freud, 1936). Transferring to London at the onset of the Second World War, she continued her work, establishing first the Hampstead Nursery and then the Hampstead Child Therapy Course and Clinic.

Erik Erikson (1902–94)

Erikson studied psychoanalysis in Vienna, moving to Harvard Medical School, USA in 1933. His interests were broader than Sigmund Freud's but, like Freud, his findings were constructed from individual case studies rather than large-scale surveys. This led to generalised concepts that are difficult to define and test (Bee and Boyd, 2012). Focused on personality and identity, Erikson saw development as the resolution of a series of successive conflicts and challenges. His eight psychosocial stages describe progress as a set of binaries, expanding Sigmund Freud's stages beyond the psychosexual: stage 1 (babies, birth to one) is characterised by *trust vs mistrust*; stage 2 (toddlers) by *autonomy vs shame and doubt*; stage 3 (pre-school) by *initiative vs guilt*; stage 4 covers the primary years (5–11) and is characterised by *industry vs inferiority* as children learn or fail to learn; in stage 5 (adolescence), the conflict is *identity vs confusion* as teenagers strive to develop stable personalities; stage 6 (early adulthood) covers *intimacy vs isolation* as people seek to form significant relationships with others; stage 7 (later adulthood) is characterised by *generativity vs stagnation*, differentiating between adults who engage with careers, families and communities, and those who remain solitary; in stage 8 (old age), adults are believed to reflect back on their lives with *integrity or despair*, depending on whether they view their lives as successful or wasted (Erikson, 1963).

Melanie Klein (1882–1960)

Unlike Erikson, Klein's views brought her into conflict with the Freuds. Born in Vienna, she studied psychoanalysis in Budapest as a mature student. She was encouraged to psychoanalyse her own children and in so doing developed the techniques of 'play therapy' that are used in psychotherapeutic interventions. She published *The Psychoanalysis of Children* in 1932 (Klein, 1932), but this led to a very public controversy with Anna Freud around whether children could be psychoanalysed. Nevertheless, Klein's work played a significant part in bringing mother–child and other interpersonal relationships into the development debate for she saw that actual relationships played a significant role (Segal, 2004), whereas Freud's work centred on biological drives and mental constructs. Klein views the split psyche as rooted in early childhood. The young baby cannot differentiate between self and other, so when needs are met and the baby is warm, fed, and cuddled, the baby sees both self and mother as 'good'. Conversely, when these needs are unmet, both are viewed as 'bad'. To survive psychically the baby learns to hive or 'split off' these negative feelings and to project them onto the mother who is then seen as negative (Gittins, 1998).

Together, psychoanalytic approaches make an important contribution to our understanding of the complexities of personality development, for they demonstrate how children's 'perception' of the events they encounter can be as important as the events themselves (Seligman, 2005).

Behaviourism

In comparison, behaviourism deals with the tangible, what can be 'observed and measured' (Santrock, 2011: 26). Behaviourists sought to understand cause and effect, setting up controlled laboratory experiments where they could minimise unwanted inputs. Schaffer (1996) claims that behaviourist ideas originate in the Lockean philosophy that the child is born a 'blank slate' (see Chapter 4), which parents can mould and shape into the child they desire, but within the animal domain practical experiments are usually traced back to the Russian physiologist Ivan Pavlov (Pavlov, 1904) who was himself influenced by Darwin and Sechenov.

Classical conditioning

Ivan Pavlov's (1849–1936) interest in the functioning of human organs led to experimentation with dogs' digestive processes, and his insights into how stimuli could cause conditioned reflexes (associational biological responses). These ideas were taken up in America by John B. Watson (1878–1958) who demonstrated that classical conditioning can occur in human beings through his experiments to induce fear in a child (little Albert) (Santrock, 2011). Classical conditioning centres on reflex responses to stimuli but later behaviourists demonstrated that responses can be induced through voluntary behaviour too (Birch, 1997).

Operant conditioning

Edward Thorndike's Law of Effect (1911) states that pleasant consequences encourage behaviour to be repeated and, conversely, unpleasant ones discourage repetition. He demonstrated how cats quickly learned to pull a string to escape from a box once they had done this accidentally, calling this 'trial-and-error learning'.

Burrhus F. Skinner (1904–1990), from his position in the Department of Psychology at Harvard University, experimented with this notion, terming 'operant conditioning', the process whereby different kinds of reinforcement could encourage particular behaviours in rats (Skinner Foundation, 2012). Skinner found that continuous reinforcement is most effective in inducing learning quickly but partial reinforcement is more likely to cause the behaviour to continue after the intervention stops (Birch, 1997). These ideas underpin the notion of behaviour modification when children are encouraged to behave in certain ways by the careful application of rewards and, sometimes, sanctions. These techniques are most successful when the teacher ignores undesirable behaviour to encourage its extinction and rewards the positive to encourage repetition.

Social learning theory

The extrapolation of ideas from animal to children's behaviour must be approached with care, for children have many others ways of learning. Children learn through language and observation, as well as trial and error, and social learning theory attempts to bring observational learning (imitation) into the frame of behavioural change.

Albert Bandura (b. 1925), the American psychologist, is most closely associated with this work. Like the earlier behaviourists he also carried out 'controlled experiments' but focused on human learning. In 1961 Bandura (with Ross and Ross) devised an experiment to see whether children copied aggressive behaviour (Bandura et al., 1961). He found that children who watched a rubber 'Bobo' doll being thumped (either live or on screen) treated a 'real' doll more aggressively than a control group. In a later experiment, Bandura (1965) showed that children can learn behaviour but choose not to copy it.

Three groups of children were shown film of a model acting aggressively but shown different consequences. Those who saw the model punished demonstrated the least aggressive behaviour themselves. When all three groups were offered rewards, they all acted aggressively, demonstrating that children can 'acquire' behaviour but do not automatically 'perform' it. The learning process involves thought as well as imitation, so social learning theory offers a link between behaviourism and cognitive development (see below).

Cognitivism

While psychoanalytic theories emphasise the unconscious and consequently children's emotional development, cognitivism focuses on conscious thought and the exploration of real objects, and is exemplifed by Jean Piaget's work.

Jean Piaget (1896–1980)

Born into an academic family, Piaget was initially a student of the natural sciences but as an adult his interests turned to the human mind. For a period he worked on intelligence testing with Alfred Binet in France. Later, as Director of the J.-J. Rousseau Institute in Geneva, he focused on children, reasoning that their development might reveal how humans acquire knowledge (Smith, 2000). His concern was whether a child could perform operations (internalised mental actions) or needed to test ideas empirically in order to understand change (Santrock, 2011).

After closely studying his offspring, Piaget identified four stages of thought processing.

- In the *sensorimotor stage* (birth to two), children learn through sensory experience and movement. Reflexes give way to controllable schemas as the child learns how to act on the world (make things happen). A child who understands that objects have permanence is clearly able to hold a mental image.
- In the *pre-operational stage* (two to seven), children can represent the world in words and pictures but are unable to imagine consequences or see the world from other people's perspectives. Developmentally, they are egocentric.
- From 7 to 11 children enter the *concrete operational stage*. They can carry out calculations with physical objects to manipulate and understand that quantities do not change even if they change shape (conservation), unless you add or remove material.
- Between 11 and 15 the *formal operational stage* of adulthood commences. Children can manipulate ideas mentally, reason and think in the abstract (Smith et al., 2003).

Piaget envisaged that mental capacity develops through *adaptation*. Children *assimilate* new ideas that align with existing beliefs, and through *accommodation*, modify their beliefs to take account of new ideas that challenge their existing knowledge, reaching a new mental *equilibrium* when these contradictions are resolved (Santrock, 2011).

As Director of the International Bureau of Education in Geneva from 1926–67, Piaget took on the challenge of linking his ideas to pedagogy. His student and biographer, Munari, claims that Piaget's annual director's speeches 'forgotten by most reviewers' offer an explicit account of his educational credo. According to these, Piaget believed education to be the saviour of society and that this was best achieved without coercion and through active participation 'by a process of trial and error, working actively and independently, that is, without restriction and with ample time at their disposal' (Piaget, 1959, in Munari, 1994: 4).

As a theoretician, Piaget was 'a giant' (Santrock, 2011: 188) but later psychologists criticised the rigidity of his work, seeing children's development as gradual and individualised. Many researchers have demonstrated that Piaget's clinical findings were based on experimental designs that confounded children (Bryant, 1974; Borke, 1975; McGarrigle and Donaldson, 1974), thereby affecting his results. Dunn (1998), too, found that children in their home environment were able to decentre much earlier than Piaget believed possible. Nevertheless, Piaget's work profoundly influenced child development theory.

Lev Vygotsky (1896–1934)

Vygotsky was born in the same year as Piaget but work published in Russia only reached the West in the late 1960s so his ideas seem far more recent. Rather than focus on the biological like Piaget, Vygotsky viewed 'sociability' to be the primary human characteristic. As early as 1932 Vygotsky was explaining the importance of the adult, for the developing child can learn from 'asymmetric' relationships: 'Absolutely everything in the behaviour of the child is merged and rooted in social relations' (Vygotsky, 1982–84, 4: 281; in Ivic, 1994: 3).

Ivic (1994: 3) describes Vygotsky's work as a 'socio-historico-cultural theory of the development of higher mental functions'. Vygotsky views language as internalised thought and this enables 'psychic organisation' of the mind. However, it is social contact that enables the increasing sophistication of verbal expression that underpins learning. Adults impart to children the knowledge and understanding that prevails in the culture to which they belong (acculturisation), and socialise children to behave in certain ways even as they learn to talk and think. Dialogue allows the adult to support a child's learning, but internalised as 'inner speech', it helps the child to learn to self-regulate behaviour (Santrock, 2011).

Education becomes the 'artificial development' of the child (Vygotsky, 1982–84, 1: 107; in Ivic, 1994: 6). S/he can be helped to learn by an adult who offers appropriate support for a task that is within the child's grasp – in the zone of proximal development (ZPD). Individuals can also take command of their own learning through metacognition and social constructivism. *Metacognition* refers to an individual's awareness of his/her own processes of thinking and learning. *Social constructivism* is the individualised conversion of social learning into internalised new knowledge.

Contemporary researchers increasingly support Vygotsky's theories, as there is evidence that the areas of the brain governing social functions mature earlier than other parts. For example, the parts of the brain that govern the baby's perception of human faces and voices develop early in life, giving early 'sociability' a biological provenance (Ivic, 1994). In 1963, Fantz found that two-day-old babies chose to look at patterned stimuli like faces rather than coloured discs and later research also supports this preference for the human face (Balas, 2010; Cashon, 2010; Quinn et al., 2009; all in Santrock, 2011).

Jerome Bruner (b. 1915)

American psychologist, Bruner was asked to write the introduction to Vygotsky's *Thought and Language* in its first English translation in 1962. This led him to consider how Vygotsky's ideas could be used within education. With colleagues Wood and Ross (in 1976) he developed the practice of *scaffolding* whereby the teacher contingently applies a range of strategies to enable the child to learn within the ZPD, withdrawing support as the child became more able to complete the task alone (Wood, 1998).

Scaffolding is a flexible, child-centred strategy to support learning and this is in keeping with Bruner's educational philosophy that children progressively acquire adult thinking skills. Bruner (1977 [60]) believed that children learn through investigation – discovery learning – and developed a four-stage theory of instruction (Bruner, 1966) centring on: a predisposition to learn; structured knowledge; modes of representation; and effective sequencing. Perhaps influenced by Piaget's stages, Bruner (ibid) identified three stages of cognitive development associated to the modes of representation: physical action in the *Enactive* stage (birth to one); mental images in the *Iconic* stage (one to seven); symbolic systems, language, number, music in the *Symbolic* stage (seven plus). Bruner refuted Piaget's notion of readiness to learn, believing, like Vygotsky, that the adult role was to promote learning. His 'spiral curriculum' captured the idea that it was possible to introduce concepts to children in simple ways at a stage before they could formally understand them, embellishing them later: 'any subject can be taught to any child at any age in some form that is honest' (Bruner, 1977 [60]: ix).

Barbara Rogoff

Barbara Rogoff (1995), with colleagues, developed Vygotsky's ideas of *acculturisation* and Bruner's notion of scaffolding into the concept of *guided participation*. She revealed how adults worldwide support children in acquiring the skills needed to take part in the traditional activities of their local communities, physically helping them to do the work rather than explaining how to do it verbally. Studying American Girl Scouts at a cookie sale, she developed three planes of analysis: at the level of the community; the interpersonal; and the individual (ibid). Nowadays we take for granted the importance of relationships in shaping children's development but this was not always so clearly understood, even at the level of human dependency and attachment, an idea initially conceptualised by Bowlby.

Attachment

John Bowlby (1907–90)

Bowlby entered psychiatry in a period when psychology was dominated by a 'one-body' perspective. The child was viewed as a potentially autonomous individual who needed to be encouraged to become independent to develop 'ego-strength'. After Klein, s/he was also the vessel in which adult repressions and suppressions developed. Reeves (2007), a former associate, explains how Bowlby's views challenged these approaches, for he believed from the outset that environment and social context were important as was a 'caring' attitude towards children. His work with 'difficult' children in residential schools and child guidance clinics led him to develop a 'two-body' theorisation around the mother–child relationship, which challenged the dominant paradigm. Bowlby first recognised attachment in terms of loss – maternal deprivation – when children lived without family. He refuted the contemporary psychoanalytical view that fantasy shaped development. For Bowlby, it was children's lived experiences – nurture – that underpinned their psychological well-being.

Bowlby's work was timely. Despite significant losses in battle, considerable numbers of men returned home and needed work at the end of the Second World War, work that women had been carrying out in their absence. The government needed to encourage women back into the home, to return to domestic duties and help re-stabilise society. Supported by trends within psychoanalysis, Bowlby's theories contributed to the 'post-war celebration of home and hearth' (Burman, 1994: 78).

Theories of attachment, so central to the care of the next generation, continued and continue to challenge scientists. Bowlby (1982 [1969]) himself, further theorised that the child develops expectations for future relationships from the one s/he experiences with the primary carer and this becomes an 'internal working model' that affects all subsequent social interactions.

Also in the 1960s, Schaffer and Emerson carried out a longitudinal study of the first 18 months of 60 babies' lives (Schaffer and Emerson, 1964). They found that babies made indiscriminate attachments in the first three months but that at four months of age they demonstrated set preferences. By seven months the child was found to focus on a single attachment figure, but by nine months was able to cope with multiple attachments. These findings are now known to relate only to a Westernised context where society privileges 'monotropic' (one carer) relationships.

Ainsworth and Bell (1970) devised the 'strange situation' to test the theory that sensitive mothering fosters security in the young child. This was a sequence of episodes that enabled observation of infants' responses to the arrival and departure of their main carers. One hundred American families were observed in controlled conditions in order to examine the nature of the infant's separation anxiety, willingness to explore, stranger anxiety and reunion behaviour. From this work, Ainsworth identified three attachment styles: secure; ambivalent; and avoidant. Others tested these findings, and later observers, Main and Solomon (1986) added a fourth style – disorganised.

Throughout the 1980s researchers continued to study mother–child interactions, identifying how young children learn to focus and take turns through joint involvement episodes with their main carer (Tomasello and Todd, 1983; Schaffer 1989, 1992; in Schaffer, 1996). However, Bowlby's work was also criticised.

Michael Rutter (b. 1933)

Michael Rutter (1972), reassessing attachment theory, made a case for infants developing multiple attachments and international evidence supports this view, as we saw in Chapter 2. Rutter also pointed out that Bowlby failed to distinguish between 'privation' (the absence of an emotional bond) and 'deprivation' (the loss of an emotional bond), claiming that privation can cause physical and intellectual growth impairment and later antisocial or psychopathic behaviour. Lack of stimulation and social interaction compound the problem, and children need specialist care to escape long-term consequences. The fall of the Ceausescu government provided an exceptional opportunity for empirical research into attachment theory and Professor Rutter became coordinator of the English and Romanian Adoptee Study (Nuffield Foundation, 2014), a naturalistic study of deprivation established in the early 1990s when Romanian orphans were brought into England for adoption. To date this has followed the attainments of some 165 children at the ages of 4, 6, 11 and 15. It finds that the effects of early malnourishment are mostly recoverable and that children make rapid developmental gains once they are adequately cared for. However, those adopted after 6 months of age continue to show significant deprivation-specific concentration and social functioning problems (Nuffield Foundation, 2014);

Rutter et al., 1999; Colvert et al., 2008), confirming the connection between early privation and long-term problems of attachment.

Contemporary advances in genetics identify that the situation is more complex than first thought. Nature and nurture both pay a significant role in the development of attachment. As an example, variations in the serotonin transporter gene indicate different levels of susceptibility. In naturalistic observations focused on maternal responsiveness, children with two short alleles (alternative genetic forms) were found to be more vulnerable to external influences than those with two long alleles who appear to develop security regardless of the type of care they received (Barry et al., 2008).

Donald Winnicott (1896–1971)

Winnicott, a near contemporary of Bowlby's, accepted the prevalent one-body model, seeing the mother and baby as a single unit with the baby as a 'patient' to be nursed and nurtured until competent to act agentively. Thus the relationship is an asymmetrical one with the baby needing support if bonding does not occur spontaneously. Winnicott became aware of the problems of separation and deprivation following his work with evacuees after the Second World War, but rather than focusing on the inviolability of the family, he championed substitute care (maternal and/or paternal). Winnicott advocated the establishment of small residential units where children could experience 'good enough' mothering and a 'primary home experience' (Reeves, 2007). He also observed (Winnicott, 1953) that children often sought comfort from inert substitutes; pieces of blanket, teddies and articles of parental clothing became non-social attachments. He termed these *transitional objects*, as they helped the child to move away from maternal ties and towards acting independently. Even securely attached children will take these between home and nursery to make a link between the two, or use them at bedtime to go to sleep alone (Flanagan, 1996). Drawing on Winnicott's work on *Playing and Reality* (Winnicott, 1971), many psychologists believe that children's imaginary friends are also a 'form of transitional phenomena' (Majors, 2013).

Ecological approach
Urie Bronfenbrenner (1917–2005)

Bronfenbrenner was a key psychologist, at Cornell University from 1948, who significantly influenced the study of human development across the lifespan. In particular, he led the move towards ecologically valid naturalistic observation of children, and away from laboratory study – 'the science of the strange behaviour of children in strange situations with strange adults for the briefest possible periods of time' (Bronfenbrenner, 1977: 513). Rejecting such fragmented approaches to child development, Bronfenbrenner developed an ecological theory. This draws the 'proximal processes' that mould the child into a single model, opening up child development to a broad spectrum of ideas, and making it at once both 'multidisciplinary and multiprofessional' (Lerner, 2005: ix, x). The ecological model centres children within their social context, so is discussed further in Chapter 6.

Equally importantly, Bronfenbrenner believed that new insights about childhood should be used to benefit children. Becoming 'the professional conscience of the field of human development' (Lerner, 2005: x), he put his beliefs into practice as he co-founded America's 1965 Head Start programme (which greatly influenced England's Sure Start initiative) (see Chapter 7).

Family types

As the family is traditionally the basic unit of childcare, family structures and behaviours are a key concern of psychologists. Different family practices have the potential to affect children's development in distinctive ways.

Diana Baumrind attempted to classify parental behaviours by type in 1966 and 1967 (Bee and Boyd, 2012). She identified three categories:

- *Permissive* parents who tend to indulge children or leave them to regulate their own behaviour and whose children tend towards antisocial behaviour, becoming rebellious or defiant if challenged.
- *Authoritarian* parents who control their children's actions, expecting them to accept and follow very stringent guidelines and to take on a range of set tasks. This often leads to anxious children who seek adult approval, who work hard at school and conform to society's expectations but have a tendency to give up if things go badly.
- *Authoritative* parents, a third and idealised type, who reason with and guide the child but take his/her likes and ways into consideration when making decisions. This parent potentially supports children to become lively, socially adjusted and resilient individuals who can confidently master the tasks set for them.

In 1983 Maccoby and Martin (in Bee and Boyd, 2012) saw that these categories actually denote degrees of acceptance and responsiveness, and degrees of demand and control, and that intersecting these vectors enabled the identification of a fourth type.

- *Neglectful* parents who fail to engage with the child to produce socially incompetent and immature children with low levels of self-esteem. They display a tendency to opt out that leads often to truancy and delinquency (in Bee and Boyd, 2012).

More recent research suggests that authoritative parenting creates competent children but demonstrates that the stereotypes are culturally mediated
to produce appropriate outcomes. For example, Asian child-rearing practices are often authoritarian but lead to high levels of achievement in their
children (Stevenson and Zusho, 2002; in Santrock, 2011). Similarly, Latino
children grow up to be obedient and respectful when their parents are
authoritarian (Harwood et al., 2002; in Santrock, 2011).

This discussion of family types focuses on the role of nurture when it
links children's subsequent development to the parenting style adopted. Yet,
taken too literally, this could create unfounded guilt in carers, for such claims
ignore the interactive element in parenting, minimise the role of agency in
childhood and fail to consider the possibility of biological bases to behaviour.

Biological perspectives

Scientific advances daily afford new understandings of the biological foundations of life, showing us how both nature and nurture play a significant
role in child development.

The physical body we are born with shapes our abilities just as surely
as the care and guidance with which we are raised. In contemporary science, new knowledge, materials and equipment are making it increasingly
safe and affordable to look inside the human body. Humans are beginning
to understand the complex chemical and physical activity that underpins
human thought and action, perhaps life itself.

Genetics

Human bodies are built up from cells, all of which are subdivisions of the
zygote formed at conception when a single male and female cell fuse to form
a new life. Thus our genetic inheritance is in place from the very beginning,
although there is some flexibility as not all 'options' develop. Scientists use
the term *genotype* to distinguish the material mapped in the genes from the
phenotype, the observable outcomes when genes and environment interact.
The typical human body contains 46 *chromosomes* (23 pairs, one set derived
from the mother, one set derived from the father). These hold the genetic
material that will determine our development in line with other human
beings as well as our individual characteristics. Chromosomes are long
strings of DNA – molecules comprising numerous genes that control development. Since February 2001, the position of each gene has been mapped
as part of the Human Genome Project. Twenty-two sets of chromosome
pairs – *autosomes* – have identical structures but the 23rd pair are either X
or Y chromosomes and determine the child's sex. Females have two X

chromosomes, males an X and a Y and, for this reason, females have a slightly higher chance of avoiding abnormalities as a faulty gene can more easily be replaced by an alternative (Bee and Boyd, 2012: 40).

Individual characteristics are determined by complex processes. When the instructions from the two sets of genes are the same – *homozygous* – this determines the pattern. When they differ – *heterozygous* – only one set can be selected. Some genes (like the one for curly hair) are *dominant* and will always take precedence. Others (like the gene for straight hair) are *recessive* so a child will only have straight hair if she inherits that instruction from both parents. Nevertheless the curly-haired could still carry a straight hair gene and pass that on to offspring. Some characteristics are *co-dominant*, others – *expressive* ones – vary in the degree to which they determine a characteristic. *Polygenic* characteristics, like skin colour, enable blending. Others, like height are *multi-factorial*, relying on both genetic inheritance and environmental factors. Thus, each generation is newly constructed from a broad range of possibilities, maintaining the potential for adaptation (Bee and Boyd, 2012).

These ideas are developed further in Chapter 9.

Cognitive neuroscience

Our understanding of the physiology, biochemistry, pharmacology and structure of the vertebrate brain has significantly improved over the past hundred years. Genetic advances contribute to this and, more recently, neuroimaging has made it possible for scientists to study the human brain functioning directly (Goswami, 2004). Activity occurs at both molecular and cellular levels but also at systematic levels when entire networks support intellectual and cognitive processing.

Neurons (brain cells) comprise a *nucleus* that holds genetic information, a *soma* where signals are joined and passed on, and an *axon* (or cable), sometimes insulated by a fatty (myelin) sheath, that carries information from the cell body to the numerous branching *dendrites* that end in *terminals* or *bulbs* (synapses) that can send and receive information (see Figure 5.1). *Neurotransmitters* are chemical messengers that transmit information from cell to cell by crossing the gap between synapses. These can be *excitatory* (increasing the probability that a neuron will fire) or *inhibitory* (discouraging the neuron from firing). Whether or not firing occurs is determined by the stimulation rate achieved by an electrical signal travelling down the axon. If sufficiently strong, the signal triggers a release of chemical neurotransmitters into the synaptic gap that are taken up by the opposing dendrites and reconverted into an electrical signal. This is a delicate process and explains how, by overwhelming the natural functioning of the neurotransmitters, diseases and drugs can so easily affect brain functioning (Wolfe, 2010: Chapter 4). Thus, thinking and action are controlled by chemical reactions on human matter and magnetic resonance imaging (MRI) scanners can see this happening inside the human brain, increasing our knowledge about the parts responsible for different activities and the nature of the brain activity itself (see Wolfe, 2010: Chapter 1).

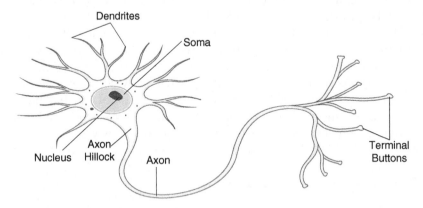

Axon: the long fibre that connects the cell body to the terminal buttons and transmits the signal.

Axon hillock: a control at the end of the soma that determines whether a signal is strong enough to activate the neuron.

Dendrites: the branching paths that enable multiple linkages with other cells.

Nucleus: the central mechanism to maintain the neuron and ensure functionality.

Soma: the space where signals from dendrites are joined together and passed on.

Terminal buttons: the means of sending signals across the synaptic gap to other neurons.

Figure 5.1   The structure of a neuron

The brain is divided into four main sections (see Figure 5.2):

- the *occipital lobes* lie at the base of the head and largely deal with visual information
- the *temporal lobes* are at the side of the brain and deal with auditory inputs
- the *parietal lobes* crown the back of the head and deal with pressure, touch, pain and the position of the limbs. Their posterior parts monitor inputs to create spatial awareness
- the *frontal lobes* perform the most complex functions and are associated with reasoning, higher-level cognition, expressive language and motor skills (Wolfe, 2010: Chapter 3).

However, in young children the different sense areas are initially linked and this may help them to develop complex understandings (schemas) like number, time and intensity, which do not neatly fit into a sensory area. For this reason, young children respond well to multi-sensory teaching methods (Goswami, 2004).

By seven months gestation the foetal brain has developed almost all its neurons (Goswami, 2004). In the last few months of pregnancy, glial cells develop. These hold the neurons together and give the brain form and structure (Bee and Boyd, 2012). Once born, brain development is almost entirely a growth process. Synaptogenesis is the process whereby axons, synapses and dendrites (fibre connections) grow. The visual and auditory cortexes develop rapidly. By 4 to 12 months they have a density of around 150 per cent of the adult level and are pruned back to 100 per cent by age four. The pre-frontal cortex (associated with planning and reasoning) develops more slowly, peaking after 12 months, and is pruned to adult levels between 10 and 20 years. Brain metabolism (an indicator of functioning) peaks at about

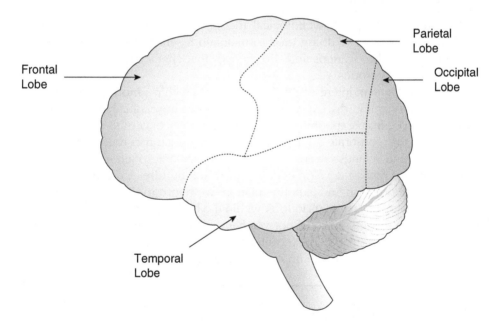

The frontal lobe: associated with reasoning, motor skills, higher level cognition and expressive language.

The parietal lobe: associated with processing tactile sensory information such as pressure, touch and pain.

The occipital lobe: associated with interpreting visual stimuli and information.

The temporal lobe: includes the primary auditory cortex, supports interpretation of sounds and language.

Figure 5.2   The structure of the brain

150 per cent of the adult level at around four to five years, reducing to adult levels at about ten years. These figures demonstrate the child's brain to be maximally flexible but plasticity continues in adulthood, enabling recovery from injury and the acquisition of new learning. Sensitive periods for learning exist but are more flexible than once thought, enabling deprived children to develop elementary skills but possibly not to progress to higher levels of functioning. Brains vary considerably, functions are localised, and different individuals need different numbers of neurons to carry out identical functions. As neurons are interchangeable in immature brains, dramatic environmental differences can result in very different outcomes. This flexibility enables development to vary but differential activity can compensate for the effects of extreme conditions, minimising negative outcomes (Goswami, 2004). Neuroscience is discussed further in Chapter 9.

Summary

This chapter grouped psychological theorists according to their underpinning beliefs and in so doing tried to maintain a sense of historical development, despite the overlaps and divergences that characterise individual lives and career trajectories.

It sets the human interest in their own species within a more general interest in life and scientific discovery, and demonstrates how initially the interest in children arose from experiments with animals and a concern to understand the processes that constitute adult behaviour. In late Victorian times, science was empirical, and scientists were interested in observable phenomena, debating the origins of human development in nature and nurture. A century later, after intensive theorisation and experimentation, we return to direct observation as new technologies enable us to look within the body, and particularly its neural structures to identify *what*, if not yet *how*, different elements cause different outcomes. It is to enable greater understanding of these future developments that this chapter ended with an outline of the biology of human life.

Points for reflection

- Which aspects of psychological theory can *you* apply to real life? How is this of benefit?
- When you were a child, how closely did your parents' behaviour model a single family type?
- Reassess your stance towards the nature–nurture debate in light of recent scientific discoveries. (The Goswami (2004) and Perry (2002) articles could be helpful here.)

Further reading

Bradbury, D.E. (1937) The contribution of the child study movement to child psychology. *Psychological Bulletin*, 34(1): 21–38.
Offers an explanatory historical overview.

Shuttleworth, S. (2010) *The Mind of the Child.* Oxford: Oxford University Press.
Considers Victorian developments in literature, science and medicine to create new insights.

Music, G. (2011) *Nurturing Natures: Attachment and Children's Emotional, Sociocultural and Brain Development.* Hove: Psychology Press.
Updates child development theory in light of more recent neurological advances.

Goswami, U. (2004) 'Annual review: neuroscience and education', *British Journal of Educational Psychology*, 74: 1–14.
Goswami, U. (2006) 'Neuroscience and education: from research to practice?', *Nature Reviews: Neuroscience*, 7(5): 406–11.
Perry, B.D. (2002) 'Childhood experience and the expression of genetic potential', *Brain and Mind*, 3: 79–100.
Bee, H. and Boyd, D. (2012) *The Developing Child*, 13th edn. New York: Allyn and Bacon.
Accessible accounts of brain activity. Bee and Boyd (2012: Chapter 2: Prenatal Development) systematically explain the biology.

Beilin, H. (1992) 'Piaget's enduring contribution to developmental psychology', *Developmental Psychology*, 28(2): 191–204.
Robbins, J. (2007) 'Young children thinking and talking: using sociocultural theory for multi-layered analysis', *Learning and Socio-cultural Theory: Exploring Modern Vygotskian Perspectives International Workshop 2007*, 1(1) [Online]. Available at http://ro.uow.edu.au/llrg/vol1/iss1/3 (accessed June 2014).
Stroebe, M. and Archer, J. (2013) 'Origins of modern ideas on love and loss: contrasting forerunners of attachment theory', *Review of General Psychology*, 17(1): 28–39.
Twemlow, S.W. and Parens, H. (2006) 'Might Freud's legacy lie beyond the couch?', *Psychoanalytic Psychology*, 23(2): 430–51.

(Continued)

(Continued)

Watrin, J.P. and Darwich, R. (2012) 'On behaviorism in the cognitive revolution: myth and reactions', *Review of General Psychology*, 16(3): 269–82.
Succinct discussions of specific psychological traditions.

Websites

http://psychology.about.com
Comprehensive coverage of key concepts, fields and people.

www.psychologytoday
Magazine spin off with useful articles sorted by topic stream.

www.victorianweb.org
A nodal network of key material on Victorian times.

www.ibe.unesco.org/en/services/online-materials/publications/thinkers-on-education.html
Lists articles, for example on Freud, Piaget and Vygotsky, in Prospects, *the quarterly journal of comparative education, 1993/1994, UNESCO.*

To gain *free* access to selected SAGE journal articles related to key topics in this chapter, visit: www.sagepub.co.uk/hazelrwright.

CHAPTER 6

SOCIOLOGICAL PERSPECTIVES

Overview

This chapter uses Bronfenbrenner's ecological theory to show how the development of an individual child is affected by macro-level policies through a series of nested systems. It then outlines key perspectives that underpin sociological thought:

- Marxism and critical theory
- functionalism and socialisation
- capitals, habitus and social reproduction
- poststructuralism and postmodernism
- globalisation, late modernity and structuration
- feminism, intersectionality and postcolonialism.

The chapter adopts a three-part framework to apply theoretical perspectives to:

- the family – changing family structures, looked after children
- society – models of inclusion: medical, social and affirmative
- childhood – the new sociology of childhood, social constructionism, and constructs of childhood.

It offers concise overviews of complex concepts and examines how these relate to our understanding of childhood.

When we talk about childhood many of us will conjure up a vision of a discrete family unit with parents who work to provide and care for their children, and children whose lives are bounded by play and schooling.

In recent times the traditional gender, age and power divisions within Westernised societies have flexed and stretched but remain recognisable. Many of us will hold a modernised – but still stereotypical – view of childhood that sees different family structures as variants rather than established alternative forms. This chapter will trace some of the changes and variations that shape our contemporary understandings of family, community and society to help us to think more broadly, but it starts by describing some key theoretical perspectives common within the discipline of sociology to provide a spatial and historical lens through which to gaze.

As a discipline, sociology can be traced back to the work of key theorists who formulated new ways of studying social behaviour. Initially the focus was to emulate scientific approaches and in the 1930s Auguste Comte (1798–1857) advocated *positivist* approaches, the objective collection of empirical evidence to determine how aspects of the real world are causally connected. Emile Durkheim (1858–1917) used such approaches in his studies of suicide (1897), division of labour (1893) and religious life (1912), listing the *social facts* (for example, family, class and religion) that constrain the ways that society functions. Karl Marx (1818–1883) continued this *structural* study of society, focusing on economic capital and social class (see below), but Max Weber (1864–1920) developed an interest in understanding 'why' people do certain things and how they display *agency*, introducing a less positivist approach in his studies of religion and bureaucracy. Later, sociologists developed specific ways of studying society: Alfred Schultz (1967 [1932], phenomenology), G.H. Mead (1967 [1934], symbolic interactionism), Garfinkel (1984 [1967]) ethnomethodology), influenced by Goffman's (1971[1959]) concern with the social self. Thus, there is a broad range of sociological theory and research methodology to explore in future.

Sociological imagination

American sociologist, C. Wright Mills (2000 [1959]), made the case for developing a 'sociological imagination' by which he meant that sociologists should relate personal struggles (agency) to public (structural) issues important within society (Fulcher and Scott, 2011). 'The sociological imagination enables us to grasp history and biography and the relations between the two in society' (Wright Mills, 2000: 6). This linking of micro-level (local and personal) needs to the macro-level (societal) enables us to better understand the world in which we live.

Ecological theory

Ecological theory provides a framework in which to make these links. In the scientific work of the American developmental psychologist, Urie

Bronfenbrenner, dating from 1979, this takes the form of a concentric ring model that places the child at the centre of his/her universe.

- The *microsystem* describes the relationships, roles and events the child experiences daily within the family, peer group or substitute care setting.
- The *mesosystem* delineates the interactions between two or more settings in the microsystem, so between the family and day care, family and peers, and/or peers and day care. Thus, it is a system of microsystems.
- The *exosystem* delineates interactions that may only indirectly influence the child, such as between the nursery and the parental workplace.
- The *macrosystem* describes activity within the larger culture, for example beliefs, knowledge bases, resources.
- The *chronosystem* offers a means of incorporating the effects of change over time (for example, on affluence, economic recession, ways of living, gendered expectations) (Bronfenbrenner, 1994: 39–40).

McDowall Clark (2010) portrays the different spheres as cogs that interact, and in moving away from the nested circles, stresses the intersection of spheres rather than the inner/outer movement across boundaries. This interpretation fits more neatly with postmodernist perspectives (see Figure 6.1).

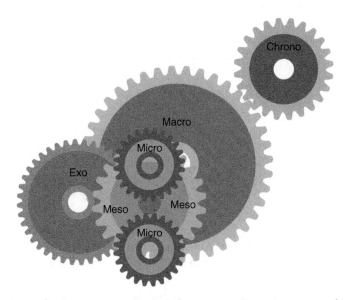

Figure 6.1   Bronfenbrenner's ecological theory as a dynamic system of interactive cogs

(source: McDowall Clark, 2010)

Key sociological perspectives

Marxism

This economic and social system derived from the theories of Karl Marx and his companion Friedrich Engels (1820–1895). They were concerned with the contradictions within *capitalist* industrial societies that divided people into wealthy employers (the *bourgeoisie*) and workers who 'sold' their labour (the *proletariat*). Marx believed that workers internalise the social mechanisms that bound their lives, an idea later termed *false-consciousness* (Lukàcs, 1971 [1920]), and this prevents them from challenging their oppression. He believed that to understand society required criticality not just observation. Activity is complex and unity only achieved when opposing views are reconciled through a process of *dialectic* analysis. Believing that philosophers should try to change the world not merely observe it, Marx and Engels envisaged a communist society in which the working class would overthrow the governing classes, ending class struggles and inequality as all workers are paid according to their need. Marx's *Das Kapital* (Volumes: 1 (1867), 2 (1885) and 3 (1894)) explored these ideas in detail, and the *Communist Manifesto* (co-written with Engels in 1848) was intended as a blueprint for this new egalitarian society (Bilton et al., 2002). However, despite its longevity in Cuba, experiences in Russia and the Soviet Block, and in China, North Korea and Vietnam suggest that equality is not that easily achieved through communism. Under these regimes, many families have lived in extreme poverty with children who were hungry, poorly housed and clothed, and expected to comply absolutely with the dictates of the regime.

Critical theory

In the twentieth century critical theorists associated with the German Institute for Social Research (founded 1923) sought to understand why Marx's predicted socialist revolution failed to occur, and to reconstruct the logic of Marxism in line with twentieth century capitalism. Members of this 'Frankfurt School' – philosophers like Adorno, Horkheimer, Marcuse, and later, Habermas – argued that false consciousness is so deeply embedded within society that people believe the existing system is both rational and inevitable. External exploitation and internal self-disciplining lead to *domination*, people conforming to social expectations rather than seeking liberation, settling for the freedoms of *consumer choice* rather than socio-political and economic liberty. Critical theory promotes the *dialectical imagination*, the ability to view the world as having the potential to change. Habermas (in *Theory of Communicative Action*, 1987 [1984]) offered a new discursive approach, *reflective communication,* which encourages citizens to develop a consensual approach to social policy through constructive discourse (Agger, 1991). This highly theoretical debate engages with childhood mainly through trying to radicalise educational systems in order to challenge inequalities within societies.

Functionalism and socialisation

While sociologists with a political bent considered how society could be changed others sought to understand the world as it is. The functionalist perception derives from the work of the sociologist Emile Durkheim and his interest in how society maintains stability. It deems this to be achieved when institutions and individuals have a defined role to play, and conform to the expectations of that role. This perspective was dominant in American sociology in the 1940s and 1950s with Robert Merton and Talcott Parsons as key advocates. Merton developed the notion of *manifest* (intentional) and *latent* (incidental) functions. So, when people choose to hold a street party, its manifest function is to celebrate a public occasion. Its latent function could be a corresponding improvement in social relationships in a residential street. Merton also considered the nature of *dysfunction* and its work in promoting change through resolution of conflict. Talcott Parsons, who applied functionalism to the family, is seen to have 'unduly stressed factors leading to social cohesion' (Giddens, 2006: 22). The functionalist family was a nuclear one with the father as the main (or only) breadwinner, and the mother as full-time carer and housewife. This ensured children received attention but possibly from frustrated women. Boys were granted greater freedom and more educational opportunities than girls, perpetuating gender inequality and disadvantaging children from single-parent families. Functionalism is criticised by feminist sociologists for over promoting the division of labour within the family to the detriment of mothers' freedom to work beyond the domestic sphere.

Capitals, habitus and social reproduction

Pierre Bourdieu (1930–2002) developed Marx and Engels' views of capital (*Das Kapital*, (1867, 1885, 1894), recognising that there were multiple ways that this can be acquired. Rather than using the term *human* capital that had come to represent an individual's value in terms of labour, Bourdieu (1986) coined three main types of capital: *economic*, which is directly 'convertible' into money and readily 'institutionalised' through property rights; *cultural*, which is often institutionalised as educational qualifications; and *social*, which is formed from obligations ('connections') perhaps in the form of a hereditary title. *Cultural* capital is seen as an 'embodied' characteristic, one that is fundamental to a person's *habitus*, his/her position in the world.

Cultural capital captures the notion of *social reproduction* whereby parents pass their advantages down through the generations, and offers an additional explanation for the maintenance of divisions and structures within society. Children from wealthy families are often multiply endowed as all three types of capital bestow benefit and those who have one tend to have access to the others, too.

Capital is a useful way of labelling the attributes that individuals, and groups of individuals, can muster for self-advancement, and researchers continue to define new forms. *Emotional capital* (Reay, 2000) refers to ways in which mothers can privilege their children by using emotional support to further their achievement and well-being.

Maternal capital (Wells, 2010) is used by health scientists to describe the child's genetic (phenotypical) inheritance that predisposes survival and growth. More controversially, *erotic capital* (Hakim, 2011) describes how women can/do use their looks and charms to restore gendered power imbalances in their favour.

Poststructuralism and postmodernism

By the mid-1960s most radical thinkers no longer believed that the transformation of capitalist society was imminent. Many turned away from political activism, focusing instead on ways of challenging the status quo by changing its discourse (ways of thinking and talking). Some continued in the critical theory tradition but others followed the French philosophers in *deconstructing* (unpicking), and thereby challenging, accepted norms. There are considerable overlaps between the terms *poststructuralism* and *postmodernism* and some philosophers contributed to both idioms. This is, perhaps, to be expected given that these are both approaches that aimed to disrupt accepted ideas. As Agger (1991: 112) says: 'Perhaps the most important hallmark of all this work is its aversion to clean positivist definitions and categories'. Sara Wilson (n.d.) claims Foucault's book *The Order of Things* (Foucault, 1966) to be a 'key text' in the development of poststructuralism, and in *Archaeology of Knowledge* (Foucault, 1969) Foucault called for thinkers to 'disconnect the unquestioned continuities by which we organise, in advance, the discourse that we are to analyse'. However, Foucault was interested in both discourse *and* practices, applying his ideas to institutions (for example, prisons, 1977) and human characteristic (for example sexuality, 1978, 1985, 1986) to see how these are constituted. His interest lies in the social world (Agger, 1991) not just the language that describes it so Foucault is also a central figure in postmodernism.

Despite the overlaps, a distinction can be made between poststructuralism and postmodernism.

Poststructuralism is essentially a theory of knowledge and language, centred on deconstruction of texts, after Derrida (1974 [1967, in French]). Derrida claimed that every text can be read at a superficial level but this misses the layers of hidden meanings that lie in the choice of words and ideas that are used in the writing. At an everyday and simple level, for example, our reading of text often slides over the use of words like 'history', 'mankind', 'manpower', which demonstrate the continuing patriarchal nature of society despite feminist challenges to de-gender language. For Derrida, every definition needs clarifying and every clarification needs further clarification so meaning remains elusive. Such 'deconstruction' is ably demonstrated in Stronach and Maclure's *Educational Research Undone* (1997), which continually unpicks its own claims. For example, the poststructuralist legacy is that it has taught people to question the significance of political manifestos and policy documents rather than accept what is offered at face value. In effect, it asks us to read between the lines. Taking a Foucauldian approach to poststructuralism, MacNaughton (2005) shows how critical reflection can be applied to early years settings to examine and challenge the taken-for-granted discourses that disempower children.

Postmodernism is a broader theory of culture, history and society, claiming the writings of Foucault, Barthes, Lyotard and Baudrillard as seminal sources. Lyotard's (1979) *The Postmodern Condition* is one of its core works (Agger, 1991). Like critical theory and poststructuralism, postmodernism rejects the idea that representations can be taken purely at face value and, instead, argues that every aspect of knowledge is subject to cultural and historical interpretation. Different subjects occupy different positions so there can be no universal truths that hold good for all society. Thus postmodernism rejects the *grand narratives* (overarching theories) that were once considered true for all times and places, favouring instead the multiple narratives of smaller groups whose knowledge is *situated* (specific to their context). In its most extreme forms, postmodernist theory challenges the existence of centralised knowledge, declaring that everything is relative, continually shifting in space and time. In its less extreme forms it asks us to question our values and actions and to think more carefully before we act. In the early years sector Dahlberg et al. (2007 [1999]) applied a postmodern analysis to issues of quality in 1999, questioning the reduction of value judgements to a series of measurable outcomes, and expounding the virtues of diversity and the importance of minority voices and localised action. They believe that, in favouring pedagogical documentation over child observation, the educator places the powerful child at the centre of his/her learning rather than assessing him/her against expectations and norms and thereby focusing on deficiencies and needs.

Globalisation and late modernity

Postmodern society signifies one which is abruptly different from the society that preceded it, one in which people have lost confidence in progress.

It is one where they no longer believe that the application of scientific principles will solve the world's problems, one which is profoundly globalised, challenging the traditional powers of the nation state. Towards the end of the twentieth century this radical disjuncture was widely acclaimed but Vandenberghe (1999) dismisses it as 'the fad of the Eighties' and Anthony Giddens (1991), less radically, claimed that the world is experiencing not postmodernity but late modernity, a formulation that embraces change while allowing continuity. Giddens captured Harvey's (1990) postmodern notion of 'time-space compression' in terms of differences of scale. He views life as 'contextually situated in time and space' but believes that the 'intrusion of distance into local activities' marks radical change, for 'phenomenal worlds for the most part are truly global' (Giddens, 1991: 187ff).

Giddens had already offered a resolution for another fundamental issue within sociology, the structure–agency debate.

Structuration

Some sociologists attribute problems to *structural issues* (how a society meets the economic and social needs of its people and how it deals with restrictive categories like race, class, gender, age, wealth) while others give more weight to *agency* (the degree to which an individual works to control his/her own destiny). Postmodern thinking refutes such oppositional notions, and, seeking an alternative way of resolving this dichotomy, Giddens posited the notion of *structuration*, which recognises the interaction of these two influences (Giddens, 1984). Giddens explains how human beings are continually making and re-making the social structure. Patterns of activity and behaviour are predictable because humans act in similar ways. However, humans are empowered to act in certain ways through their knowledge of the social structures within which they live: they know what is acceptable. Thus, language exists because it *is* socially structured. Without rules and shared meaning, language is reduced to noise. Yet language only exhibits structural qualities because humans understand, use, reinforce and modify the rules of language.

Feminism

Another significant 'voice' in the twentieth century is that of women, for too long invisible in historic and political accounts unless exceptional. The first phase of feminism is commonly traced to the late nineteenth century when the suffragettes campaigned for votes and equal rights for women (Walby, 1990), but in the 1790s Mary Wollstonecraft was arguing that it was 'irrational' not to regard women as 'rational' beings (1792, in Bilton et al., 2002: 488). Second Wave feminists of the 1960s and 1970s, following the lead of the American Betty Friedan, made a distinction between sexual difference and socially constructed gender differences, arguing that gender distinctions in education, in the workplace, and in politics should be redressed in order to enable women full access to the public sphere. Women grouped under the banner 'the personal is political', focusing on those aspects of life that were previously reserved for the private sphere: the division of labour in the home, sexual relationships, pay and discrimination in the workplace, rape and domestic violence (Bilton et al., 2002). In the UK, in *The Female Eunuch* (1970) Germaine Greer called for 'revolution' rather than 'reform', and women teachers took their views into schools in the 1970s and 1980s, encouraging girls' involvement in traditional male subjects (Arnot et al., 1999). However, different groups of women hold different views of feminism and this has tended to dilute the power of women to change society.

Third Wave feminists of the post-1990s rationalised some of these differences in terms of the intersectionality of race, gender and class, raising awareness that people who belong to more than one minority group have to consider where their interests are best served and, conversely, reminding groups of the need to recognise the diversity of their members (see 'Intersectionality' below).

Children and childcare are a significant cause of factions within feminism as women group according to whether to have children, whether to work as mothers, and how to find solutions to childcare issues. This is clearly tabulated in Jones' book on women and work (2012). There is evidence that many women choose part-time work as a compromise (Hakim, 2004; Wright, 2011), but in America, choosing not to work is labelled 'opting out' (Belkin, 2003; Jones, 2012), the prerogative of those who can afford not to work. For more radical feminists, women who make this choice are seen to be undermining attempts to create family-friendly conditions in the workplace, 'choice' being only a new name for 'privilege' (Elliott, 2009).

Intersectionality

Intersectionality, a term coined by Kimberley Crenshaw (1989), indicates how categories like race, class and gender overlap, making visible the multiple oppressions to which some individuals are subject. The term is not confined to the three main categories, to women, or to adults. Children are also subject to these oppressions, often directly and indirectly through the treatment of their parents. The need to consider inequality holistically is officially recognised even if redress is slow to achieve. For example, the Australian Human Rights and Equal Opportunities Commission (2001: 2; in Yuval-Davis, 2006) describes how 'aspects of identity are indivisible' and how 'speaking of race and gender in isolation from each other results in concrete disadvantage'. Care must be taken to avoid interlinking characteristics to construct an even more complex hierarchical access to different resources (Yuval-Davis, 2006).

Butler's (1990) conceptualisation of gender as an act of performativity supports a different approach to challenging inequality. If we concur that people do indeed choose to act in gendered ways, then change lies in their own hands in that they can choose to act differently. This supports a view of gender as a continuum rather than a dichotomy, but fails to address material issues and expectations at the macro-level.

Postcolonialism

Chapter 3 mentioned the legacy of inequality deriving from the European colonisation of the world, and within literary and cultural studies, attempts have been made to redress the balance and give voice to minority groups. Within the social sciences, intersectionality serves a similar purpose. Not all groups seek integration into mainstream society, however. Amy Tan (2003) describes how some Asian-Americans protect their marginalisation, seeing it as the basis for collective empowerment. Tan claims her right to recognition as an American rather than an American-Chinese writer, someone who writes fiction rather than books with a multicultural message. She describes a 'new and insidious form of censorship' hidden beneath a 'cloak of good intentions and ethnic correctness' that creates an expectation that fiction about other cultures must portray an accurate and positive picture at all times lest it be deemed racist (ibid: 309).

The perspectives outlined above deal with society at the theoretical and macro-level. At the meso- and micro-level, children are more visible in their families and communities, their homes and schools.

Applying the perspectives

The family

The family is usually the unit of provision and care for the child. This is often a nuclear family even though this has been the dominant social structure for a relatively short time. Nicholson (1997: 27) claims that the 'traditional' family is 'not all that traditional' but a middle-class phenomenon becoming common with industrialisation with the advent of waged work. It was the development of factory work that led to the division of labour, with men going out to work (free to enter the public sphere) and women left in the domestic sphere to care for the home and family. In a functionalist society, this became idealised as a norm whereas in reality there were many poorer families who could never afford the 'luxury' of a non-working wife/mother (Jackson, 2008).

During the twentieth century the notion of family was much debated and changes were conceptual, practical and legal. Conceptually, the idea of 'families of choice' (Weston, 1991, in Ribbens McCarthy and Edwards, 2011) captured the notion of commitment rather than legality, emerging in response to the HIV/AIDS crisis and the needs of lesbian, gay, bisexual and transgender (LGBT) people for friends to take on the role of provider and carer. The term was later extended to adoptive families, too (Benavente and Gains, 2008), making a distinction between elective bonds and 'families of origin'. In contrast, Ulrich Beck and his wife Elizabeth (Beck and Beck-Gernsheim, 1995) explained the instability of contemporary families as a continual quest for love in a world where competing needs to procreate and work are difficult to reconcile, leading to the 'battle of the sexes'; a view that favours the adult relationship over the means of generative reproduction. David Morgan (1996) offers the notion of 'family practices', seeing a family in terms of what it does together rather than set roles and personnel. This adjectival usage of the term family makes it both more practical and more flexible, and this is reflected in the key legal changes described below.

Changing family structures

During the twentieth century, it became easier to dissolve adult partnerships. From the mid-1960s Western countries began to introduce 'no fault' divorce laws. In the UK the Divorce Reform Act was passed in 1969 and came into effect in 1971, leading to a rise in lone-parent households, described by Giddens (2006: 224) as 'an overwhelmingly female category'. Figures for the UK show that one of the fastest growing family types in the 1990s was single, never married mothers who constituted nine per cent of families (*Social Trends 30*, 2000, in Giddens, 2006: 226). This category is not available for comparison in *Social Trends 41* (ONS, 2011) but the number of lone mother families increased (12.7 to 14.1 per cent) while lone father families remained constant (2.1 per cent). In 1993, the Child Support Agency (CSA) was set up to ensure that separated fathers contributed to the cost of bringing up their children. Its enforcement is poor even after reformulation as a Child Maintenance Group, under the UK Department of Work and Pensions in 2012. However, its existence reinforces the notion of accountability for children for life.

Social Trends data also shows that between 2001 and 2010 the number of married couple families decreased slightly (from 72.4 to 68 per cent), but cohabiting couples increased slightly (12.5 to 15.3 per cent). The proportion of same sex cohabiting couples stayed the same (at 0.3 per cent) while a small number of civil partner families appeared in the statistics (0.2 per cent) in 2010. This followed a number of status changes. A ruling in 1999 in the UK enabled homosexual couples in a stable relationship to be classed as

families, and in the US judges allowed a gay male couple to be jointly registered on a birth certificate in the same year (Giddens, 2006). In the UK the
Civil Partnership Act of 2004 came into force in December 2005 (ONS, 2013)
and the 2010 Equality Act made sexual orientation one of the characteristics
'protected' against discrimination in law. Despite some resistance from Church
organisations, the Marriage (Same Sex Couples) Act became law in July 2013.

These figures take no account of the growing informal networks of
extended families that occur as parents remarry or go to live with new partners, amalgamating families and adding new layers of *de facto* relations at
the head of the family. Nor do they take into account the consequences
of extended life expectancy. Brannen (2003, in Giddens, 2006) talks of the
'beanpole' family: as people live longer, families become long and thin as
three or four generations co-survive. Mothers of the 'sandwich generation'
(Zal, 1992) are expected to care for both children and elderly parents, even
grandparents, and this can add to stress and reduce the time devoted to
children. As Apter claims (1997), the 'cluttered nest' has replaced the 'empty
nest' syndrome. Many children fail to move out of the family home even
when they become parents themselves. Thus, children become subject to
multi-generational 'caring' and this can be a source of harmony, conflict or
confusion depending on the quality of relationships.

Looked after children

Not all children are brought up within their family of birth. When family
circumstances make this impossible, the state steps in. This may be a temporary or permanent arrangement and can be a voluntary arrangement or
due to a court order under Section 31 of the 1989 Children Act if a child is
deemed to be suffering, or likely to suffer, significant harm. According to the
NSPCC (2014b), there were 92,000 children in care in the UK, and in general,
outcomes for children in care are 'poorer' than for the wider population in
terms of educational attainment, mental health and homelessness. Also, 'a
minority are at continued risk of abuse or neglect' (NSPCC, 2014a).

Even the government admits that the historical development of the child
'care' system in England has been reactive, evolving from the workhouses
of the 1834 Poor Law and 'often precipitated by scandals and their impact
on public opinion' (HoC, 2009a: 22). Concerns about abuse in residential
homes in the 1990s led to a spate of legislation in the new millennium, the
Care Standards Act 2000, the Children (Leaving Care) Act 2000, the Adoption
and Children Act 2002 and an emphasis on adoption when possible. The
2006 Care Matters Green Paper provided further recommendations, leading to the Children and Young Persons Act 2008. Perhaps one of the more
significant changes relates to the obligation on local authorities to engage
in 'corporate parenting' and 'approximate more closely the care of birth

parents' (ibid: 15). A significant improvement here is the 'staying put' policy that has enabled many children to have a continuing relationship with foster parents between the ages of 18 and 21, thereby having a base from which to leave home whether to work or study (HM Government, 2013).

The Munro Review of Child Protection, which made a final report in May 2011 (DfE, 2011c), called for a more child-centred system that recognises social workers' expertise, dislodging the 'compliance culture'. The proposals were accepted by the coalition government but progress was slow. New multi-agency inspections were supposed to commence in June 2013. However, in April 2013, the Chief Inspector of the Office for Standards in Education, Children's Services and Skills (Ofsted) decided to abandon such plans after pilot inspections drew attention to problems (Ofsted, 2013). Instead they adopted a single inspection framework that covers both child protection and services for looked after children in December 2013. This U-turn was controversial, leading to debate around both light touch and integrated inspections (Ofsted 2014a,b). Such changes demonstrate how plans that appear to meet the needs of individual children are not easily converted to public policy.

Society

The philosophical and legal changes relating to children, family structures and substitute care demonstrate how the UK (and other countries too) are attempting to become more inclusive of their populations, and this includes attitudes to disability. Society is moving away from the classifications and categorisations favoured in the scientific and psychological realms, and is beginning to recognise the value of individuals and their right to fulfilling lives whatever their physical, social, intellectual or emotional abilities and needs.

Models of inclusion

The *medical model* of disability defines people in terms of their medical condition. It is a deficit model that regards disability as an individual problem and focuses on the way that the professional can support the individual to find a 'cure' or other means of compensating for his/her condition. For children, it turned their condition into a deficit and led to a segregated education within special schools. Even as late as 1980 the World Health Organization (WHO) created an International Classification of Impairment, Disabilities and Handicaps that focused on loss of or reduced function (ETTAD, 2007).

In the 1970s, disabled citizens began to challenge their marginalisation (Shakespeare and Watson, 2002), demonstrating that they were often excluded from participation by society's practices and the assumption that most people were able-minded and able-bodied. The *social model* of disability sees that it is not an individual's needs that exclude him/her but the expectations and provision within normative society. It is not the wheelchair that disables the child but the narrow doorways, stairs and steps in our environment. It is not the inability to see that excludes the blind child but the privileging of visual clues and the lack of aural, sensory or human support. The social model focuses on removing barriers to inclusion rather than 'curing' individuals. For children, this led to inclusion within mainstream schooling after the Warnock Report (Warnock, 1978) called for an end to segregation. In practice, 'people are disabled both by social barriers and by their bodies', a postmodern view that makes an 'essential connection between impairment and embodiment' (Shakespeare and Watson, 2002: 15, 28). Both models are important as children need personalised support, additional resources *and* a classroom that is accessible to all. Importantly, they also need recognition.

The *affirmative model* (Swain and French, 2000) offers an alternative to the view of disability as personal tragedy. People are born with or develop a set of characteristics and abilities, and these bound their opportunities in life, sometimes restricting, sometimes enhancing what they experience and can do. Our impairments are a core part of us and we all need the opportunity to enjoy to the full the capacities we have, rather than pity for what we cannot do. An affirmative view of childhood promises all children, whatever their needs and abilities, a fruitful and productive life, and is altogether more positive.

Childhood

New sociology of childhood

These theoretical perspectives form the historical backdrop to our changing views of childhood but Vygotsky's work (for example, Vygotsky, 1978), with its stress on culture and social relations, also played a significant role. Postmodernist challenges to traditional and universal viewpoints led to recognition that there are multiple childhoods that vary with spatial and historical context. Vygotsky's *social constructivism* in its claim that children's progress is mediated by relationships and culture afforded opportunities to understand development as situated rather than universal, thus psychology also contributed to the ascendance of a new sociology of childhood.

Social constructionism

Currently, both family and childhood are commonly viewed as social constructs. The term *construct* implies that humans are taking responsibility for the way their world is viewed rather than describing an innate reality. When 'construct' is prefaced by 'social' this enforces the notion of a group of people shaping the framework of their lives collectively so it is a term that recognises the power of human agency and the multiplicity of possible frameworks. Specific labels may be applied internally by participants, or externally by theorists, either a single or a group of individuals. Thus, when we talk about constructs of childhood we are referring to views of childhood that vary with context: childhood is 'constituted through the discourse' (James and Prout, 1997: xi). We can talk in general terms about childhood as a social construct but also about different constructs of childhood, and the latter groupings enable us to study diversity over time and place without getting lost in individual detail.

The unfolding paradigm

In 1982 Batsford published *The Sociology of Childhood* edited by Chris Jenks (Jenks, 1982). This collected together key writing about childhood from the 1950s, 1960s and 1970s and demonstrated how theories of childhood started from a desire to explain children in relation to the adults they will become. As Jenks (ibid: 23) explained: 'the child is constituted purposively within theory'. Thus, Piaget set out to identify how the child becomes a rational adult, Parsons considered how the child is socialised into becoming an acceptable citizen, Freud saw the 'difference of childhood... as pathological' (ibid: 19) and in need of repression. Jenks is critical of these dominant interpretations as they turn the child into 'a device through which to propound versions of social cohesion' (ibid: 13). Referring to excerpts from the works of Aries, Coveney and DeMause reproduced in his 1982 book, Jenks shows how images of childhood have evolved throughout history and called for a recognition that childhood itself is socially constituted, depending on the context in which it is immanent. Jenks prepared the ground for change with his 'recommendation' that a 'sociology of childhood should emerge from the constitutive practices that provide for the child and the child-adult relationship' (ibid: 24).

In 1990 Alison James and Alan Prout edited *Constructing and Reconstructing Childhood* [James and Prout, 1997 [1990]), tracing the interest in childhood to the International Year of the Child of 1979, and UNICEF and WHO media coverage of children whose lives were very different to those of the affluent West. Daily images of poverty, war and famine unsettled the traditional view of the child protected by family and society. By the time the second edition was published in 1997 (ibid: ix) the authors were claiming of the sociology of childhood that 'the field had cohered remarkably' and was making good the way that family sociology 'had, rather surprisingly rendered children almost invisible', reinforcing the point that children should be seen as 'social actors' and childhood regarded as 'a part of society and culture rather than a precursor to it'. The new sociology of childhood focuses on children as 'beings' rather than as 'becomings'.

This new paradigm put the active child at the centre of his/her life, shifting notions of childhood away from the traditional view that children are social-ised into the ways of society for 'socialization acts as a kind of suppressor of childhood's present tense.' (ibid: 28).

Constructs of childhood

If childhood is socially constructed, this bequeaths to the researcher of child-hood the task of identifying and grouping the different constructs, and theo-rists have risen to this challenge, creating their master lists of constructs of childhood. In 1990, Hendrick, a contributor to the seminal *Constructing and Reconstructing Childhood,* listed seven different constructs initially, but by 1997, had expanded this to 11 types. His first typologies are still listed in Hill and Tisdall's text (1997) and have a clarity that makes them easy to assimi-late. The romantic child; the sinful child; the factory child; the delinquent child; the school child; the psycho-medical child; and the welfare child, are all labels that convey the characteristics they encapsulate. The modified labels in the 1997 edition are less stereotypical but also less memorable because of this.

In *Theorizing Childhood,* James et al. (1998) together attempted a more systematic classification, dividing categories into *pre-sociological* (traditional) and *sociological* (more contemporary), with schooled and urban children as additional groups. The pre-sociological categories reflected perspectives already discussed in earlier chapters: the *evil* child tainted by Adam's original sin; the *innocent* child depicted by Rousseau; the *immanent* child, Locke's impressionable child whose mind is a blank slate; the *naturally developing* child typified by Piaget's views on innate development; and the *unconscious* child who owes existence to Freud's work on psychoanalysis.

To create the more innovative sociological categories, childhood was considered in relation to common tensions within society. A systematic co-comparison of several dichotomies enabled the derivation of four typologies: the *social structural* child who is seen as a constant structural category with a defined place in society; the *minority group* child who also has a clearly defined status but occupies a marginalised position; the *socially constructed* child, in contrast, represents a more perspectival view, a child who is a prod-uct of a specific time and context; the *tribal* child, a highly localised category, a child who creates a niche within an isolated society.

These are complex categories and later theorists reverted back to applying labels to recognisable aspects of childhood rather than attempting a system-atic analysis. Jenks (2005 [1996]) drew upon classical literature to depict the evil child as *Dionysian*; the good child as *Apollonian*. Dahlberg et al. (1999) adopted lengthy titles that gave a composite overview of the category they were describing, reflecting their postmodern stance. Mills and Mills (2000) classified children as innocents, apprentices, members of a distinct group, vulnerable, and as animals.

There is currently a strong Australian interest in constructs of childhood. Sorin (2005) lists ten constructs representing historical (the innocent child, the noble/saviour child, the evil child) and contemporary viewpoints. Sorin's *snowballing child* is over-indulged and makes constant demands on busy parents for material goods and attention, while the *out-of-control* child captures extreme behaviour patterns. The *child as commodity* reflects the commercialism of childhood, and the *child as victim,* the abuses and bullying that occur on the domestic scene as well as the global problems of warfare, poverty and famine. The *agentic child*, is a positive construct referring to the 'strong child' who enjoys legal rights and a voice in his/her own affairs, unlike the *miniature adult* and *adult-in-training*.

A more recent treatment, again from Australia, returns to four simple constructs (Whiteman and De Gioia, 2012). The *silent child* evokes those historical views of children where childhood was passively constructed: Aries' invisible child, Locke's blank slate. These children needed moulding by adults as recommended by Rousseau, Pestalozi and Froebel so placed an immense burden on the carers and educators to do this correctly. The *individual child* is the child of modernity, the scientific child of the maturationists (Stanley Hall, Gesell and Piaget) who direct the educator to provide developmentally appropriate practice (DAP) in order to encourage innate development, or in the case of the behaviourists (Pavlov, Watson and Skinner), to apply sanction and rewards to condition children to behave appropriately. The *social child* is the Vygotskian child who learns through social interaction, whose agency is promoted through the rights granted by the UNCRC (UNCRC, 1989) (see Chapter 7) and further promoted in pedagogical practices like Malaguzzi's Reggio Emilia (see Chapter 8). The *cultural child* develops from the ideas of Vygotsky and Malaguzzi, but also Bronfenbrenner's and Rogoff's beliefs in the significance of the broader community. This is the child with rights who actively engages with the world, empowered through partnership to challenge social justice, diversity and inclusion.

Summary

This chapter has provided succinct overviews of the main theories posited to explain how society functions, from Marxist concerns with economic dominance to more recent challenges to mainstream power. Minority views, encouraged by the poststructuralist, postmodernist and postcolonial attempts to challenge universalism have created spaces for new interpretations of family and childhood. Structures previously seen as fixed are seen to be constituted by human beings, and made up of a mix of generalised and localised characteristics. Importantly, this 'deconstruction' of social relationships has enabled a new paradigm of childhood that seeks to empower the child to take an active role in the decisions that influence his/her own life.

Points for reflection

 With a real child in mind, specify the key influences within each layer of Bronfenbrenner's ecosystem. (You could do this for your own childhood.)

 Imagine yourself committed to *either* Marxism, functionalism, feminism or postmodernism. How would this affect your expectations for children?

 Develop a personal construct of childhood. Consider the different frameworks and determine how *you* view young children. Can you present this diagrammatically?

Further reading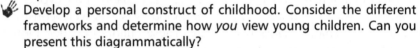

There are useful overviews in: Fulcher and Scott (2011); Ribbens McCarthy and Edwards (2011); James and James (2008) (see References).

Corsaro, W. (2011) *The Sociology of Childhood,* 3rd edn. London: Sage.
Mayall, B. (2002) *Towards a Sociology for Childhood.* Maidenhead: McGraw-Hill Education.
Smith, R. (2010) *A Universal Child?* Basingstoke: Palgrave Macmillan.
Wyness, M. (2011) *Childhood and Society,* 2nd edn. Basingstoke: Palgrave Macmillan.
These texts offer broader sociological perspectives. Mayall's (2002) research-based study pays particular attention to gender issues.

Agger, B. (1991) 'Critical theory, poststructuralism, postmodernism', *Annual Review of Sociology,* 17: 105–131.
Crenshaw, K. (1991) 'Mapping the margins: intersectionality, identity politics and violence against women of color', *Stanford Law Review,* 43(6): 1241–99.
Clear and comprehensive overviews of complex topics.

Websites

www.statistics.gov.uk/hub/index.html
Up-to-date figures from the Office of National Statistics (ONS).

www.marxists.org/archive/ Marxists Internet Archive Library
*Hosts links to works of many philosophers and scientists of
international repute.*

To gain *free* access to selected SAGE journal articles related to key
topics in this chapter, visit: www.sagepub.co.uk/hazelrwright.

CHAPTER 7

ECONOMIC AND POLICY PERSPECTIVES

Overview

This chapter considers how decisions are made within society. It starts with a broad base before focusing on childhood.

It considers key economic philosophies underpinning government:

- *laissez-faire* (market) and redistributive economies
- means of determining redistribution: by utility, right and by capability

It then examines political systems and power:

- local, regional and global
- British systems of government
- political change over time

Lastly it lays out policy and practice around childhood in England:

- New Labour policies, 1997–2001, 2001–2005, 2005–2010
- coalition reviews and policies, 2010 onwards.

Modern governments need systems for making decisions on behalf of the people they rule, and how to rule fairly is a notion that has long occupied the minds of the economists and political philosophers upon whose guidance governments depend. This chapter will look briefly at the economic philosophies that underpin governance, ways that governments distribute resources and at the consequent political systems that arise from these phi-losophies. It focuses particularly on the British situation. It will then consider the legislation and policies that have profoundly affected the nature of child-hood for youngsters growing up in Britain in recent times (defined as after the Second World War), focusing later on the English context.

Economic philosophies underpinning government

Laissez-faire (market) versus redistributive economies

Laissez-faire economics is one of the guiding principles of capitalism. It refutes the *redistributive practices* of earlier societies, of communist states, and left wing parties, whereby those in power directly control the allocation of goods to the people they rule. It represents the view – prevalent in the eighteenth century – that rather than intervene, governments should leave market forces (supply and demand) to balance the economy. Market econo-mies are inherently competitive as suppliers seek to realise profit and con-sumers to cut costs. Commodities take on aspects of their value as if these are inherent characteristics, a process known in Marxist terms as *commodity fetishism* (Cunningham, F., 2005). For example, silk becomes a desirable item simply because it costs more than wool. People strive to purchase goods because they *can* rather than because they need them, giving way to exces-sive consumerism. As Marx claimed, they forget that others have had to toil to produce their surplus purchases (Cunningham, F., 2005). In Chapter 9 we consider how consumerism shapes children's expectations.

Capitalist society *commodifies* labour, too (Fulcher and Scott, 2011). A wage is payment for work done but, under capitalism, rates of remunera-tion reflect scarcity and skill but not necessarily effort. Earlier, in industri-alising Britain, workers were numerous, opportunities few, and the *laissez faire* economy allowed exploitation. Children were employed as 'scavengers', crawling under spinning mules to clear up cotton waste; 'trappers', manning the doors alone in the dark in the coal mines; 'jiggers' and 'dippers', handling toxic glazes in the potteries; milliners' apprentices, sewing in cramped condi-tions in the fashion industry; lace makers, agricultural labourers and chimney sweeps (Wilkes, 2011). There were few regulations to protect children or the adults they worked alongside during the industrial revolution so they often risked their lives in order to eat. In a truly *laissez-faire* economy there is no formal regulation: all are 'left to fend for themselves' (Humphries, 2010: 305).

By the nineteenth century it was becoming apparent that self-regulation was divisive: the rich were becoming richer at the expense of the majority. Governments needed to curb the excesses of the market, and redistribute some resources to the poorer members of society. Traditionally, Labour governments favour a *welfare-state model* that provides benefits (health care, education, employment and pension rights) to the entire population regardless of individual wealth. This is funded through a system of 'progressive' taxation, whereby the wealthy pay higher taxes to reduce the effects of inequalities in earnings. In contrast, Conservative governments prefer a *market model* that means-tests benefits, allocating them only to the very poor and needy. Others are expected to buy services, contributing to pension and health schemes from their income (Fulcher and Scott, 2011).

Successive changes of government and the accompanying policy swings led to a recognition that neither model was entirely appropriate to shape global decision making in a period of rapid change and economic recession. Poorer families, and the children in them, experienced waves of hardship as benefits were bestowed then later reduced or removed entirely, sometimes with little advance warning. Prominent political sociologist, Anthony Giddens (1998), proposed a *Third Way* of governing, one that strove to bridge the extremes of the two existing models. He called for a strengthening of civil society and the creation of meaningful partnerships to link private and public resources, and reinforce the processes of democratic decision making. This was to offer individuals a sense of both responsibility and possibility.

Redistribution of wealth

Whatever model a government adopts, it needs a means to determine policy and how to do this fairly has been much debated. Three distinctive philosophical perspectives are worth considering in the abstract: utilitarianism; human rights; and the capability approach.

Utilitarianism

In the UK, policy is top down – those in power make the decisions and still use a utilitarian argument to justify this. Adopting Jeremy Bentham's (1748–1832) belief that morally right actions are those that create 'the greatest amount of good for the greatest number' (UCL, 2013), policy makers estimate the probable benefits of different strategies and choose the one that appears to be most beneficial. It is assumed that, as human beings are rational, this is the option that the majority would have chosen for themselves. Thus, decisions are based on assumption and can be simply wrong or manipulated, for power remains in the hands of an elite minority. Ordinary people are rarely consulted in advance, children even less commonly. Nevertheless, the principles, that each individual's satisfaction is equally valuable and that the majority view matters, are fundamental to a fair society. Bentham's view that laws should be beneficial rather than oppressive is important, so too his belief that one should always ask of a policy – 'what use is it?'. Recall these values when we consider early years policy later in the chapter.

Rights-based policy

In contrast, rights-based policy seeks to remove inequality by empowering individuals and persuading government(s) to commit to threshold entitlements and shared goals. The UN *Universal Declaration of Human Rights* (UN, 1948) laid down standards to guide development based on key principles: universality and inalienability, indivisibility, interdependence and interrelatedness, non-discrimination and equality, participation and inclusion, accountability and the rule of law. Collectively, the standards affirm that all individuals possess equal rights. These cannot be refuted and must be upheld by those in power.

The UN *Programme for Reform* (UN, 1997) prioritised 'rights' over 'needs' and the standards were clarified in a *Statement of Common Understanding* in May 2003 (UNICEF, 2003). The move from needs to rights is explicitly political. An unfulfilled 'need' is a source of dissatisfaction whereas a 'right' not respected is a violation for which 'redress or reparation can be legally and legitimately claimed'. The reform gives the UN a mandate to instigate changes worldwide (UNFPA, 2008) and this empowers governments to intervene if a country neglects or abuses its children. A rights-based approach calls for fairer resource allocation and action to be taken against severe violation even if only a few are affected. A needs-based approach is much weaker. It focuses on the procurement of extra resources to provide services to groups who are without, and is open to utilitarian arguments about the number of individuals affected (Cornwall and Nyamu-Musembi, 2004: 1417).

Capability approach

While rights-based policy makers were championing international reforms, economic philosopher Amartya Sen was seeking a basis for policy making that was less deterministic than utilitarianism and considerate of individual needs. Sen believes it is the 'life we lead and what we can or cannot do, can or cannot be' that really matters (Sen, 1987: 16) and the capability approach (CA) argues that individuals should have control over their lives (Sen, 1999). Sen demonstrates that politicians can enable choice if they focus on the 'potential' to achieve (capability) that people have rather than what they do achieve (functioning). Instead of imposing a single optimum solution, policy makers can offer choices and let people take the options that are 'useful' to them.

Sen argues against an egalitarian distribution of resources, seeing this to be both unfair and wasteful. First, it treats all members of a household (or community) collectively, enabling dominant individuals to take more than their nominal allocation of resources. This deprives weaker members, the ill and elderly, women and children. Second, it distributes goods whether or not this makes sense. Inevitably some will receive and squander goods they do not want and do not value.

Sen's notion of 'usefulness' has been taken up by the World Bank, which now considers development in terms of the Human Development Index (HDI), a measure of what people are able to do. Earlier measures, Gross Domestic Product (GDP) or Gross National Income (GNI) were primarily indicators of spending power. The HDI combines measure of life expectancy (health), years of schooling (education) and income (living standard) into a single indicator (running from 0 to 1) that more closely captures the quality of life (UNDP, 2013). CA is increasingly used in studies of education and children's well-being. The focus on 'potential' is particularly apt when considering how children can be empowered to grow into mature adults, and being able to choose supports individual agency, differentiation and diversity (Biggeri et al., 2011).

Political systems and power

When we talk about government we still talk about 'the nation'. This implies a group of people with a strong collective identity, and often an identifiable ethnic and cultural background (Fulcher and Scott, 2011). As society became more settled, alignment of cultural, territorial and political boundaries gave rise to the 'nation state' where groups of citizens took control of their own affairs, developing laws to configure rights and responsibilities and organisational structures to enforce their implementation. Sometimes, particularly in Europe, this was the result of the emergence of distinctive groups of peoples. Sometimes, the artificial creation of state boundaries when new lands were settled or colonised led to a reversal of the process, with governments forced to actively create a sense of national identity among the people they served. Thus the term was always 'problematic' and remains so; 'hard to sustain in the face of global networks' (Singh, 2007: 37).

In earlier times European countries were ruled dynastically. Powerful families controlled territories whose boundaries and allegiances were subject to change when family members intermarried. Ordinary people were seen to be subjects and answerable to whichever family was in power at any one time; the right to rule granted by 'divine right'. Much earlier still, the first nations emerged as different tribes of people settled in different areas and developed their own languages, cultures, and religious practices, often based on the worship of ancestors and myths created to explain their existence (Smith, 1994). Thus, although a nation is only an 'imagined community'

(Anderson, 1991) as its members can only ever know a small proportion of their fellows, national identity can be deeply entrenched.

Political hierarchies
The nation state

The nation state is one in which the cultural and political boundaries align. Nations claim the right to decide their own destinies and the adjective 'national' identifies any services or functions run by a country's government. We saw in Chapter 3 how the British nation evolved over time. Once a collection of individual tribes, assimilating successive invasions of Celts, Romans, Saxons, Vikings, Normans, the United Kingdom of Great Britain was formed through the unification of England, Wales, Scotland and Northern Ireland by individual Acts of Union in the eighteenth century. Its joint status has been frequently challenged. In 1998 there was a significant devolution of political independence to Scottish, Welsh and Northern Irish parliaments and the Scottish National Party (SNP) would still like an independent Scotland. Thus, when we talk about political systems and policy prior to 1998, it is possible to talk about British systems, but from that date we are discussing English, sometimes English and Welsh initiatives.

Regional alliances

In addition to internal groupings, nations often form external alliances to achieve greater stability and power within the global framework. This takes various forms. Some groupings are enforced. Britain ruled its Empire, colonised from the late sixteenth to the nineteenth century, only allowing a gradual transition into the more egalitarian *Commonwealth of Nations* as member states demanded independence during the twentieth century. Some groupings are consensual. Thus, in 1949 Britain, Canada and other European nations aligned with America in the North Atlantic Treaty Organization (NATO), making a joint commitment to 'safeguard the security of its members through political and military means' (NATO, 2013).

In contrast, the European Economic Community (EEC) (formed 1957) was originally a trade organisation, evolving out of the European Coal and Steel Community into a powerful institution with around 27 member states, a Council, and a Parliament (directly elected from 1979). Becoming the European Union (EU) in 1993 it acquired further responsibility for shared governance through the European Commission (EC) (its executive body) and the Court of Justice based in Luxembourg. (This deals with legal disputes between EU governments and institutions, and is not to be confused with the United Nations International Court of Justice in the Hague.) The EU continues to support economic policy, adopting a single currency, the Euro, in

2002 (EU, 2013). It works alongside the Council of Europe (CoE), a looser organisation of some 47 countries based in Strasbourg, administered through a Parliamentary Assembly and aligned with the European Court of Human Rights (founded 1959). Countries wishing to join the EU first have to become members of the CoE (CoE, 2013).

International organisations

Many of the key contemporary international organisations formed after the Second World War when countries recognised the need for common policies and cooperation.

The Organisation for Economic Co-operation and Development (OECD) operates at a global level as a forum for governments to share problems and seek international solutions. It was formed in 1961 (from a 1948 European prototype), with the aim 'to promote policies that will improve the economic and social well-being of people around the world' (OECD, 2013). It collects international data and seeks to set global safety standards. Its membership reflects its European origins but it is currently reaching out to the Brazil, Russia, India and China (BRIC) states as these rapidly growing countries command market share. OECD is actively involved in planning strategies for efficient childcare (see *Starting Strong* and *Quality Toolbox*, OECD iLibrary, 2013).

The United Nations was established in 1945, replacing the League of Nations (founded 1919). Fifty-one countries signed its Charter so it is truly international. Its remit is to promote world peace, to develop respect and friendly relations among nations and to help them work together to conquer hunger, disease, illiteracy and poverty (UN, 2013). In 1948 the World Health Organization (WHO) was established to provide leadership on global health matters (WHO, 2013), and in the same year, as we have seen, the Universal Declaration of Human Rights established expectations for fair treatment of the world's citizens.

In 1953 the United Nations International Children's Emergency Fund (UNICEF), set up in 1946 to feed the starving children of Europe, became a permanent part of the UN with a mandate to help children worldwide. Through the 1959 Declaration of the Rights of the Child it articulated children's rights to protection, education, health care, shelter and good nutrition (UNICEF, 2013) developing these further through the 1989 UNCRC (see later).

Multilevel systems of governance create checks and balances that curb abuses of power but also necessitate careful alignment of policies. In the human rights arena, the hierarchies are very visible and the influences both upwards and downwards. Britain, for example, has a long history of human rights legislation, first passing a Bill of Rights in 1689. France too sought *Liberté, Egalité et Fraternité* during the French Revolution (1787–99). After the Second World War, Britain supported the European Convention on

Human Rights (1950), the European Commission of Human Rights (1954–98) and European Court of Human Rights (1959). Yet, only in 1966 were UK citizens given permission to take their individual grievances to the European Court in Strasbourg, and in 1998 government passed a British Human Rights Act intended to make this process unnecessary (BBC News, 2000).

The British context
The British political system
Britain has a distinctive political system: the Westminster model, shaped over several centuries (Dunleavy, 2006).

Members of Parliament (MPs) and local councillors align with a party and are elected to power in single member districts. The leader of the largest party becomes Prime Minister (PM) and appoints the cabinet. Together they control foreign and economic policy and limit the role of the judiciary (courts) but the government collectively holds responsibility for major policy. Individual ministers are accountable for specific departments with civil servants responsible for implementation of policy.

The party (often Conservative or Labour) with the majority in the House of Commons has powers to legislate and execute decisions, subject only to approval by the unelected House of Lords. Government 'whips' expect MPs to support the party line when legislation goes to a vote and the only scrutiny is through question time, backbench rebellions, select committees with a specific mandate and parliamentary audit. Decision making is centralised and local government dependent on central finance.

Pre- and post-millennium legislation concerning children and childcare reached unprecedented levels, and remodelling continues, so it is important to understand the processes involved. Potential new legislation passes through a series of set stages being challenged and redefined until Parliament is satisfied it is fit for purpose, so there is usually considerable delay between identification of a need for change and implementation of a new law. For example, the Children and Families Act (passed March 2014) implements new policy for children with special educational needs in September 2014, yet these ideas were first promoted in the Green Paper, *Support and Aspiration*, in March 2011 (DfE, 2011b).

The British legislative process is as follows:

- a *Green Paper* is drawn up and made available for public consultation.
- a *White Paper* is made available for public consultation. This usually discusses proposals in more detail and incorporates public feedback and the findings from any research that the government commissioned.
- a draft law or *Bill* (or several Bills) is drawn up for reading in the House of Commons. Bills are presented for a first reading (no debate) and a

second reading (for debate). A Standing Committee considers the Bill clause by clause and reports back to the House to agree changes. A third reading grants final approval.

- these processes are repeated with the Bill in the House of Lords, which can recommend amendment, rejection or approval. The Bill returns to Commons and the Houses negotiate amendments (called 'ping pong'). If both Houses vote to pass the Bill it becomes an Act of Parliament but still requires notional Royal Assent to become law.

Sometimes Acts of Parliament include powers for regulations or subsequent secondary legislation to take care of the detail behind the principles in the Act. If Bills originate in the House of Lords, they are processed there before passing to the Commons.

Since the 1970s, delegated power is a feature of national government. Both Conservative and Labour governments have established quasi-independent non-governmental organisations (quangos) like trusts, commissions, councils and corporations, to implement and manage government policy. These enable people to 'bypass' the elective processes fundamental to representative government, to carry out executive, advisory and tribunal functions on behalf of government, a process that has become so commonplace that its validity is rarely even questioned. Yet, it has the effect of distancing governments from the decisions they make and diminishing the power of local authorities, as it places an intermediate tier between national and local bases (Bochel and Bochel, 2004). Ofsted is a quango, so too was the New Labour Children's Workforce Development Council set up to reform the face of childcare (disbanded in March 2012).

A British overview

Classical economic theory was dominant in the eighteenth century but the visible injustices of a *laissez faire* economy prompted change thereafter. In the nineteenth century, British governments passed a succession of Factory Acts to curb exploitation of the workforce and consumer protection laws to prevent the growth of monopolies. Reform continued throughout the Victorian period and during the 1930s recession governments redoubled their efforts to break up monopolies. After the Second World War, significant attempts were made to construct a welfare society that provided benefits for all, 'irrespective of income' (Fulcher and Scott, 2011: 564).

In the UK, traditionally a two-party political system with parties claiming consecutive periods of power (Childs, 2006), the pendulum had swung away from 'welfare' towards the 'market' model by the 1970s. Governments were removing trade barriers and deregulating industry to let prices find their market level. Conservative governments in power from 1970–74, and again from 1979–1997 (led by Margaret Thatcher, and later, John Major) sought to 'roll back' the state and restore freedom and choice to individuals by reinstat-ing market factors. Such policies are termed *neo-liberal* for they appear to offer choice (hence, liberal) but in reality this is modified, beset by economic restrictions (thus, neo). The Thatcher government believed that the state 'should retreat from interfering in the family' to encourage a break with the 'dependency culture' (Winter and Connolly, 1996: 30). Under Thatcher's rule the divisions between rich and poor 'surged' (Eaton, 2013) and continue to grow, and this represents a serious fracture in the social fabric. Under the late Conservative administration, the poor were vilified. Lone parents were con-strued as 'scroungers' on the state (McIntosh, 1996) in a *moral panic* dispro-portionate to their cost to society (Linné and Jones, 2000) and many children were consequently relegated to lives of extreme poverty as benefits were cut.

Blair's New Labour government came to power in 1997, determined to tackle exclusion through education. It embraced the American notion of *workfare*, the idea that social policy should encourage a return to work rather than dependence on welfare (Fulcher and Scott, 2011: 565). This led to a focus on skills and vocational training to increase individuals' market effectiveness and make Britain a more successful player in the global market. Workfare relies on a move away from 'entitlement' to one where the right to benefits increasingly carries conditions, a process that Dwyer (2004) calls *creeping conditionality*. Thus, lone parents saw their entitlement to ben-efit become a right to claim job seeker's allowance provided they attended interviews and actively sought work. The duration of benefit eligibility was repeatedly reduced. In 2008 mothers of children aged 12 and above were required to find work. In 2009 the age was lowered to ten, and then to seven in 2010 (dropping with minimal notice to five under the coalition govern-ment in May 2012).

The Third Way

Traditionally the Labour Party stood for collectivist policies and state direc-tion of the economy. The Conservative Party, in contrast, championed 'enter-prise, market discipline, consumer choice and freedom' (Fulcher and Scott, 2011: 577), and under Thatcher, this took the form of privatising industry and services. The New Right rejected the 'nanny state' in favour of individual responsibility and morality, often invoking popular anxiety to challenge union militancy, immigration, crime and the permissive society.

Future government needed to find a way to rise above these contradictions and enable Britain to effectively engage with the global economy and the Blair government, New Labour, adapted Giddens' notion of the Third Way. However, on coming to power in 1997, the party did not altogether abandon redistribution. They introduced a minimum wage, and policies to support those in poverty, particularly children and the aged. The cross-departmental Social Exclusion Unit comprised 18 separate teams all tasked to work with the neediest in society, but there was little attempt to reduce the difference between rich and poor, and this gap continued to grow (Cribb et al., 2012).

Policy and practice around childhood

In the early twentieth century legislation for children was limited, often focused on schooling rather than the young. Exceptions were the 1904 Prevention of Cruelty to Children Act that gave the NSPCC a statutory right to intervene on behalf of children; the 1918 Maternity and Child Welfare Act that provided free antenatal care and medical attention for children under five; and the 1948 Children Act that appointed local authority Children's Committees and Children's Officers to oversee the care of 'orphaned' and 'delinquent' children.

In 1959 the UN took up the cause of children. With the Declaration of the Rights of the Child it claimed for children, a moral right to maternal protection, health, food, shelter and education but it was only in 1989 that the rights of children were enshrined in international law in a comprehensive document that covered all ages up to 18.

The UNCRC grants every child the right to:

- a childhood (that is, protection from harm)
- be educated (that is, all girls and boys completing primary school)
- be healthy (that is, to have clean water, nutritious food and medical care)
- be treated fairly (that is, to change unfair laws and practices)
- be heard (that is, to consider children's views).

This is the most complete statement of children's rights ever produced and is the most widely ratified international human rights treaty in history. In the UK it was enacted through the Children Act 1989 (in force in 1991), which radically moderated the relationship between the child, parents and the state. The Act made the welfare of children paramount where previously their needs had been subsumed within the family. Children were given the right to participate in decisions that concerned them with advocates to make their case. The concept of parental responsibility replaced that of parental rights and local authorities were charged with providing services for children in need, including accommodation, fostering or day care if that represented the child's best interests. Children were to live with family unless separation was necessary and removal was to be carefully controlled. As ever, local authorities were required to intervene if a child was deemed to be at risk of significant harm and all cases were to be reviewed at regular intervals. The courts were to expedite matters concerning children to avoid delays and required to consult a checklist that clearly set out the child's circumstances and his/her personal wishes. There was a strong focus on collaboration and cooperation that was continued in later calls for multi-agency working.

This new focus on children and their rights made them a central focus for policy, whereas in the past it was usually voluntary bodies that spoke out on behalf of children: the Pre-school Playgroups Association, now Pre-school Learning Alliance (1961), the National Children's Bureau (1963), the Child Poverty Action Group (1965), National Daycare Trust (1980), Kids' Club Network, now 4Children (1985) (Baldock et al., 2013).

Labour reforms
New Labour arrives: 1997–2001

The New Labour government of 1997 saw childcare as key to their economic and social justice agendas. The National Childcare Strategy (1998) tasked local authorities to set up Early Years Development and Childcare Partnerships (EYDCPs), to expand and extend provision to cater for after school and holiday periods, developments often funded through the Big Lottery's New Opportunities Fund. The 1998 Comprehensive Spending Review established the Sure Start programme, to work in the community with young children (birth to three) and their families, aiming to break the cycle of disadvantage. From 1998, all four-year-olds were entitled to a funded early education place (DfE, 2014b). The designation of Ofsted as the regulatory body in 1999 (enacted in the 2000 Care Standards Act) signalled a policy orientation towards education, enabling standardisation of provision and greater opportunity for data collection. However, the separation of the regulatory and advisory roles galvanised some local authorities to establish support services for settings, parents and the children in their care, reintroducing a welfare element into early years provision (Baldock et al., 2013).

Prime Minister Tony Blair attended the Millennium Summit in September 2000 and like other world leaders made a commitment to support the achievement of eight Millennium Development Goals by 2015. These underline the very different scope of global problems faced by children. The goals are to:

1. eradicate extreme poverty and hunger
2. achieve universal primary education
3. promote gender equality and empower women
4. reduce child mortality
5. improve maternal health
6. combat HIV/AIDS, malaria and other diseases
7. ensure environmental sustainability
8. develop a global partnership for development.

New Labour consolidates: 2001–05

During Labour's second period of office, changes for children gained pace. Staff training was standardised under the auspices of the Council for Awards in Children's Care and Education (CACHE), the Qualifications and Curriculum Authority (QCA) and the National Early Years Training Organisation (NEYTO). The *Curriculum Guidance for the Foundation Stage* was published (QCA, 2000) (see Chapter 8). National standards for childcare provision were established in 2001 and a specialist Early Years Directorate drawn up within Ofsted to monitor these. The Neighbourhood Nurseries Initiative of 2001 focused expansion in the poorer areas and New Opportunities Funding of £100 million was made available for this purpose in England alone (Big Lottery Fund, 2005). In 2004 entitlement to a funded nursery place was extended to all three-year-olds (DfE, 2014b). Nursery businesses replaced many community settings. By 2012 small chains and stand-alone private-for-profit childcare businesses accounted for 75 per cent of the private childcare sector (Lloyd, 2012). Commercialisation made childcare more visible and sometimes more professional. Common branding reduced the range of choices available to parents even as it increased the number of potential places. Commercial nurseries tend to be more detached from the localities they serve and this reduces the traditional role of childcare settings in supporting the family and local community even as Children's Centres were established to promote this function, hardly evidence of joined-up thinking.

The Strategy Unit's Inter-Departmental Childcare Review, *Delivering for Children and Families* (Cabinet Office, 2002) set out a vision for childcare in 2010, with coordinated services, an additional 250,000 places (especially) for three-year-olds, and one-stop Children's Centres (offering childcare, family support and health services) in disadvantaged areas. The expansion of childcare drew attention to the lack of educational guidance for children under three and this deficit was bridged by the *Birth to Three Matters* framework (DfES, 2002) that set out the principles of supporting the development of: a strong child, a skilful communicator, a competent learner, a healthy child.

The *Laming Report* (HoC, 2003) into the death of Victoria Climbié gave the government a timely justification to advocate radical structural changes to services for children. The Green Paper *Every Child Matters* (ECM) (DfES, 2003b) heralded a long-term plan to create 'joined-up' practices to prevent children falling foul of gaps between services. The ECM paper presented a national framework for change that required local authorities to define their own plans based around the five national outcomes: be healthy; stay safe; enjoy and achieve; make a positive contribution; and achieve economic well-being. It outlined the essential components of a Children's Trust, a Common Assessment Framework (CAF) and multi-agency workforce strategy, setting a framework for implementation.

Key aspects of ECM came into force in the 2004 Children Act. This aimed to improve and integrate children's services, promote early intervention, provide strong leadership and bring together different professionals in multi-disciplinary teams in order achieve positive outcomes for children and young people and their families. To do this, it established new roles, powers and responsibilities.

- New roles included: a Children's Commissioner for England to speak out for children; a Director of Children's Services in each local authority to encourage accountability; lead members in each service to enable inter-agency working; local safeguarding children boards to coordinate child protection issues.
- Government claimed powers to: set up a new database with information about children (later refuted); intervene in failing authorities; establish a framework for inspection and joint area reviews.
- Under new responsibilities, agencies were to: cooperate; safeguard and promote the welfare of children; produce children and young people's plans; promote the educational achievement of looked after children; ascertain the wishes and feelings of children before making decisions that could affect them.

Some initiatives were supported by additional legislation. For instance, the Local Government Act of 2000 gave local authorities the power to promote well-being and local area agreements supported cooperation and collaboration between services (Baldock et al., 2013). However, the success of local implementation was to be assessed by the achievement of the five Every Child Matters outcomes.

New Labour completes: 2005–2010

The *Ten Year Strategy for Childcare* (HM Treasury, 2004) focused on providing childcare options for parents that were sufficient, flexible, affordable and to a high level of quality. These matters were addressed in the 2006 Childcare Act, which formalised the strategic role of the local authority. A set of new duties required them to: improve outcomes for all pre-school children and reduce inequalities; secure sufficient childcare for working parents; provide a better parental information service; provide information, advice and training for childcare providers. The Ten Year Strategy had also established a rationale for extending funded early years provision to two year olds and this was piloted from 2006. After detailed evaluation it was decided that provision should be extended in September 2013, and rolled out further in 2014, with priority given to those children who would most benefit (Maisey et al, 2013).

A new Early Years Foundation Stage Curriculum for children aged birth to five was mandated, to come into force in September 2008 (see Chapter 8).

By 2010 each local community was to have a Sure Start Children's Centre and guaranteed all-year out-of-school care from 8am to 6pm. Much of the work in these areas was orchestrated through the Children's Workforce Development Council (CWDC) set up in 2005 and this quango launched the Early Years Practitioner Status (EYPS) in 2007, monitoring its progress until CWDC responsibilities passed to the teaching authorities in 2012. The 2006 Act also reformed and simplified early years regulation and inspection arrangements, providing for a new integrated education and care quality framework (for pre-school children) and a new Ofsted childcare register.

Gordon Brown replaced Tony Blair as Prime Minister in 2007, ironically the year in which UNICEF research found children in the UK to rank lowest among industrial nations in terms of well-being (UNICEF, 2007). Brown planned to coordinate children's services further, but this never progressed beyond the division of education to create a Department for Children, Schools and Families (DCSF), which separated the issues for young children from those affecting further and higher education (Baldock et al., 2013).

The coalition makes changes, 2010 onwards

It was ominous for Every Child Matters when the coalition government uploaded banners onto the DCSF website distancing themselves from policy introduced by the previous government that was still obligatory. Indeed, writing in 2013, Baldock et al. claimed that 'the Labour Party's attempted revolution in Early Years services is faltering' (Baldock et al., 2013: 25). There was dissent for the universal status of Sure Start initiatives even before the election, and under the coalition, the core purpose of Children's Centres was redefined. In written evidence to parliament in December 2012, The Children's Society (2012) expressed concern that this focus on 'the most disadvantaged and reducing inequalities' would lead to Children's Centres becoming 'an extension of social care'. Nevertheless, Statutory Guidance issued in April 2013 (DfE, 2013b) talked of the need 'to reduce inequalities between families in greatest need and their peers' (ibid: 7). It expected local authorities 'to target children's centres services at young children and families in the area who are at risk of poor outcomes' (ibid: 9), making a distinction between provision of centres and services.

Reviews affecting children

There was a policy vacuum while the coalition government gathered data to enable evidence-based policy making. In 2010 it commissioned a number of independent reviews.

The Munro Review of Child Protection: Final report (DfE, 2011c) recommended a less bureaucratic system with a better-trained workforce to enable senior social workers to exercise their professional judgement.

The Foundation Years: Preventing Poor Children Becoming Poor Adults (Field, 2010) proposed a set of *life chances indicators* to assess outcomes for children and a foundation years education system geared to support poorer families to nurture their children, paid according to its successfulness. In April 2011 these issues were addressed in the Child Poverty Strategy.

In *The Early Years: Foundations for Life, Health and Learning*, Dame Clare Tickell (2011) recommended a continuing but simplified curriculum framework, a greater role for parents and carers, revised training routes and further investigations into staff ratios.

Graham Allen, MP, was commissioned to carry out an independent review of early intervention in 2011. This reported in two stages. In January, *The Next Steps* (Allen, 2011b) made a strong case for early intervention, favouring quality pre-school education, parenting support and the establishment of an Early Intervention Foundation to coordinate provision. In July, *Smart Investment, Massive Savings* (Allen, 2011a) investigated how to fund new programmes through private sector financial instruments coordinated by a jointly funded foundation and set out to 'change the culture at the heart of government' (ibid: viii). This report carried endorsements from Tickell, Field, Munro, and Joyce Moseley who had worked on an earlier Cabinet Office 'Big Society' investigation into *Resolving Multiple Disadvantage* from April to September 2011 (Allen, 2011b; LTCW, 2011).

Government responses and actions

The government response to these reviews appeared as *Supporting Families in the Foundation Years* (DfE, 2011b). The most significant commitments were to increase the number of health visitors, revise the EYFS and the Code of Practice and retain the network of Sure Start Children's Centres. Other foci were early intervention, changes to the workforce and greater support for families in terms of flexible working and additional online support services.

An Early Intervention Foundation was formally launched on 15 April 2013 supported initially by the charities 4Children and Achievement for all 3As and the Local Government Association. It is Chaired by Graham Allen (staffed by Carey Oppenheim, Donna Molloy and Leon Feinstein among others), and tasked to deliver the three As 'Assessment, Advice and Advocacy of Early Intervention' (Howard, 2013).

A further significant review, the *Nutbrown Report* (Nutbrown, 2012), was handled separately.

The early years review and the aftermath

Cathy Nutbrown (2012) was commissioned to review the early years and her report, *Foundations for Quality* contained 19 recommendations, including progressively greater ratios of higher and more broadly qualified staff, and suggested improvements to training, mentoring and induction. The government response, the *More Great Childcare* (DfE, 2013a) headed by the Minister for Children, Elizabeth Truss, sought to raise the status and quality of the workforce, expand provision, improve regulation and give more choice to parents, but planned to fund this by relaxing adult:child ratios when a staff member had higher-level qualifications.

These plans were highly criticised by practitioners and academics, and by Nick Clegg, Deputy Prime Minister. In a powerful response, Nutbrown (2013: 10) claimed that most of her recommendations were rejected or transformed into strategies that would 'shake the foundations of quality provision'.

The reform of special needs education

Special needs education was an early target for legal reform and the DfE (2011a) announced plans in the Green Paper, *Support and Aspiration*. This dismantled the graduated response mechanisms previously in force, focusing resources on children with severe and complex needs. Such children became eligible for an education, health and care (EHC) plan rather than a statement with a personal budget to be overseen by parents/carers to fund the child's specific needs. The budget can be spent on education in a specialist institution or in the mainstream if a local school can meet the child's needs without affecting the education of other children in the class. Children who would previously have commanded Action or Action Plus support are to be catered for through normal classroom provision and no longer require an individual education plan (IEP). School-based coordinators – special educational needs coordinators (SENCOs) – are to manage the school's needs, buying in advice from specialists as required, whereas previously there was a state-managed infrastructure to access at will. These changes were 'heralded as the biggest shake-up of the SEN system in 30 years' (SENmagazine, 2014) as, special educational needs are to be streamlined and marketised, becoming self-financing. Schools, and clusters of schools and settings, are to manage their own training and provision, supported for the first two years, at least, by Early Support, a team based at the Council for Disabled Children at, the National Children's Bureau.

The changes form part of the Children and Families Act 2014 that also legislates for revisions to the care of adopted and looked after children, the family justice system, childcare, shared parental leave, antenatal leave, flexible working and the Office of the Children's Commissioner (OCC). They are implemented through a new Code of Practice (DfE, 2014a), in force from September 2014. Some schools were viewing the funding arrangements with concern even before they came into practice (for example, Read 2014).

Public concern

These are significant changes that raise some concern. There are fears that the new special educational needs (SEN) policy is dismantling an official system and replacing it with voluntary support. The Nutbrown Review (Nutbrown, 2012) provoked criticism that the government is not listening to the experts it deploys. Increasingly, practitioners worry that early years is now finance-driven and, despite high expectations for the sector, only services for the most disadvantaged receive funding. The charity Action for Children, headed by Dame Tickell, now evaluates how annual changes in government spending impact on children, young people and families, publishing their findings in *The Red Book* (Action for Children, 2011, 2012, 2013). Practitioners can consult this directly (online) to develop informed views that avoid political and media-induced bias.

Summary

This chapter started broadly and progressively focused on contemporary early years policy. At the outset, it considered how economic philosophies underpin collective decision-making to illuminate the options open to governments when they decide how to share out scarce resources. It then looked at the practical aspects of government – how, at the macro-level, globalisation has created hierarchies of power and how, at the micro-level, the UK determines its governance. A historical overview showed the direction of change over time. Finally, the focus took a childhood orientation, considering international and local policy in a shared context before looking specifically at the New Labour initiatives around *Every Child Matters,* and the coalition government's dismantling of this agenda, their extensive review of particular sectors and the coming together of overall policy, some of it highly contested. Inevitably, this chapter abruptly stops mid-process so readers should be mindful of the timescale when using it as a source. For that reason, it attempts to describe rather than explore or explain policies.

Points for reflection

- Visit one of the websites below and explore the wealth of material it makes accessible. How can you use the site to support your studies?
- Consider how society is trying to make life better for children. Will the changes benefit *all* children?
- If you had to advise the government on quality, affordable childcare, what issues would you need to consider and which would *you* prioritise?

Further reading

Miller, L. and Hevey, D. (2012) *Policy Issues in the Early Years.* London: Sage.
*A useful overview that complements Baldock et al. (2013) (see
References).*

Frost, N. (2011) *Rethinking Children and Families: The Relationship
   Between Childhood, Families and the State.* London: Continuum.
Lee, N. (2001) *Childhood and Society.* Maidenhead: Open University Press.
Oswell, D. (2013) *The Agency of Children: From Family to Global Human
   Rights.* Cambridge: Cambridge University Press.
*General texts that consider the power relations between adults and
children, the individual and the state. Archard (2004), too, focuses on
children's rights (see References).*

Pugh, G. (2010) 'Improving outcomes for young children: can we narrow the gap?', *Early Years*, 30(1): 5–14.
Good overview of the early years reforms under New Labour.

Taguma, M., Litjens, I. and Makowiecki, K. (2012) *Quality Matters in Early
   Childhood Education and Care: United Kingdom (England).* OECD.
*OECD overview into how England does and can encourage families
and communities to support better quality childcare.*

Websites

www.un.org/en/ – the UN website.
www.unicef.org.uk/, also www.unicef.org – UN information on children.
www.who.int/en/ – WHO website.
www.oecd.org/unitedkingdom/, also www.oecd.org/ – OECD website.
*These official sites are packed with definitive information and links to
further material.*

Many OECD policy documents can be read online on the OECD iLibrary.
Search under 'early childhood' or 'starting strong' at www.oecd-
ilibrary.org.

To gain *free* access to selected SAGE journal articles related to key
topics in this chapter, visit: www.sagepub.co.uk/hazelrwright.

CHAPTER 8

EDUCATIONAL PERSPECTIVES

> **Overview**
>
> This chapter summarises key educational developments in England through time and across sectors.
>
> - Early developments include education's religious foundations, elementary education and its extension, and in culmination, the 1944 (Butler) Education Act that established the structure of state education in the twentieth century.
> - For the compulsory sector, the account traces developments prior to, and after, the 1988 Education Reform Act.
> - The early years pathway examines the transition from pioneering nursery initiatives, through voluntary provision, to state intervention.
> - For post-compulsory education, vocationalism and the development of the further and higher education sectors are key themes.

This chapter offers an overview of educational developments in England. For the early period this may include other countries in the British Isles, too. The intention is to identify key developments within different educational sectors but also to maintain a sense of chronology, mindful that important government legislation tends to cut across sectoral divisions.

Early developments in education

In English society, formal education was initially associated with ecclesiastical learning. A limited number of grammar and song schools existed by 600

AD, the first Oxford Colleges were set up from the 1200s onwards, and independent schools like Winchester and Eton were founded around 1400. Kelly (1992: 9) describes education in the medieval period as 'education for salvation', claiming that 'the desire to read the words of Holy Scripture became for centuries one of the greatest incentives to literacy among humble people'. Adult literacy was important and priests had a duty to teach their parishioners to read so that they could learn from religious tracts. The advent of the printing press in 1476 and the availability of an English Bible from 1535 made this imperative. In the seventeenth century there was a strong Puritan expectation that parents should have their children learn to read and write. Families were often taught together in Sunday school classes but by the early eighteenth century some children attended charity schools run by organisations like the Society for Promoting Christian Knowledge (SPCK), which also established night schools to educate adults.

By 1660 a growing interest in scientific learning among religious nonconformists, excluded from Oxford and Cambridge by their beliefs, led to the establishment of 'dissenting academies'. These taught secular subjects – law, medicine, commerce, engineering and the arts – providing limited higher education opportunities for adults. Such practices continued and expanded during the eighteenth century and local initiatives were boosted by learned travellers giving adult public lectures (Fieldhouse et al., 1996).

Elementary education

The nineteenth century saw the development of more universal education. For adults this was largely philanthropic or collegial, centred in the mechanics institutes and numerous mutual improvement societies that flourished in local communities. For children, provision was more formal but geographically very uneven. Local Dame schools were often little more than childminding services, serious instruction still aligned with religion. The 1807 Parochial Schools Bill secured some provision for the labouring classes and in 1811 the Church of England National Society made plans to set up a school in every parish. The dominance of the Church of England was challenged, however. Nonconformist supporters of the Quaker, Joseph Lancaster, formed the Royal Lancasterian Association (1810) which became the British and Foreign School Society in 1814. Lancaster ran an effective nonconformist school in Southwark, its progress watched by the 'wonder-waiting eyes' of foreign princes, Jews and Turks, among others (Corston, 2014 [1840: 11]). This used a monitorial system, whereby teachers educated the older and abler children who, in turn, taught groups of younger children, in a process that enabled a small number of trained teachers to cascade learning to significant numbers of students. The system is commonly associated with Lancaster but may have been influenced by the work of clergyman Andrew Bell in India (Barnard, 1961).

We saw in Chapter 3 that John Pounds began to teach poor children in 1818. This encouraged other philanthropists to set up 'ragged schools' in underprivileged communities, many of which used the monitorial system. In 1833 the government awarded the National and British and Foreign School Societies £20,000 to fund 50 per cent of the cost of new school buildings, a grant that became an annual award, marking a first stage in the development of compulsory education (ibid). In 1836 (after the 1832 Reform Act gave an additional million people the vote) the Central Society of Education was set up to minimise religious influences on schools and in 1839 a Privy Council, chaired by Dr Kay (later Sir James Kay-Shuttleworth), was established 'for the consideration of all matters affecting the education of the people' (ibid: 99).

This early state intervention clearly threatened church authority as Barnard describes a number of incidences where Kay was unable to introduce schemes due to religious dissent. When Kay circumvented disagreement by establishing a private teacher training establishment in 1840 with a colleague, Tufnell, the Church quickly responded, establishing similar colleges as quickly as possible – some 22 church training institutions in England and Wales by 1845. This created a pattern of residential training for teachers in private colleges that continued for 50 years. Perhaps because of the power issues, probably because of the costs involved too, state schooling was introduced piecemeal. Rather than abandon the existing monitorial system of teaching, Kay decided to improve both the standards and quantity of trainees by indenturing pupil teachers from 13 to 18 into a five-year training scheme that served as an apprenticeship for future teacher training in college. The Newcastle Commission (1858–61) into elementary education decided to offer capitation grants to existing provision rather than to develop new schools and, concerned to curb inefficiency, brought in the system of payment by results.

It was this piecemeal system that the Liberal Gladstone government sought to change with Forster's Education Act in 1870 and its extension to infant provision (five to seven) a year later, an arbitrary decision that made five the start age for compulsory schooling. In effect, Forster's Act endorsed the contiguous development of secular board and voluntary church schools that continues to exist today. The new school boards accounted for only a third of new provision between 1870 and 1876 (ibid: 119); the Church maintained its majority. It was the State, however, that enabled and enforced children's school attendance. We saw in Chapter 3 how a series of Factory Acts attempted to take children out of the workforce and into education. Only in 1880 was attendance to ten years of age made compulsory.

The early twentieth century saw small-scale but significant reform and from 1899 this was superintended by a Board of Education. The 1902 Education Act established local education authorities (LEAs), introduced a more universal secular curriculum, and attempted to extend provision beyond elementary level. The 1906 Act allowed LEAs to provide meals for undernourished children. The 1907 Act introduced medical inspections. The 1918 Education Act focused on older students and adults but also instituted ancillary services: medical inspections, nursery schools and centres for pupils with special needs.

In the inter-war period the Hadow Committee carried out six comprehensive reviews of compulsory schooling (Gillard, 2006) covering:

- differentiation of the curriculum for boys and girls (1923)
- psychological tests of educable capacity (1924)
- the education of the adolescent (1926)
- books in public elementary schools (1928)
- the primary school (1931)
- infant and nursery schools (1933).

Together these informed the content of the 1944 Education Act. Three of the reports were narrowly focused. The 1923 report on gender called for a greater focus on aesthetics and elementary hygiene and domestic skills. The 1924 report thoroughly examined the role and utility of intelligence and attainment tests in light of the significant developments in the field. The 1928 report considered the provision and function of books in schools and at home.

The remaining three reports considered overall structures in light of contemporary knowledge of child development. The 1926 report recommended the division of schooling into primary and secondary phases at age 11. *The Primary School* (1931) report supported an experimental pedagogy for 7- to 11-year-olds; reviewed teacher training, staffing, examining, the needs of 'retarded' children, premises and equipment. The 1933 report made parallel recommendations for five- to seven-year-olds. It included recommendations for emotional development from Cyril Burt and Susan Isaacs (Gillard, 2006).

Education beyond the elementary

Secondary education was seriously demarcated along class lines (Ball, 2008) and largely confined to those who could afford to pay. It had been offered on an *ad hoc* basis by some school boards but the *Newcastle Report* (1861) found against extending schooling provision for the working classes. Males from wealthy families were traditionally sent to fee-paying public schools and these were reviewed separately, in the *Clarendon Report* (1864). In 1868 the *Taunton Report* addressed the 'needs' of the growing middle classes and recommended a national system of secondary education based on the existing endowed schools (White, 2006). This led to the passing of the 1869 Endowed Schools Act for England. Wales progressed more slowly, establishing a Welsh secondary education system by 1869. In 1894 the Bryce Commission was asked to plan a coordinated system for England, consequently the 1902 Education Act mandated local education authorities to organise both secondary and higher education. LEAs were empowered to train teachers, provide scholarships and to pay the fees of students in colleges or hostels (Barnard, 1961).

In 1904 Secondary Regulations introduced a subject-based curriculum and in 1907 the Education (Administrative Provisions) Act created a scholarship/ free place system. The Victorians had determined under the 1889 Technical Instruction Act to separate technical education from secondary schooling but in 1938 the Spens report, *Secondary Education with Special Reference to Grammar Schools and Technical High Schools,* recommended a tripartite system of secondary schools – the grammar school, the technical school and the skills-based secondary modern – and this pattern of provision was further endorsed by the 1943 Norwood report, *Curriculum and Examinations in Secondary Schools* (ibid).

The 1944 (Butler) Education Act

The 1944 (Butler) Education Act brought together many ideas mooted earlier and established the structure of English state education. A parallel Act in 1945 set out the system for Scotland. Butler's Act established LEAs and formally replaced the term *elementary*, introducing the primary, secondary and further education sectors. It raised the school leaving age to 15 and called for provision for all pupils whatever 'their different ages, abilities and aptitudes' (McKenzie, 2001: 176). This led to the introduction of an 11 plus examination to select pupils for grammar, secondary modern and (nominally) technical education but the Act did not legislate for such divisions, nor for the GCE examinations (1951) that privileged some children over others (ibid: 189). The Act anticipated localised curriculum and pedagogic decisions by headteachers and LEAs. It established a non-denominational daily act of worship in schools but allowed exemption without prejudice (ibid: 182). It stipulated free education with support (clothing, boarding allowances, milk, meals, transport) to those who needed it (ibid: 176). LEA development plans were to include children then termed 'handicapped' at both primary and secondary level. Under the Handicapped Pupils and School Health Service Regulations 1945 children were to undergo medical assessment to allocate them to a place within a rigid 11-category framework (Gillard, 2011). Thus the Act's achievement in terms of removing class, religious and meritocratic barriers within education was very limited despite creating a universal system. The 1944 Act also established Central Advisory Councils for Education (CACE) in England and Wales (ibid: 176), which later produced the significant Crowther, Newsom and Plowden reports.

Compulsory education

In 1967 the CACE enquiry into *Children and their Primary Schools,* led by Lady Plowden and a team of Her Majesty's Inspectors (HMIs), convened to examine primary education in England 'in all its aspects' (CACE, 1967). Typical of its time, it took a Piagetian view of education, supporting active and individualised learning and stating clearly its belief that: 'At the heart of the educational process lies the child' (ibid: 7). The Plowden Report continued to inform primary practice and educational philosophy even after guidance on *The School Curriculum* (DES, 1981) tried to put the curriculum 'at the heart of education'.

While educators embraced progressive practices with enthusiasm others took a more utilitarian view. Many employers felt that school leavers were unable to scribe letters and compute numbers adequately. Their concerns were set out in the *Black Papers,* a series of tracts that criticised standards in education and called for reform of the system – a return to traditional teaching methods. They were five in number, published between 1969 and 1977. Three were written by Brian Cox and Tony Dyson; two by Cox and Rhodes Boyson (Gillard, 2011).

1978 saw the start of a series of official enquiries into education, fulfilling the recommendation of the Plowden Report that provision should be surveyed at least once every ten years. Five HMI surveys reported across the age range between 1978 and 1985. *Primary Education in England* (1978) commissioned the National Foundation for Educational Research (NFER) to test the reading and mathematical achievement of classes of 5, 7, and 11 year-olds in more than 540 schools. This provided a measure of the efficacy of primary education in England in the period 1975 to 1977 to assess against the claims made in the *Black Papers* (Gillard, 2011).

Viewing the summaries on the *Education in England* website, it is interesting to note that amidst recommendations for teaching improvement, *Aspects of Secondary Education in England* (DES, 1979), the second survey, reminded schools that public examination results should neither limit nor dominate the school experience. The report on 80 first schools in England, *Education 5 to 9* (DES, 1982) was generally complacent and supportive of the integrated primary school. Taken together, recommendations suggested a need to extend and integrate learning and to apply rather than merely practise skills. The report on *9–13 Middle Schools* (DES, 1983) recommended greater coordination and continuity across the curriculum, more active and in-depth learning opportunities with greater differentiation to match pupil's needs, and advised that falling rolls might require schools to amalgamate to enable subject-specialist teaching. The title *Education 8 to 12 in Combined and Middle Schools* (1985) is misleading, as it studied 33 schools that cover this age range and a further 16 that catered for 5- to 16-year-olds (Gillard, 2011). Like the previous one, this report called for greater curriculum coherence; also for more active teaching methods, more effective assessment and better equipped teachers (DES, 1985). The failure to contrast the combined and middle schools suggests that inspectors failed to find differences that would support a clear policy direction for the optimisation of school age structures.

Curriculum and assessment were extensively debated in this period, and plans made to increase parental participation and school control of budgets. These discourses culminated in the 1988 Education Reform Act, a Conservative restructuring of education at all levels. Before we consider this in detail, we need to consider the evolution of secondary schooling in the period since 1944.

As stated, the 1944 Education (Butler) Act indirectly enabled the grammar/secondary modern dichotomy to become the common pattern (McCulloch, 2002). A technical pathway appeared costly and, instead, the *Crowther Report* (CACE, 1959) was tasked to consider further education opportunities for children 15–18.

During the 1960s, growing concern over the education of less able 13- to 16-year-olds led governments to consider the merits of a single educational pathway. The 1964 (Boyle) Education Act enabled middle schools and reallocation of school buildings, anticipating changes to the normative structure of grammar and secondary modern schools. The *Newsom Report, Half our Future* (CACE, 1963) identified significant problems within secondary modern provision. Together, these paved the way for the 1965 Labour call for local authorities to submit proposals for comprehensive education (Circular 10/65) (Gillard, 2011: Chapter 6). This was revoked by the following Conservative government (Circular 10/70) but reinstated in 1974 and enforced through Labour's 1976 Education Act, only to be repealed and replaced by the Conservative's 1979 Education Act that allowed LEAs to maintain selective systems (Gillard, 2011). These successive policy changes left different localities with very different patterns of provision, state secondary schools randomly distributed, and schools vulnerable to criticism. Powerful elites were determined to enact change and this was achieved in 1988 following the business- and media-led campaign to raise achievement embodied in the *Black Papers*.

The Education Reform (Baker) Act 1988 and the national curriculum

The 1988 reforms changed the nature of education. Ostensibly empowering parents, 'marketisation' became a ploy to reduce the power of schools and LEAs (disbanding the Inner London Education Authority entirely) and invest significant powers in central government. The Act created new forms of school, grant maintained and city technology colleges, to introduce selective education in new ways. Central allegiance was reaffirmed in a requirement for conformity to a broadly Christian religious ethos. Local management of schools (LMS) undermined dependence on county-level support networks (Chitty, 2004). Schools now managed their own buildings and staff, with budgets allocated according to pupil numbers, ages and degree of special need. The Act established curriculum and assessment councils to oversee cumbersome Standard Assessment Tests (SATs) at the end of each key stage (7, 11, 14 and 16) and a reformed inspection service geared to raise standards (Gillard, 2011). At pupil level, the national curriculum was possibly most significant. Written by a government quango rather than by practicing teachers, this presented curriculum content for each subject for each year group in a series of folders, and required planning and progression to be monitored against multiple attainment targets assessed at ten levels. Teaching was reduced to curriculum 'delivery', with significant time spent on planning, documentation and record keeping.

The curriculum proved unworkable and was continually challenged. A teacher boycott of SATs in 1993–4, forced the government to make revisions in 1995. As national SATs results were used to create league tables, this led to schools teaching to the test, and excluding challenging children. The 1995 revised national curriculum was condensed into a single document for each sector, covering all ten curriculum areas. Teachers still found it too content based so in 1999 New Labour belatedly published 'handbooks' setting out curricular aims. The revised primary curriculum slimmed down non-core programmes to embed the National Literacy and Numeracy Strategies, introduced a year earlier, and interdisciplinary study of citizenship and personal, social and health education (PSHE) (Cassidy, 1999).

The debate around literacy was heightened when the government commissioned Jim Rose to review the teaching of early reading. Rose (2006) recommended a synthetic phonics approach over all others even though this contradicted 'the powerful body of evidence accumulated over the last three years' (Wyse and Styles, 2007).

The primary curriculum remained highly contested and in 2009–10 was subjected to three major reviews (Gillard, 2011). Robin Alexander's, *Cambridge Primary Review* (CPR) produced a two-part interim report in February 2009 (Alexander and Flutter, 2009; Alexander, 2009b), and a final report in October (Alexander, 2009a). It called for a broader, balanced and enriched curriculum reinstating the arts and humanities but was overshadowed by the government's own review, headed by Jim Rose (2009), which made a provisional report in February, final report in April 2009. Rose called for a curriculum founded on six areas of learning, offering some continuity from the early years curriculum. The House of Commons Children, Schools and Families Committee (CSFC) report on the national curriculum, suggesting a slimming down, was also published in April (HoC, 2009b). It is notable that CPR recommended raising the school starting age to six yet the Labour government decided to offer all four-year-olds a place at school or nursery. In practice, the impending general election prevented most changes and the coalition government abandoned the 2010 revised primary curriculum, ostensibly to 'save' £7 million (Williams, 2010).

The secondary curriculum was also to be modified but the 2007 proposals were removed from the public domain after the election. The coalition government 'sought' expert views in 2011, and told schools to 'disapply' the curriculum in 2013–14 but be ready to phase in a new framework in 2014. This appears to privilege formal learning in English, maths and science over other subjects. Independent school and academies are to be exempted from this new curriculum, further fuelling professional dissent. The Prime Minister describes the new curricula, in place in September 2014, as 'tough and rigorous' (Adams, 2013).

The reform of 16–18 qualifications has also been subject to debate and modification under both Labour and coalition governments. Curriculum 2000 introduced AS-levels as an independent but integral stage but new plans include a standalone AS level decoupled from the A-level (Ofqual, 2013). Proposals for overarching frameworks were also made but not adopted. One of the significant trends in the twenty-first century is the freeing of schools from local authority control. Academies receive state funding directly from central government rather than at county level. Trust schools remain within the remit of the local authority but additional support is provided by a charitable partnership from business or other expert groups. Free schools are state-funded, all-ability schools set up in response to local demand by teams who come together to create an acceptable education plan. They have independent governance and can decide their own curriculum, attendance patterns and how they spend their budget, but are still subject to Ofsted inspection.

Early years pathway

Nursery education, much neglected by the state, has a significant history that offers insights into contemporary childhoods.

Early developments: the nursery tradition

In Britain, Robert Owen's nursery school at the New Lanark Mills stands out as visionary. Socialist, Owen, took over the management of these Scottish cotton mills from his father-in-law, David Dale, in 1800. Dale had traditionally used workhouse children from Glasgow in his mills. Unlike many contemporaries he had treated them well, housing them on the upper floors of one of the mills and providing them with suitable clothing, washing facilities, food and a basic education, but they still worked long hours without wages. The New Lanark Trust for Education claims that a typical diet included beef or cheese, occasional fresh herrings, barley broth and bread, potatoes and porridge served with milk in summer and 'swats' (a molasses and beer concoction) in winter. Dale employed teachers to educate the children in the early evening (from 7pm to 9pm) and expected them to attend church on Sundays.

Owen was determined to phase out child labour and committed to improving the living conditions of his workforce, building them a village with doctor, school, cooperative store and community centre – the Institute for the Formation of Character, opened in 1816. He set up a 'sickness' fund, educational and recreational facilities and public baths, and provided children with school clothes (a white tunic). From 1817 an infant school catered for children able to walk. Here they were encouraged to play, run around and socialise, rather than set to book learning. For older children, teachers provided a progressive education encompassing music, dancing, nature studies, history, geography and drawing, in addition to the essential '3Rs': reading, writing and arithmetic. Corporal punishment was banned (far in advance of the 1987 ban in English state schools, 1998 ban in the independent sector). The school was taken over by the Parish Board in 1876. Relocated in 1884, it continues as a community school despite the mill closure in 1968 (New Lanark Trust, 2001).

Nursery pioneer, Samuel Wilderspin left a very different legacy. He supported the local establishment of some 150 nursery schools in a decade, actively travelling the country to give public lectures on education. In contrast to Owen's socialist model, Wilderspin's schools were concerned with mass instruction, setting a pattern for rote learning and repetition but with some practical resources, playground activities and religious learning. Wilderspin set out his ideas in a treatise of 1823 that became the universal pattern for nursery education. Under the Reverend William Wilson this slipped into 'preparation' for entry into national schools (Whitbread, 1972).

Other early nursery provision developed out of European movements. The Home and Colonial Society was formed in 1837 to train teachers in Pestalozzian techniques and Bertha Ronge opened the first Froebelian kindergarten in London in 1851. Kindergartens began to spread across the country in the 1860s with societies based in Manchester and London by the 1870s (Brosterman, 1997). Some 900 'revisionist' Froebelians, inspired by Pestalozzi, too, met at the Sesame Club to discuss how to 'educate' their children. A subgroup formed the Sesame League with the intention of setting up a model kindergarten in 1890, but this soon dropped any pretense of catering for all classes. The first free kindergarten opened in Woolwich in 1900 as part of the Toynbee Hall Settlement, a socialist endeavour to support the working classes (Brehony, 2000).

As part of its superintendence, the Board of Education commissioned a report on School Attendance of Children Below the Age of 5, the Acland Report (HMSO, 1908). This found that at least a third of children aged three to five were registered for elementary education, a practice perceived as inappropriate. It considered that home 'affords advantages' when 'the mother does her duty by her children' (ibid: 16). Drawing on comparisons with settings in Belgium, France, Germany and Switzerland, the report recommended standards of provision for less advantaged youngsters but little changed as implementation was left to the discretion of local authorities. Between 1900 and 1910, 12 free kindergartens opened in England and Scotland, and together with Margaret McMillan's Deptford Nursery these became the first funded nursery schools following the 1918 Education Act. By 1923 there were still only 24 nurseries in England so a group of influential socialists formed the Nursery School Association of Great Britain and Ireland. Its officers included Ramsey MacDonald, (Prime Minister in 1924); socialist philosopher, Bertrand Russell; and educators Grace Owen and Lillian de Lissa. Margaret McMillan was the first president. Lack of funding amid political crises restricted further development. The association managed to open eight emergency open-air nurseries by 1934 and gained agreement that schools be established in areas of housing reconstruction, but there was little attempt to create universal provision either before or after the Second World War. Development was piecemeal – individuals set up nurseries when and where they could. The Cambridge Malting House School that employed Susan Isaacs from 1924 to 1927 was very much in this tradition. Susan, herself, had been trained by Grace Owen at Manchester University (Brehony, 2000).

Maria Montessori's ideas for nursery education offered a 'scientific' basis for pedagogy and were initially lauded as 'a catchword of educational innovation'. The Montessori Association included prominent educators such as Edmond Holmes, Michael Sadler, Albert Mansbridge and Lord Lytton, yet Montessori's work was 'soon marginalized by the educational establishment' (Cunningham, 2000: 204). She was not open to 'revision' to accommodate other theoretical perspectives, and this rigidity and her commercial development of teaching materials was unpopular, limiting her impact.

Steiner nurseries, too, made little impact on numbers of children served, but Great Britain did have a Waldorf school at the time of Steiner's death in 1925, one of the first four to open (Uhrmacher, 1995). Despite piecemeal expansion by committed individuals, it was only in 2004 that the English government funded an investigation into the merits of the Steiner philosophy. It commissioned a team from the University of West of England to determine the possible benefits of establishing Steiner provision alongside mainstream education (Woods et al., 2005). The focus was on the 23 schools rather than the more numerous nurseries.

The middle phase: volunteers step in

By the 1950s some part-time provision was made available but, generally, it was developments in the voluntary sector that compensated for the dearth of public provision. Belle Tutaev, an American moving to Britain from Jamaica, noticed the isolation of young families. She decided to establish a group where her pre-school-age daughter could make friends with other children but found hall managers reluctant to lend rooms for children's play as this might damage the fittings. She and three friends had to start attending the local church, to influence the decision from within, but eventually gained permission to use the hall. They 'borrowed' their children's toys to resource the first playgroup meetings and thus began the process of sessional 'setting up' and 'tidying away' that still constrains many children's play provision.

Tutaev demonstrates the power of timely social action. Finding a lack of regulatory advice, she contacted a charity manager (at Save the Children) and a government minister (Department of Health) for guidance. She then published a letter in *The Guardian* in 1961 (Tutaev, 1961) to encourage other mothers to follow her lead. The public response was enormous, some 150 letters per week for many weeks. By August 1962 a national group was able to hold an annual general meeting (AGM) for the Pre-school Playgroups Association (PPA), with 150 members present.

Both the Plowden report and the Urban Aid programmes supported nursery expansion and for a short while it appeared that Margaret Thatcher, as Minister of Education in 1972, intended to develop provision but other economic priorities took precedence (*Early Education* website). The 1972 White Paper *Education: A Framework for Expansion* (Margaret Thatcher Foundation, 1972 provides a summary statement) planned education for 90 per cent of four-year-olds, and 50 per cent of three-year-olds but was unable to proceed to policy (National Commission on Education, 1993). The voluntary sector continued to fill the gap. By 1978 PPA membership stood at 13,500, organised through a network of national and regional branches (Playgroup Movement, 2014). The movement flourished in the 1970s and 1980s. It supported playgroups, trained staff and published guides to promote these endeavours.

However, a growing interest in pre-school education, after the 1988 Education Reform Act, heralded increasing government intervention. In the early 1990s, four significant studies focused on quality in the early years, bringing increasing pressure to regulate and standardise provision, and forcing the PPA to adapt to continue in an increasingly government-controlled sector (Henderson, 2011), changing its name to Pre-school Learning Alliance (PLA) in 1995 (Pre-School Learning Alliance, 2014).

The state takes over: early childhood education and care

The first of these national reports, the Rumbold report *Starting with Quality* (DES, 1990) found early years provision very uneven and recommended more attention to planning and monitoring children's needs, better staff training and service coordination. Anticipating changes in school provision, it recommended a curriculum based around eight areas of learning: aesthetic and creative, human and social, language and literacy, mathematics, physical, science, spiritual and moral, and technology. *Learning to Succeed: A Radical Look at Education Today and a Strategy for the Future* was a report by the National Commission on Education (1993), a consortium of the British Association, the British Academy, the Royal Society and the Fellowship of Engineering, funded by the Paul Hamlyn Foundation, with a broad remit to consider the overall state of education in the UK. This devoted a chapter to 'a good start in education' and recommended national standards, local reviews and publicly-funded, good quality education for all three and four year-olds. *Start Right* (Ball, 1994, for The Royal Society of Arts) made similar recommendations and specified an appropriate curriculum; well-trained permanent staff; high staff-to-children ratios; customised buildings and equipment; and a partnership role for parents. Prior to the introduction of a voucher scheme to fund education for four-year-olds (in 1996) the Audit Commission (1996a) was asked to review the costs and benefits of early years education. Its report, *Counting to Five* recommended a 'sticks' and 'carrots' approach to expansion. A companion management handbook, *Under Fives Count* (Audit Commission, 1996b) set out standards for good practice within the sector. Together these reports clearly signposted a concern to change early years provision.

Chapter 7 traced the key policy initiatives affecting the sector so here the focus is on curriculum development in the early years. Up to 1996, there was no set curriculum for early years. Many individual groups did plan for children's learning but based their ideas on resources published for primary schools, or by the Pre-school Playgroups Association. Audrey Curtis and Sheelagh Hills' *My World* (1979), a themed resource book written for the teacher of the 'socially handicapped' child, held a much broader appeal. By 1986, Curtis's new book *A Curriculum for the Pre-school Child* offered suggestions grouped around skills and competencies. In America David Weikart and colleagues developed the High/Scope Curriculum for public (state) schools in Ypsilanti, Michigan in the 1960s and 70s and some English establishments adopted aspects of this philosophy. High/Scope is an open framework that supports educators in encouraging children to construct their own knowledge (High/Scope Educational Research Foundation, 1991). Children are offered choices about what they do and encouraged to verbalise their problems and solutions within a practice often summed up as 'plan, do, review'.

However, in 1996, just prior to losing the general election, the Conservative government intervened formally, publishing the *Desirable Learning Outcomes* (SCAA, 1996) to accompany the introduction of the nursery vouchers scheme and Ofsted inspections (Kwon, 2002). In 1997 the New Labour government rebranded these as *Early Learning Goals*, setting them in a broader framework as *Curriculum Guidance for the Foundation Stage* (QCA, 2000). Principles for early years education, stepping stones to achieving goals for three to five-year-olds and practice guidance were provided to enable practitioners to assist children and monitor their progress. This document placed reception classes firmly within the early years curriculum and justified the inclusion of outdoor play (Edgington, 2007) but it was easily converted into checklists for progress. Early years settings were overwhelmed by paperwork as they planned for and monitored children's progress, and many schools attempted to 'get ahead' by formally teaching reception class children to read and write. Reacting to this, many early years settings championed the creative approaches of the Reggio Emilia nurseries. These are named after the Italian locality where they were developed as part of a grass-roots initiative for community development after the Second Word War. The visionary behind this approach, Loris Malaguzzi, believed that children possess a 'hundred languages' through which to express their views and that it is the educator's duty to nurture this creativity rather than to distill education into formal learning. In Reggio, children are encouraged to learn through 'long-term engrossing projects, which are carried out in a beautiful, healthy, love-filled setting' (Gardner, 1998: xvi).

Birth to Three Matters (DfES, 2002) introduced a curriculum for younger children, centred on four aspects: a strong child; a skilful communicator; a competent learner; a healthy child. Keen to create a seamless progression from birth to five, the government sanctioned the formation of the Early Years Foundation Stage in 2008, complete with a goals-based curriculum broken down into levels of progression that supposedly reflected the wide range of ages at which individual children would achieve different landmarks of development. This introduced four guiding themes: the unique child; positive relationships; enabling environments; learning and development. It is, and was, intended to reinstate the principles of a play-based curriculum with an early years workforce that, fearful of negative Ofsted outcomes, had become overly focused on paper-based planning and reporting.

Structurally there is evidence of several international influences within its design. On paper, the 2008 EYFS followed a set of principles, intended outcomes and learning goals equivalent to New Zealand's *Te Whariki* curriculum (New Zealand Ministry of Education, 1996). However the similarity is superficial. *Te Whariki* was 'developed in response to initiatives from the early childhood sector' and formed around a set of strongly held ethical and spiritual values, which represented the interlacing of two cultural traditions as equal and mutually dependent partners, embodied through the metaphor of a woven mat. In contrast, the EYFS was essentially goals-led, other attributes added later. In the emphasis on outdoor play, the 2008 EYFS was also influenced by good practice within the Scandinavian countries and in particular the *Forest School* philosophy developed in Denmark in the 1950s and brought into the UK after a visit by Bridgwater College in 1994 (Knight, 2009).

These active and flexible approaches to learning contradict the primary initiatives to achieve early literacy through formal phonics training so a further readjustment was inevitable and this, the responsibility of the Conservative-Liberal Democrat coalition, was introduced in September 2012. The EYFS now has seven areas of learning but three – communication and language; physical development; and personal, social and emotional development – are 'prime'. The additional four 'specific' areas are literacy, maths, understanding the world, and expressive arts and design. The document is more directive than the 2008 version and its overall tenor more formal. The literacy element promotes phonetic support for reading and writing, and clearly sets out the requirements for assessment and safeguarding

Post-compulsory education

Policy decisions affecting early years and compulsory schooling nest within more general educational discussions. The economic downturn made unemployment and vocational skills significant educational targets in the twentieth century, as now, and this was publically acknowledged in Callaghan's 1976 *Great Debate* speech. The Manpower Services Commission, established 1973, was already attempting to coordinate employment and training initiatives (Chitty, 2004), supporting the 1983 Technical and Vocational Education Initiative (TVEI) to bring vocational training into the compulsory sector from 14 onwards. 1986 saw the introduction of modern apprenticeships. Also the founding of the National Council for Vocational Qualifications tasked to establish a coherent framework of National Vocational Qualifications (NVQs) with five levels of difficulty based on competences agreed with relevant professional bodies (Trowler, 2003).

This opened up a system of workplace training for early years workers that later fed into sector-endorsed foundation degrees, enabling many experienced childcare staff to legitimise their experiential knowledge. Attempts to bring vocational training into the compulsory sector were more difficult to implement as schools lacked practical expertise and resources. The Dearing Review (Dearing, 1996) identified three separate pathways for post-16 education: the occupational path linked to NVQs; the vocational path linked to General National Vocational Qualifications (GNVQs) of September 1995; and the academic linked to A- and AS-levels (Chitty, 2004). For a short time, following the 14–19 Green Paper (DES, 2002) and the follow-up strategy document (DfES, 2003a), it looked as if the government might incorporate a matriculation diploma offering academic and vocational elements in a single framework, but successive governments were loath to risk undermining the status of the A-level. (Yet the independent sector employs the International Baccalaureate and Cambridge Pre-U Diploma to good effect.)

Rising expectations that all will gain higher levels of qualification led to expansion of the tertiary sector throughout the modern period. Exeter, Hull, Leicester and Southampton received university charters in the 1950s, followed by seven further universities in the early 1960s (East Anglia, Essex, Kent, Lancaster, Sussex, Warwick and York). The *Robbins Report* (Committee on Higher Education, 1963), anticipating a doubling of student numbers, launched a major expansion programme to include universities, colleges of advanced technology (CATs) and research institutes, but the Labour government curtailed this plan (apart from establishing The Open University in 1969). Instead, it introduced a binary system, an autonomous university sector and a 'public' sector that kept CATs and teacher training colleges under local authority control. It was only with the Conservative 1988 Education Reform Act that a Polytechnic and Colleges Funding Council was established. This removed 30 polytechnics and 50 colleges from local authority control, paving the way for the 1992 Further and Higher Education Act that abolished the Council for National Academic Awards and enabled conversion to 'university' status (Chitty, 2004).

This move was in keeping with Kenneth Baker's call for widening participation. Targets for 30 per cent attendance, set in 1989, increased to 50 per cent by 2010 when New Labour came to power in 1997. However, developments were to follow an economic model, students must support their own studies not the state. Thus the 1998 Teaching and Higher Education Act established arrangements for the introduction of student loans, introduction of tuition fees and the abolition of maintenance grants. The White Paper, *The Future of Higher Education* (DfES, 2003c) planned to raise tuition fees to £3,000 in 2006 with some financial support for lower-income families. It also included the two-year foundation degree in its targets for 50 per cent participation, encouraging support for the early years and childcare and education course (Chitty, 2004). The public outcry seemed risible when fees rose to £9,000 a year following the recommendation of the Browne Review of Education (BIS, 2010).

Summary

For students and staff working within education, the subject has significance at both a professional (those we teach) and personal (how we learn) levels. The changes from elementary to primary, secondary and nursery sectors were important for children's education; the expansion of the post-compulsory sector important in opening up opportunities to qualify for work.

From an early years perspective, the growing focus on vocational edu-cation, the growth of NVQs and the introduction of the foundation degree from 2003 onwards were highly significant. The move towards widening participation – and particularly the expansion of the university sector in 1992 – facilitated the growth of a range of new degrees focused on non-traditional subjects. The bid for quality in the early years focused on both children's education and the training of adults, and in 1992 a group of advisers and early years workers began to meet regularly at the National Children's Bureau to discuss the development of the sector. In 1993 the Early Childhood Education Forum (ECEF) was launched, some 40 national organisations coming together to discuss change (Abbott and Pugh, 1998). One of their priorities was to 'develop the climbing frame' for early years qualifications and this group played a significant role in championing the development of early childhood studies degrees, both BAs and Masters, and sector-specific initiatives like the early years professional status (EYPS), introduced in 2006 and replaced by early years teacher status (EYTS) in 2013, and early years initial teacher training (EYITT) in 2014.

Points for reflection

- Reflect on your own education. How will it have differed from that of your parents and grandparents?
- Consider why there are still so many different types of nursery school. Which aspects of provision do you think will most benefit children?
- In what ways can contemporary educational philosophies – High/Scope, Reggio Emilia, *Te Whariki*, Forest Schools – enhance provision within the English EYFS (or another national framework)?

Further reading

Abbott, I., Rathbone, M. Whitehead, P. (2012) *Education Policy.* London: Sage.
Up-to-date policy, education history in the making.

Aldrich, R. (2002) *A Century of Education.* London: RoutledgeFalmer.
Good thematic approach to twentieth century educational development but no early years chapter.

(Continued)

(Continued)

Bates, J., Lewis, S. and Pickard, A. (2011) *Education Policy, Practice and the Professional.* London: Continuum.
Provides a detailed overview that looks across the sectors.

Blundell, D. (2012) *Education and Constructions of Childhood.* London: Continuum.
Shows how education shapes childhood as a concept.

Nutbrown, C., Clough, P., and Selbie, P. (2014) *Early Childhood Education: History, Philosophy and Experience,* 2nd edn. London: Sage.
Focuses on the lives and philosophies of the main early childhood pioneers.

Tomlinson, P. (2013) *Early Years Policy and Practice: A Critical Alliance.* Northwich: Critical Publishing.
Offers a critique of early years policy since 1900.

Websites

www.educationengland.org.uk
Details the history of English education.

http://teacher.scholastic.com/products/ect/roots.htm
Offers free resources.

www.communityplaythings.co.uk/learning-library
Information on pioneers under articles and philosophy.

www.tactyc.org.uk/reflections-papers.asp
Access to key papers by early years professionals.

http://ecrp.uiuc.edu/index.html
Access to early childhood journal and additional papers.

www.froebeltrust.org.uk
www.montessori.org.uk
www.steinerwaldorf.org
www.pre-school.org.uk
Provide current information about the nursery groups and some historical data.

To gain *free* access to selected SAGE journal articles related to key topics in this chapter, visit: www.sagepub.co.uk/hazelrwright.

CHAPTER 9

CONTEMPORARY PERSPECTIVES

Overview

This chapter focuses on current concerns about children in Western society.

- The *neurological child* looks at genetic mapping and imprinting, and contemporary knowledge of the child's developing brain capacity.
- The *institutionalised child* examines how real and exaggerated fears encourage parents to overprotect their children, and how society constructs the child as 'at risk'.
- The *pampered child* discusses how affluence leads to health issues and separation from the natural environment.
- The *precocious child* considers the impact of technology, the media and marketing.
- The *included child* reviews the changing perception of children with different capabilities.

In national terms, policy development was continuous from 1997 to 2010 under the regime of New Labour although the Every Child Matters framework set out in 2003–4 announced concerted plans for change. In global terms, however, the new millennium signalled new beginnings and this was reflected in a revived interest in children's development. A consortium of government departments and the Economic and Social Research Council agreed to fund the Millennium Cohort Study managed from the Institute of Education (IoE) (IoE, 2014). This is to track 19,000 children born in the UK between September 2000 and January 2002 at regular intervals. It is a significant study, with a carefully constructed sample to enable generalisation to the wider population, and built-in oversampling of significant sub-groups to enable extrapolation of sector-specific findings. Despite a change of government, its work continues to be funded.

On a smaller scale, the BBC and The Open University collaboration *Child of Our Time* follows a group of 25 children born in 2000 through the first 25 years of their lives (BBC1, 2014). This project creates a visual record with analytical commentary for the children, their homes, families and varied lifestyles. Together the programmes offer a multicultural view of contemporary childhoods, individually they offer vignettes of individual lives.

Over time these holistic studies will record real lives unfolding but observers can already identify patterns that set contemporary childhoods apart from those of earlier generations. Childhood is shaped and constrained by the same processes that mould our broader society, the scientific and technological developments that alter all our lives. Thus, we focus again on the role of nature in development as we learn more about the functioning of brain and body (the neurological child), and witness childhood transformed by social processes (the institutionalised and included child) consequent upon affluence and innovation (the pampered and precious child).

The neurological child

Chapter 5 outlined the structure of the human brain and the basic physiological processes whereby characteristics are transmitted from one generation to the next. Recent advances in medical, and particularly neurological science, have enabled a better understanding of both children's physiological inheritance and the interplay of physical and non-physical attributes in their overall development. New techniques reveal the activity occurring within the body or brain and the micro-level triggers that cause the child's body to change and adapt in certain ways.

Genetic mapping permits scientists to identify the tasks of specific genes, and, sometimes, to ascertain the sites that predict abnormality. This suggests the potential to prevent or cure conditions in the future, building on research that is already underway. Autosomal disorders are normally present from birth and in the UK all newborn babies are routinely screened for phenylketonuria (PKU), a rare genetic disorder that leads to brain damage if untreated. Many conditions – Tay-Sachs, Huntington's, sickle-cell disease – are race specific. Some disorders – colour blindness, haemophilia and fragile-X syndrome – are sex linked. There are also more than 50 identified chromosomal anomalies. Most result in miscarriage but some children survive with reduced mental capacity. This is the case with Down's syndrome children (who carry an additional copy of chromosome 21) and with sex-chromosome anomalies like Klinefelter's (boys with XXY), and Turner (girls with XXX) syndromes. Research into developmental disorders increases knowledge of genetic inheritance. For instance, the gene FOXP2 is known to link to severe language problems and a number of neural markers have been identified, for example N600 for processing meaning, P600 for processing language structures (Goswami, 2004). However, abnormality also arises from drugs, toxins, diseases and dietary deficiencies that affect the mother at periods of embryonic vulnerability (Bee and Boyd, 2012).

Genetic (or genomic) imprinting is another important discovery. This is a process whereby some genes are biochemically marked when the ova and sperm develop in the parents. Imprinting can 'turn off' the normal development process, 'turn on' atypical ones, and cause certain condition to pass only through the male or female line. This process is significant in the development of late-onset conditions like cancer, heart disease and Type 2 diabetes, the pre-disposition for which are now known to be traceable from birth (Jirtle and Weidman, 2007). We know that children can also inherit genes from mitochondria, structures found in the fluid that surrounds the nucleus of the ovum. Thus, a mother can pass on problems that do not directly affect her (Bee and Boyd, 2012).

Psychiatrist, Bruce Perry (2002: 82) reminds us that both social and physical environment are important for, 'in a few short years, one single cell – the fertilized egg – becomes a walking, talking, learning, loving, and thinking being'. He stresses the strong interplay between physical and non-physical causes and effects. Paediatricians have long recognised the condition 'failure to thrive', whereby a child's development is globally delayed (delay evident over a range of characteristics, physical and intellectual). This may result from an underlying medical condition but when none is present can be indicative of neglect (Corby, 2006). Recent research verifies and explains this association. Perry (ibid: 92–94) publishes scans that reveal how the brains of neglected children are smaller, less dense and slower to grow. These show how understimulation causes atrophy (shrinking). As he observes 'experience literally provides the organizing framework for an infant and child' (ibid: 88). Multi-sensory deprivation, abuse, and even the more invidious neglect that arises from people living busy lives, affect the growth of children's brains. This gives a biological underpinning to Bowlby's and Rutter's studies of deprivation, explaining the origins of the developmental problems that such children encounter.

Thus, genetic mapping and brain scanning together create the potential to develop targeted teaching programmes that might modify brain activity to compensate for other problems (Goswami, 2004). However, Goswami (2006: 2) also talks of the 'current gulf between neuroscience and education' and the 'pervasive "neuromyths" that have taken root in education', suggesting we should be wary of the numerous commercial packages that claim to be based on brain science. Neuroscience reveals the parts of the brain involved in specific activities and this enables us to understand that learning is complex and so is the potential for problems. To date, our knowledge is limited and derived from comparisons between distinctive groups of people. It seems that children learning a language early use a different part of the brain than adults coming late to a language and this possibly explains how children learn new languages so rapidly. Comparison between literate and non-literate women shows that learning to read and write in childhood changes the functional organisation of the brain. Studies of dyslexic children reveal that they have an immature rather than a deviant phonological system. Taken together, these findings create a case for early remedial intervention.

Studies of numeracy demonstrate that this, too, develops in several different regions of the brain. Verbalisation and rote learning of numbers resides in areas linked to language. Number comparison and quantification develop in a separate region and this supports our observations that children can learn to count without understanding number. Complex calculation involves visuo-spatial regions of the brain: a distinctive parietal-premotor area becomes active when people finger count and when they calculate, leading to a suggestion that counting on the fingers may encourage computational skills in children. Goswami (ibid) describes, too, how fear and stress disrupt learning. The emotional system in the brain lies within the limbic system (the amygdala and hippocampus) whereas reasoning and problem solving take place in the front cortex. Learning is optimal when the two systems work together. Stress triggers the amygdala to focus on 'survival', disrupting the connection with the frontal cortex.

In her article, Goswami (ibid) refers to a seven-year OECD study that published a full report in 2007, as *Understanding the Brain: The Birth of a Learning Science*. This refutes popular neuromyths: humans do not have a predominately left or right, a male or female brain. Most but not all activities require the two hemispheres to work cooperatively. Other myths remind us to be wary of overly directing children's activity. Young children have periods when they embrace certain ideas more easily but these are sensitive rather than critical. Learning is not lost forever if opportunities are missed. Children have the capacity to learn more than one language simultaneously and bilingualism is beneficial: it does not inhibit development. We should be aware, too, that minor memory loss is normal: people, children and adults, need to forget in order to remember new things. Learning and memorising are active processes not capacities acquired during sleep. Sleep is a time when, in periods of rapid-eye movement (REM), the brain sorts and consolidates new knowledge and bodies heal, not a time for subliminally absorbing extraneous material. In their book, *The Learning Brain,* Sarah-Jayne Blakemore and Uta Frith (2005) offer an accessible discussion of many of the ideas introduced in this section.

The institutionalised child

Sociologist Frank Furedi believes that childhood has become a site for 'competitive scaremongering' creating a culture that 'denigrates parental competence' (Furedi, 2008: 16), in a society that generates fear and anxiety rather than trust. In raising issues of trust he is echoing concerns expressed elsewhere. In a statement that can be equally applied to Britain and Europe, Putnam (2000: 21), studying social capital in America, explains how a society where people support each other functions more efficiently than a distrustful one for 'trustworthiness lubricates social life'. Without it, the social fabric of society is impaired.

It is 'normal' for parents to worry about their children. However, in *Paranoid Parenting*, Furedi (2008) claims that anxiety is disproportionate to the risks. In the past, problems were contained within the family, now parents feel out of control and fear the public safety of their child. Small-scale anxieties – that a child might choke on a plastic toy in a cereal packet or topple downstairs in a baby walker – have given rise to a 'hyper-alarmist orientation towards the well-being of children' (ibid: 4). Fears are floating, 'triggered by the idea that something might happen and not by specific evidence that anything has happened' (ibid: 20). Children's freedom is eroded, few play outside alone, as parents are paranoid about 'stranger danger' (ibid: 23). Yet the new technologies raise fears about safety in the family home, too; as 'virtual reality' offers unlimited scope for anxiety (ibid: 20).

Furedi believes that parents fear legal retribution. Society views parental supervision as a virtue and there is an 'implicit threat of sanction' to those who deviate and an expectation that children younger than 13 will be regularly supervised even though there is no statutory age to mark the division between competence and immaturity (ibid: 25). Equally important is what Furedi terms the 'erosion of adult solidarity', the public responsibility for the welfare of children within local communities so that, in the absence of a parent, another responsible adult will step in to curb a child's excessive behaviour. This confidence that people you know will help you may be misplaced. Nowadays, even teachers, who stand in *loco parentis*, fear touching or comforting a child lest this is seen as abusive. Yet fieldwork suggests that children themselves still see their local communities as safe places, their familiarity making them qualitatively different from the public sphere (Harden, 2000). Parents distrust the family too as it is now construed as a site for abuse and domestic violence when once it was 'idealized as a haven from a heartless world' (Furedi, 2008: 33). There is a tendency to blame the media for the problem but Furedi believes that its role is secondary for it shapes and disseminates society's concerns rather than causing them.

As early as 1984, Finkelhor (Colton et al., 2001: 139) hypothesised a four-stage process through which abusers must pass to commit abuse:

s/he must be motivated to abuse a child; must overcome internal inhibitions; external impediments; and the child's resistance. Reciprocally, this
model suggests four ways that the incidence of abuse might be reduced.
Preventative policies can seek to alter the motivation of the potential abuser,
strengthen his/her internal inhibitions, create external impediments to abuse
and strengthen the child's resistance. Recent government initiatives have targeted external impediments and children's resilience rather than the potential abuser. Campaigns like the NSPCC, 'Pants', aim to teach children to keep
themselves safe. Suitability checks, restrictions on sole working practices
and regular training, target childcare staff. Mass publicity campaigns aim
to raise public consciousness of the possibility of abuse, but in so doing,
have created a fear culture that severely curbs children's autonomy and prevents many individuals from volunteering to work with children. The adult–
child interaction in local community groups 'has in effect been stigmatized'
(Furedi, 2008: 34).

Fears of abuse and abduction heighten existing concerns about road safety
and the perils inherent in the natural environment. In many families, parents
ferry children door-to-door to care provision that allows them to work without
worry: breakfast and afterschool clubs, organised classes and activities as well
as school itself. In 1990, Hillman and colleagues carried out a comparative
study of independent mobility in Germany and England, collecting data from
children (in England) in schools whose pupils had been asked similar questions in 1971. They found that in the English sample, only 35 per cent of parents
said that their children were allowed to travel home alone in 1990 compared
to 86 per cent in 1971. Figures for 7- and 8-year-old children dropped radically
over the period (Hillman et al., 1990). A much wider follow-up study sampling
similar geographical locations (PSI, n.d.) found that by 2010 only 25 per cent
of children travelled home alone and that even at weekends 62 per cent of
journeys were accompanied compared to 41 per cent in 1971. This is broadly
in line with an Office for National Statistics (ONS) report of 2003, which found
that 89 per cent of children were transported to places by car at weekends
and in the evening, and that only 33 per cent went to local shops and parks
on their own (Farmer, 2005). Such practices constrain children's independence
and reduce levels of physical activity.

Hillman et al. (ibid) believed fear of traffic to be a major reason why
parents transported their children everywhere and this finding still holds
true (Shaw et al., 2013), but the ONS study found that only 23 per cent of
children feared traffic accidents while 59 per cent feared abduction by strangers. These figures far exceed the statistical likelihood of such incidences
occurring and neither risk factor is increasing over time. In the period 1994
to 2002, the number of children killed in road traffic accidents fell by 79 per
cent (DT, 2010). The statistics for missing and abducted children are astound-
ingly tentative but abduction, at least, appears to be on the decrease since
2004–5 and the rate for children under 16 running away remained static over

the past six years (CEOP, 2011). Bad things do happen but not very often, and not often enough to justify a risk-averse culture.

The ONS study found that even when children met with friends, parents were in attendance: 21 per cent of children never went anywhere unaccompanied; a further 52 per cent were chaperoned some of the time. For many children, independent activity is further inhibited by regular attendance at an out-of-school facility. As part of the National Childcare Strategy, such care clubs increased from 350 at the beginning of the 1990s to around 5,000 in 2002, for example, and plans are afoot to expand provision, effectively institutionalising children's free time. The coalition government, under the Education Minister Liz Truss, sought to extend school hours, perhaps through parents running low-cost after-school clubs – an initiative likely to further reduce children's autonomous activity in their local communities (Peacock, 2013). In February 2014, Truss informed local authorities that the law was being changed to authorise school nurseries to take two-year-olds without separate registration, effectively lowering the age that children can be in school.

Thus, society is physically containing the next generation of children. This has a psychological element too as, increasingly, trained professionals intervene to change the way we think and act. Furedi (2004: 7) was a key player in developing this critique, writing about the therapy culture that objectifies the 'uncertainties of life' and recasts them in 'the amplified form of risk', to create a profound sense of vulnerability. Emotional responses to routine situations are pathologised, and this 'unwittingly' causes people to feel out of control. Society then provides support – through counselling or expert advice and people are schooled to subscribe to the expert view. Thus, society creates uniformity of thinking and dependence on authority among its people.

Katherine Ecclestone and Dennis Hayes (2009) applied Furedi's ideas to education. They trace the invidious nature of intervention throughout all stages from infant to life-long learning. They argue that therapeutic education encourages dependence on 'ritualised forms of emotional support' (ibid: xiii). It strips the knowledge element out of education and leaves behind spaces in which to intervene and modify children's beliefs and achievements, spaces where screening, profiling, improving practice and monitoring progress can take place. Schools no longer assess children just in terms of their mathematical and literacy skills and curriculum knowledge but in terms of their social competence too, allowing experts unwarranted control over their development.

> ... therapeutic education immerses young people in an introspective, instrumental curriculum of the self, and turns schools into vehicles for the latest political and popular fad to engineer the right sort of citizen. (ibid: 64)

The pampered child

Control of children's lives strips away their independence and resilience. Children who experience freedom, manage their own lives, are out and about in their local environment, make and break friendships with other children and interact with people in the local community. Those that lack this freedom become home-based and bored, and this leads parents to spend money on activities and resources to keep them occupied. Children who are transported everywhere by parents miss opportunities for regular exercise. One clear consequence is weight gain.

Childhood obesity

Childhood obesity was recognised as a policy priority in 2004. The National institute for Health and Clinical Excellence (NICE) established guidelines for prevention, assessment and management in 2006, and in 2008 a Cross-Government Obesity Unit was set up (Aicken et al., 2008).

In a series of reports funded by the Department of Health between 2008 and 2011, the IoE's Evidence for Policy and Practice Information (EPPI) and Co-ordinating Centre sought the child's perspective, finding that children focused on the social aspects of obesity, voicing concerns about bullying and social isolation rather than direct health effects. They found no direct link between educational achievement and weight, rather socio-economic status played a mediatory role. Literature reviews established a lack of studies focused on primary age children or community and family-based intervention. Yet it could be argued that this is where the problems begin (Rees et al., 2011). UK public health guidelines for physical activity have not previously included children under five, yet chief medical officers in the UK feel confident to recommend that they need three hours of physical activity per day (HMSO, 2011).

Recognising the serious nature of child obesity, the government took action. In 2006 it established a National Child Measurement Programme that records the height and weight of children in reception and year 6 each year to establish the Body Mass Index (BMI). A six-year analysis of this data identifies a gendered distinction to trends. Levels of male obesity are beginning to stabilise at year 6 even though the BMI is still increasing, and male BMI is decreasing slightly in reception. The average weight of girls, however, is still rising from year to year, and at year 6 the increase is statistically significant. There is also a tentative claim that obesity in both genders is more marked among the more deprived sectors of the community (NOO, 2013).

A 2013 statistical report (HSCIC, 2013) looks in more detail at the period 2010–11. It identified that in 2011, as in 2010, about 30 per cent of children aged 2 to 15 were classed as either overweight or obese. For reception class children the proportion stood at ten per cent, reaching 20 per cent by year six, showing that overeating and inactivity is endemic from early childhood and increasing steadily as children progress through school. These figures exist despite a 77 per cent involvement in competitive sport in school. We saw a fractional reduction in obesity at the younger end of the scale in 2012 (HSCIC, 2014); political intervention and greater public awareness may be starting to have an effect.

Obesity is a result of imbalance between calories consumed and calories used so lack of exercise and poor dietary habits are key. Poor diet stems from the types of food that children consume, foods that exceed targets for saturated fat, processed sugars and salt. Many such food products are designed to be especially attractive to children, something that is possible as there is a 'near absence' of ethical and legal guidelines governing commercial food production (Food Ethics Council, n.d.). The common public response is to blame the media for unhealthy consumption, but research shows that the influence of advertising is minimal compared to food cost, availability and the time allocated for shopping and cooking (Buckingham, 2005). Ofcom (2014: 11) found food advertising to be only one of many factors affecting consumer choice. Their qualitative research established that many mothers believed a healthy diet to be 'austere' and 'consequently perceived as unattainable'. Attempts to change the situation are hampered by children themselves. Buckingham (2005: 8) explains that by the age of eight children portray themselves as media-savvy so researchers find themselves in a 'slightly uncomfortable alliance' with the media industry in voicing a common belief that there is no need to regulate advertising aimed at children. This is not a universal message. The independent Good Childhood Inquiry (Rees et al., 2012) recommended a ban on all advertising aimed at British children under 12.

Material consumption

Media advertising is not only directed to children's foods. An industrialised society that sets childhood apart from adulthood, establishes an additional market for the mass production of goods specifically for children. In an affluent society, children not only command their own clothes, books and toys – they demand branded goods surplus to their actual need – just like adults. Children become consumers and this makes them both powerful and exploitable.

Martens et al. (2004) scrutinise the literature on children's consumption but express surprise at 'how little empirical research has been conducted with children' (ibid: 158). Data is often generated from pictorial and documentary evidence or from analysis of toys. Children are treated as a 'homogenous' group that is both 'impressionable' and 'pressurized', a treatment that belies differences in age, ability, agency and 'savvyness'. Analysis focuses on older children, ignoring the vast expenditure that parents and associates make on behalf of the unborn, babies, toddlers and younger children. There is also a misleading tendency to assume preferences from production trends, whereby what is made is assumed to reflect what is desired. As Best (1998: 208) says, researchers should be 'studying people – not objects', at the very least watching children at play. Martens and colleagues (2004: 162) point out that current treatments leave children 'largely invisible in theories of consumption'. In Bourdieusian terms it is assumed that children will adopt the family 'habitus' or value set, but this takes no account of peer pressure or children's resistance to parental views. Parents act as gatekeepers to what young children can obtain, and later set boundaries to their spending power when they determine gifts and pocket money. However, other children and other adults will play a role here and this may deviate from the parental norm considerably. Thus, the picture of children's role as consumers may not be fully researched but is undoubtedly significant.

Nature deficit disorder

Children's sedentary and protected lifestyles have another consequence, important for their personal well-being and for the future of the planet. They suffer from what Louv (2005) termed *nature deficit disorder*, missing out on 'the pure joy of connection with the natural world' (Moss, 2012: 2) becoming adults who do not understand how human society relies upon nature. National Trust researchers believe that technology and poverty encourage this situation. When asked why they do not explore the natural world, children offered computer games and television as reasons. The researchers also suggest that nature deprivation contributes considerably to the increasing incidence of mental health problems in the young and a decline in emotional resilience as children do not learn to take risks. Statistically, such problems are 'more pronounced' in poorer urban areas (ibid). This stratified claim is in line with the National Obesity Observatory findings discussed above (NOO, 2013). There is now global evidence that inequality within a society is detrimental to the well-being of all its members (Wilkinson and Picket, 2009), so these findings should concern us all.

The precocious child

This discourse of the precocious child also concerns the media and children's access to possessions. However, the focus moves from general ownership of goods to specific commodities that, possibly, enable children to transgress traditional child–adult boundaries. In particular, developments in technology and the media and the availability of designer clothing for children from birth.

Adults and parents control spending in early childhood so must take some responsibility if, in dressing their baby and toddler in designer gear, they establish trends that they cannot curb when children take charge of what they wear and do. Both technology and fashion are highly commercialised fields so family affluence influences children's spending power. However, inclination and know-how also play a part in spending decisions so the correlation between affluence and commodities is not a linear one. Some parents may choose to prioritise their children's requests, others may choose to regulate spending or allocate funds to other areas instead. Nevertheless, social classes that possess wealth are able to make choices that are not available to those without, so the concern that advancing technology and commodification strengthen the social divide has validity (Buckingham, 2009).

Technology

Attitudes to technology are contested: whether children are susceptible to media influences is a question that divides researchers 'quite profoundly'. Livingstone (2007: 5) expresses concern that there is not only 'little agreement' between cultural theorists and psychologists but 'worryingly, little discussion and debate'. In both childhood and media research the topic of children and the media continues to be marginalised. Uncertainty encourages people towards extreme views and whether or not new technologies like the laptop, the internet, and the mobile phone have positive or negative effects on children remains uncertain. However, fear of new inventions has been commonplace throughout history. Luddites damaged industrial machinery, ordinary citizens feared the railway, the motorcar and the aeroplane, and in more recent times, there were those who viewed the building of the Channel Tunnel with trepidation. With regard to the media, similar concerns followed the invention of the printing press, photography, the cinema, radio and television. Nevertheless, we should remember that it is not technology that brings about social change rather the human beings who invent, produce, market and regulate it, and those who buy and use it – and this includes parents (Buckingham, 2009).

Fears about new technology range from the medical (will this equipment cause physical or mental impairment?) to the social (will it encourage children to interact with other people or to isolate themselves?), from the educational (will it offer new opportunities for learning or encourage children to squander their time on meaningless activities?) to the intellectual (is multitasking a sign of enhanced skills or a failure to concentrate?). There are also fears about media violence, copycat behaviour, access to pornography, gender stereotyping, and loss of parental control and growing evidence that fears are founded. Browne and Hamilton-Giachritsis (2005: 702) claim 'there is consistent evidence that violent imagery in television, film and video, and computer games has substantial short-term effects on arousal, thoughts, and emotions increasing the likelihood of aggressive behaviour or fearful behaviour in younger children, especially in boys'; a view that supports Bandura et al's (1961) experiments with the Bobo doll. Findings with regard to older children and long-term change are less consistent.

Whether children encounter problems will depend on individual users and the choices they make as technological fixes and government regulation are proving difficult to put in place (Buckingham, 2009). Substantive research into outcomes needs a longitudinal design but the pace of change makes such designs redundant: by the time we understand the consequences of one form of technology, another will be paramount.

Media and marketing

Modern media is motivated by profitability and children's engagement with it draws them further in to the world of commerce. Children's interests are exploited as books, comics, films, CD-roms, toys, clothes and computer programmes in an extension of Disney style merchandising. In America commercialisation has taken a step further and children's television magazines are built around actors and artefacts to feed the demand for commercial spin-off products. Adults view many of these developments negatively but Buckingham (ibid: 132) warns against the 'puritanism' that desires children's pursuits be educational and improving. Media activities serve as a focus for discussion and debate among children and generate a sense of belonging.

New technologies are embedded in modern childhood and bring associated advantages. Their interactivity can be empowering. Children can access complex information instantly and can create and produce their own images, text and sounds, mixing original and existing material to create new entities. Storage problems are minimised as, increasingly, technologies are convergent (ibid) and a single item of hardware can perform multiple tasks. Mobile phones allow teenagers 'emancipation from their home', enabling interaction that is not mediated by parents. They enable activity outside the home as children can summon help quickly if needed. With them children learn to micro-coordinate their friendships (Ling, 2007) and this is socially cohesive, but implicitly carries the opportunity to bully and exclude some peers.

Research into the effects of television watching on young children suggests that this is dependent on what is watched. In a study of children birth to six, Vandewater and colleagues (2005) demonstrated that it is not viewing time that matters but the choice of programme. Children whose viewing was selected were found to imitate positive behaviours whereas those whose viewing was limited by time rules were found to imitate negative behaviours. A separate study found that programme choice was also important in terms of toddler language development. Where television characters speak directly to the viewer and there is a strong sense of narrative the programme appears to support vocabulary development and the use of expressive language, but programmes with a loose narrative structure or changing vignettes, like *Teletubbies*, fail to assist language acquisition (Linebarger and Walker, 2005). Young viewers copied the vocalisations in these programmes demonstrating, again, that children do imitate what they see on television.

Fashion and sexualisation

Society has long-feared precociousness in young children, what Buckingham (2011) terms 'age compression'. In the nineteenth century the major concern was juvenile prostitution; in the early-twentieth century, the focus was 'social hygiene'. The new, age-defined, categories of 'teenager' and 'subteen' associated with post-war expansion of the clothing market drew attention to those years when young people were neither truly children nor adult, and the regular raising of the school leaving age extended the period of quasi-immaturity. The teenage years represented a new market for consumer goods and producers use the media to exploit this new market as they would any other. Some fear that dressing youngsters in the latest fashion draws inappropriate attention to their sexuality. Fears around safeguarding and fashion become confused, the media is construed as a causal factor, and the emotive tone of the campaigners against these practices make it difficult to research the subject directly or to consider it rationally. It is another area where the children's voice is largely absent from the debate. However, an American observational study (Darien, 1998) found that purchasing decisions for children's clothes were largely collaborative with mothers and children finding garments they both liked. In a consumer society it is what sells that continues to be made in the longer term.

Gender and the media

Another challenging topic is the effect of consumerism and the media on gender equality. The 'polarised pink and blue market' (Buckingham, 2007: 20) is very evident in children's commodities. A study of British primary school children's interpretation of commercials reveals more subtle messages are being promoted. Lewin-Jones and Mitra (2009) set up a project in 2005–6 to see if advertising had lost its gendered overtones, commonplace 30 years earlier. They found that commercials for children are frequently gender-specific and that children are well aware of this. A content analysis revealed that adverts for boys are loud, active, use commanding language and talk directly to the viewer, often drawing him into an adventurous fantasy world.

For girls, the adverts are realistic, often in domestic settings, and show children playing cooperatively. The voiceover talks about the product in complete sentences or song. Background music is calm and tuneful and images dissolve and fade out rather than ending abruptly. Thus the girl is expected to be a passive observer.

Gender 'neutral' commercials usually adopt a modified version of the masculine model and have a male voiceover, and boys' commercials last longer. Thus, there are hidden messages about male dominance over and above the gender issues evident in the product choices. However, feminist standpoints may be bolstering girls against potential disempowerment. Russell and Tyler's (2002) study of the 'girlie' retail outlets 'Girl Heaven' found girls struggled to rationalise the fit between gender equality and feminine identity in the face of consumer culture but Duvall (2010) found girls more aware. Duvall explored attitudes to gender and feminism using 'girl power' cartoons with 6- to 12-year-old girls. She found them able to justify why certain cartoons were suitable for audiences of different genders and to explain clearly how violence in girls' cartoons was qualitatively different to that in boys. The girls formed supportive networks and saw themselves as equal but different to boys, thereby rising above any differences in the way that society treated them, leaving Duvall to wonder whether they might in later life engage with feminist politics or instead assume equality and act as if it exists.

The included child

The discourse of inclusion is threaded throughout this book as it underpins early years philosophies and policies. Here, a brief overview will bring these strands together, codifying national, European and international initiatives, adopted, implemented and enforced with varying degrees of commitment. Despite wavering and inconsistency, there has been a paradigm change. An acceptance that all have rights and all can contribute to and be part of our contemporary world has displaced the belief that the disadvantaged, children especially, are misfits who should be concealed from public view.

We have seen that Britain (and many other nations) took centuries to reach this point. From Elizabethan times the poor were incarcerated in the workhouse and this tradition continued well into Victorian times when philanthropic endeavours introduced the children's home, and with a strong sense of civic pride, the state built numerous hospitals, asylums and other institutions designed to protect (and conceal) the needy. British towns and cities house countless museums and heritage centres in these public buildings built to a scale and design similar to the Victorian prison. The British Empire disseminated the practice of 'institutionalisation' across the world alongside the discourses of racial and social inequality.

Within formal education, early practice *segregated* children who deviated from the 'norm'. Vlachou (1997: 12) claims that this 'masked other motives related to society's needs'. Under the medical model, disability was individualised and ordinary schooling exempted from dealing with non-standard situations. In the guise of protecting them from the harsh realities of school life, disabled children were allocated places in special schools where they could engage in humble but productive occupations, and their experience was generally one of 'exploitation, exclusion, dehumanisation and regulation' (Barton, 1986: 276).

Writing in 1972, prior to many significant changes in both equality and education in the UK, Gerheart offers a useful overview of the pre-Warnock era. The book is American but takes a broader view. Gerheart traces the legal use of descriptors to classify children, now considered to be derogatory, to Roman times. In the fifth century BC children were classified as 'fools' if ineducable. At a later date a division was made between 'idiots', children who were ineducable and unable to care for themselves, and 'lunatics' who were seen to be temporarily insane. By 1260 the statute *De praerogative regis* legalised this distinction, making idiots permanent wards of court, giving lunatics temporary protection.

In Britain, the Mental Deficiency Act of 1913 offered a four-part graduated categorisation into 'idiots' (incapable of maintaining their own safety); 'imbeciles' (incapable of managing their own affairs); 'feeble-minded' (needing care, control and supervision); and 'moral imbeciles' (retarded and potentially vicious or criminal).

These labels were used in the USA and elsewhere by the legal and medical professions. In education, Binet's IQ tests were used to divide children into slow learners, educable, trainable and totally dependent, expressed as degree of 'retardency'.

This is the world on which the Warnock report shed light in 1978. And this is why the idea that all children should be entitled to a mainstream education was so important, as children sent to special schools – whether due to physical, emotional or intellectual issues – were deprived of a full educational entitlement. Only after the imposition of a National Curriculum in 1988 were all schools supposed to provide teaching in all areas. The move towards inclusion was not perfect, many children remained segregated in special units alongside mainstream schools, in special classes or continually taken out of the classroom to be taught separately, but this was a move to recognise that all children can learn. Warnock's (2005) concerns expressed before her retirement from public life reflected on a system that was insufficiently funded, and failed to provide the specialist resources necessary for children with severe needs. Despite these shortcomings, society did become more aware and more accepting of the range of normality. We *did* adopt a social model of disability and in 2001 *did* extend the notion of inclusion to embrace all areas rather than restricting it to disability and special educational needs alone. We are moving to an affirmative model of disability, and despite the inequalities and injustices in contemporary society, there are serious attempts to change people's outlook. At times this 'political correctness' can seem excessive but radical change often needs external enforcement to bring into line those who naturally resist it. Contemporary discourse, underpinned in part by the UNCRC and the European Court of Human Rights, centres on recognising children's rights and giving children a voice in their own affairs, and this has to be an important sea change in the way society functions.

An overview of contemporary childhood

Public and political interest in childhood in the new millennium has at times been highly critical. Sue Palmer's (2006) book *Toxic Childhood* both captured and encouraged concerns that the media and popular culture was causing the loss of childhood, helped by a campaign in *The Telegraph* (Fenton, 2006). Similar concerns in 2005 prompted the Children's Society to establish their Good Childhood Inquiry; an 18-month independent inquiry that gathered evidence from more than 35,000 people through surveys, focus groups, 'my life' postcards, and the BBC *Newsround* television programme in 2007 and 2008. This proved timely as, in 2007, Britain was ranked last in an international study of children and their well-being commissioned by UNICEF. An examination of the world's 21 richest countries carried out by the Innocenti Research Centre found British childhood ill-served in a study that 'above all' sought 'to know whether children feel loved, cherished, special and supported, within the family and community, and whether the family and community are being supported in this task by public policy and resources' (UNICEF, 2007: 39).

The Children's Society published preliminary findings in 2009 (Layard and Dunn, 2009). In essence it was found that 'excessive individualism' within British society is problematic. British adults emphasise their own needs rather than foregrounding those of their children, communities and country. There is a culture of self-fulfilment rather than public service. The Children's Society concluded that children most need love and respect, and provides evidence for this claim. It also explains specifically what children want from parents, teachers, the government, the media and society at large using everyday terms that we can all understand. The messages are about cooperative interaction rather than complex strategies, incentives or deterrents. Children do not directly feel the benefits from being at the centre of major policy initiatives. What they need is to feel that they matter. Continuing concerns for children's well-being led to further research in association with the University of York (see *The Good Childhood Report*, Rees et al., 2012, in Chapter 10).

Summary

This chapter presented an overview of contemporary childhoods and looked specifically at new developments in neurological research, at fears about children's safety and developments in technology, and how these together translate into inactivity and obesity, while therapeutic interventions create dependency. It also looked at how the media and growing affluence affect children's choices. There is significant evidence that governments are concerned about children's well-being, but overall findings suggest that policy initiatives that target specific goals in isolation will not be enough to change society. Ultimately, it is human interaction that determines happiness and this depends on creating a more relaxed and caring society where inequalities are reduced and people have more time to 'be' and 'belong'.

Points for reflection

- Consider the reasons for and against giving young children access to computers. What do you conclude?
- For children, do *you* think the benefits of independence outweigh its risks? What can we do to make sure this is the case?
- 'Window shop' online for children's toys or clothes. Examine how the merchandise encourages age, class, race and gender distinctions. When is this beneficial, when is it not?

Further reading

Blakemore, S-J. and Frith, U. (2005) 'The learning brain: lessons for education: a précis, *Developmental Science*, 8(6): 459–65.
The authors summarise their book on the application of neuroscience to education.

Hofferth, S.L. and Sandberg, J.F. (2001) 'How American children spend their time', *Journal of Marriage and Family*, 63(2): 295–308.
An interesting analysis to set against own observations of children.

Zelizer, V. (2002) 'Kids and Commerce', *Childhood*, 9: 375–96.
A global consideration of children's role in production, distribution and consumption.

(Continued)

(Continued)

Bragg, S., Buckingham, D., Russell, R. and Willett, R. (2011) 'Too much, too soon? Children, "sexualisation" and consumer culture', *Sex Education*, 11(3): 279–92.
Links theory and research to show the complexity of the relationship between these issues.

Buckingham, D. (2011) *The Material Child: Growing Up in Consumer Culture*. Cambridge: Polity.
Demonstrates how the modern child is pressurised to act precociously.

Jones, P. (2009) *Rethinking Childhood*. London: Continuum.
Discusses childhood in light of contemporary concerns.

Palmer, S. (2007) *Toxic Childhood: How the Modern World Is Damaging Our Children and What We Can Do About It*. London: Orion.
Trawls contemporary research to explore how modern society and parental pressure to work combine to create a generation of out-of-control children.

Ekins, A. (2012) *The Changing Face of Special Educational Needs*. Abingdon: Routledge.
Examines and justifies the changing policy for children who need additional support.

Websites

www.thechildrensmediafoundation.org/wordpress
Not-for-profit organisation geared to ensuring children have the best possible media choices.

www.kidsmoney.org
Interactive resource to help children learn to manage money.

www.csie.org.uk
Centre for Studies on Inclusive Education website – provides authoritative information.

www.specialeducationalneeds.co.uk
Resources from Douglas Silas specialist SEN solicitors.

To gain *free* access to selected SAGE journal articles related to key topics in this chapter, visit: www.sagepub.co.uk/hazelrwright.

CHAPTER 10

FACTUAL AND FICTIONAL PERSPECTIVES

Overview

This chapter comprises two main sections.

It offers a *factual perspective* on childhood that summarises contemporary initiatives affecting children, their practitioners and the settings in which they are educated. This provides an at-a-glance overview of the key research studies and pedagogic interventions that relate to children, and is particularly helpful in attaching detail – aims, dates, personnel and findings – to projects often known only by their acronyms.

The *fictional perspective* explores childhoods over time using literary sources, as these offer easy access to a range of childhood narratives with a broad historical and geographical spread. As these are published materials, they are useful sources to share with others as part of a teaching or learning resource.

A brief historical overview sets children's fiction within a broader literary context. This covers:

- the oral history tradition
- the Romantic tradition
- Victorian times
- the end of the century
- the twentieth century and beyond.

Selective lists identify books that portray childhood to enable further reading. The lists include:

(Continued)

(Continued)

- books written for adults, sorted into autobiographical, imagined and short reads
- books written for children, sorted into classic, contemporary, short reads, picture books and stories of childhoods around the world.

In part, these books represent children's perspectives on childhood, albeit recalled through adult eyes.

Childhood: facts and fictions

By its very nature this chapter could only ever be an account of accounts. In listing factual and fictional sources it makes a fitting ending to the book for it provides a wealth of further materials to read. The factual studies provide up-to-date insights into children's lives and needs. The fictional narratives cover the entire range of childhood but focus on individualised stories, many of which are specific in time and place but universal in their messages about the nature of childhood. In the hands of skilled storytellers – artists, too, in the case of books for young children – fiction can capture the essence of childhood. Sometimes this is from an adult perspective. At others, from the perspective of the children they observe and imagine. Authors and artists do this very well, their credibility derived from the fact that all were children once.

The chapter forms a resource so the commentary is kept to a minimum. It cannot be comprehensive but does try to select wisely. Many of the projects in the factual section were funded under New Labour as part of the strategy to create an evidence base for the reform of the early childhood sector.

The lists of fiction are neither comprehensive nor fully representative. Some of the very best in children's fiction is deliberately absent from this selection as it forms a different genre. The *Chronicles of Narnia* by C.S. Lewis, *Harry Potter* series by J.K. Rowling, *Carbonel* series by Barbara Sleigh, and authors like Tolkien, Jarvis and Sendak, are omitted as they create a world of fantasy rather than supplementing our conceptualisation of childhood and what it is like to be child. Nor are the fairy tales presented here. This is not the place for the allegorical tales of Aesop or the enchanted accounts of the Brothers Grimm and Hans Christian Andersen. In passing, it is enough to recognise the value of archetypal messages of good overcoming evil and observe that tales of fairy godmothers, handsome princes and evil witches transcend time and place to create spaces in which children can explore both their vulnerability and their strengths. Missing too, are the classic but anthropomorphic stories – Beatrix Potter, *Little Grey Rabbit* by Alison Uttley and Margaret Tempest, *Frog and Toad* by Arnold Lobel – tales in which animal characters dress up as humans and do the things that humans do, but quaintly and timelessly, or in the case of *Watership Down* by Richard Adams, appear as animals but think and talk among themselves like human beings.

The book selection here is realist. It comprises biographical and narrative accounts that offer a sense of childhood as it was or is – a blend of real life histories, of fictionalised life histories, and of fictions that distil a sense of place and time and the human relationships and activities that typify childhood. Thus it brings the child's perspective of childhood into the book, capturing through narrative the diversity of children's lives. The lists cannot and should not be seen to be exhaustive, rather a starting point for making your own lists. A number of secondary reviews of literature are also listed as an additional and important resource for those who want to know more.

Between the factual and fictional accounts, there is reference to the Opie's extensive work (Opie Project, 2012). In their detailed recording and analysis of children's traditional tales, rhymes and playground games, Peter and Iona Opie uniquely captured material that lies within the oral tradition through which children's rhymes and tales were passed from generation to generation throughout history. Through such material, children made sense of events in their lives but, at times, adults appropriated the narratives and edited the rhymes and stories to better fit their views of what was appropriate for young children.

Factual research into childhood

This section briefly summaries a number of key early years research projects and interventions that directly, or indirectly, add to our understanding of contemporary childhood and the settings in which we educate our young children. The treatment is largely chronological, but at times, related studies are listed together if this makes better sense of the material. Names of key investigators help to make connections visible and distinctions clearer when acronyms include similar letter combinations.

Effective Early Learning Project (EELP) (1993-)

Christine Pascal and Tony Bertram

EELP set out to develop a cost-effective strategy to improve quality of early learning in partnership with practitioners and parents in over 200 settings, through a series of staged interventions, using the Child Involvement and Adult Engagement Scales. Fieldwork was carried out from 1993 to 1996, evaluation thereafter. Strategies were then implemented in collaboration with providers (Pascal and Bertram, 2000).

Further details at www.publications.parliament.uk/pa/cm199900/cmselect/cmeduemp/386/0061406.htm.

REAL project, Sheffield (1995 onwards)
Cathy Nutbrown and Peter Hannon

The 'Raising Early Achievement in Literacy' project was set up to promote family literacy work with parents of pre-school children.

Phase 1 (1995–96) developed the ORIM framework: *opportunities* to learn; *recognition* and valuing of their early efforts and achievements; *interaction* with adults to talk about what they do and how they feel; *modelling* by adults of behaviour, attitudes and activities.

Phase 2 developed (and tested) an 18-month long literacy programme using a random control trial design.

Effective Provision of Pre-school Education (EPPE) (1996-2003)
Kathy Sylva, Edward Melhuish, Pam Sammons, Iram Siraj and Brenda Taggart

The original European project (EPPE 3-7,1996-2003) studied the influence of pre-school education on the academic, social and behavioural development of 3,000 children in 141 settings, up to the end of KS 1. (Sylva et al., 2004).

It presented 12 case studies and found:

- visible consequences that pre-school experience benefited children;
- quality of the home learning environment was of paramount importance but did not necessarily align with visible differences in parental occupation, income or education;
- good quality provision existed in all setting types and the variation within similar types was greater than between types;
- nursery schools, and those that integrated care and education, served children best, as did settings with more highly qualified staff;
- an instructive learning environment, encouraging sustained shared thinking, played a significant role in children's achievement.

Extension projects, phased around key stage bands, monitored participants' continuing development.

EPPE 3-11 (2003-2008) studied KS 1 (see Sylva et al., 2008).
EPPSE 3-14 (2007-2011) studied KS 3 in the Secondary sector (see Sylva et al., 2012).
EPPSE 16+ (2008-2013) studies participants in year 11 and into post-compulsory education or work (see Siraj-Blatchford et al., 2011).
Further details at www.ioe.ac.uk/research/66733.html.

Researching Effective Pedagogy in the Early Years (REPEY) (2002)

Iram Siraj and Kathy Sylva

This study examined the pedagogical practices in a sample of 12 early years settings from EPPE, supplemented by an additional two reception classes to enable across-case comparisons (Siraj-Blatchford et al., 2002).

Together, EPPE and REPEY found that individual pre-schools varied in their 'effectiveness' in influencing a child's development, and that children made better all round progress in settings with:

- strong leadership and relatively little staff turnover
- warm interactive relationships between adults and children
- a complementary view of educational and social development
- sustained shared thinking encouraged through open-ended questioning
- a balance between adult-supported, freely chosen play and adult-led small group activities
- curriculum differentiation determined through individualised formative assessment
- encouragement to resolve their own conflicts by rationalising and talking through their problems assertively
- adults who have a good understanding of appropriate pedagogical content
- a trained teacher acting as manager and a good proportion of qualified staff (graduates or teachers).

Families, Children and Child Care (FCCC) Project (1998 onwards)

Penelope Leach, Alan Stein, Kathy Sylva, Jacqueline Barnes
Supported by Tedworth and Glass-House Trusts

A prospective longitudinal study of 1201 children from North London and Oxfordshire in the first five years of life. It set out to examine the effects of childcare on their development during this period. Data was collected at 3, 10, 18, 30, 36 and 51 months through visits to the children's homes. Subsequent publications are listed on the FCCC website (FCCCS, 2014).

Study of Pedagogical Effectiveness in Early Learning (SPEEL) (2002)

Janet Moyles, Siân Adams and Alison Musgrove

An ethnographic study, commissioned by the Department for Education and Employment (DfEE) in 2000, to identify the components of effective teaching within the Foundation Stage in order to create a framework of performance indicators for early years practitioners. It identified 139 key statements of competence, sorted into dimensions of practice, principles and professionalism.

As part of the Primary National Strategy, in 2005 these principles were turned into a framework to support implementation: KEEP, Key Elements of Effective Practice.

National Evaluation of Sure Start (NESS) Impact Study (2001–12)

A series of studies led by Edward Melhuish
Between 2001 and 2012 the team published 57 reports that assessed the impact of Sure Start local programmes (SSLP) on some 5,000 children surveyed at 9 months, and 3, 5, and 7 years of age, comparing their progress with others from the Millennium Cohort Study.

- The 2004 report found limited effects, mainly that mothers in SSLP areas treated their children in a warmer, more accepting manner.
- The 2005 cross-sectional study found limited evidence of better family functioning and less chaotic households but suggested it was too early to properly assess the results of intervention.
- The 2007 programme variability study found that Sure Start programmes with a holistic approach to planning and delivery better served their users.

Cambridgeshire Independent Learning in the Foundation Stage (CINDLE) (2002-2004)

Collaborative project funded by Cambridgeshire local education authority (LEA) to produce training materials for all their early years settings.
Further details at www.educ.cam.ac.uk/research/projects/cindle/news.html.

The Impact of Parental Involvement, Parental Support and Family Education on Pupil Achievement and Adjustment: A Literature Review (2003)

Charles Desforges with Alberto Abouchaar
A review commissioned by the DfES (2003) and published as RR433.

Birth to Three Matters: A Review of the Literature (2003) RR444

Tricia David, Kathy Goouch, Sacha Powell, Lesley Abbott
Available at http://webarchive.nationalarchives.gov.uk/20130401151715/
www.education.gov.uk/publications/eOrderingDownload/RR444.pdf.

National Quality Improvement Network (NQIN) (2005 onwards)

A specialist body within the National Children's Bureau

Supports quality improvement managers and policy makers who work in the early years, play and extended services to improve outcomes for children and families. Surveys the workforce to identify quality issues. Provides a holistic framework for peer support, practice development, leadership and guidance.

Effective Leadership in the Early Years Sector (ELEYS) Study (2006)

Iram Siraj and Laura Manni

A qualitative study (Siraj-Blatchford and Manni, 2007), supported by the General Teaching Council (GTC), which explored how leadership can encourage improvements in learning and achievement for children. It drew upon a sample of settings identified as 'effective' by EPPE.

The study found that contextual understanding, collaboration and commitment to children's learning were vital and suggested eight foci for training: identifying and articulating a collective vision; ensuring shared understandings, meanings and goals; effective communication; encouraging reflection; commitment to ongoing, professional development; monitoring and assessing practice; building a learning community and team culture; encouraging and facilitating parent and community partnerships.

Early Learning Partnership Project (ELPP) (2006–08)

A DCSF project headed by Maria Evangelou, Kathy Sylva, Anne Edwards, and Teresa Smith running in parallel to the statutory sector's Parents as Partners in Early Learning (PPEL) initiative

Orchestrated by the Family and Parenting Institute (FPI) and working through voluntary sector agencies, its aim was to educate parents with children at risk of learning delay to better support their young children (birth to three). The study comprised 20 longitudinal case studies and programmes included:

- Parents as First Teachers (PAFT), a six-visit home-visiting service, which derived from an American initiative.
- Parents and Early Learning (PEAL) project, a two-day training, modelling partnership in disadvantaged areas funded by DfES in 2005.
- Peers Early Education Partnership (PEEP), a two-day course, with supporting handbook, structured around the ORIM framework devised by REAL, to help parents in disadvantaged areas support their children's literacy.
- Parents' Involvement in their Children's Learning (PICL), Pen Green's framework for engaging parents through knowledge sharing.

- ICAN, an early talk programme to help staff support children with communication problems.
- Home Start used Brief Encounters (an intervention module devised by One Plus One to support health professionals and workers).
- A Bookstart initiative, Let's Find Out, used books to support learning.
- Coram provided an intervention strategy, Listening and Learning with Young Children.

The study also evaluated applications of:

- Newpin, a family play programme supporting mothers with long-term mental health problems.
- SHARE, a strategy using ContinYou's community development approaches to enhance parental support for their children's learning.
- NCH's work to develop materials to use with fathers through the Campaign for Learning.
- Thurrock Community Mothers' activities.

The University of Oxford evaluation (Evangelou et al., 2008) found that ELPP promoted significant benefits, not least the repositioning of parents as partners rather than clients. However, it expressed concerns about sustainability as such targeted work is very labour intensive.

Parents as Partners in Early Learning (PPEL) Project (2006-2008)

This was a DSCF initiative to encourage local authorities to adopt practices that encourage parental involvement in their children's learning. Phase 1 comprised a baseline audit or practice across 150 authorities. Phase 2 (2007–2008), identified 42 authorities entitled to one-year funding, to address needs revealed through the audit.

Child Poverty in Perspective: An Overview of Child Well-being in Rich Countries (2007)

Innocenti Research Centre, Report Card 7, UNICEF

A 'comprehensive assessment of the lives and well-being of children and young people in 21 nations of the industrialized world'. It used 40 separate indicators to compare child well-being under six different dimensions: material well-being; health and safety; education; peer and family relationships; behaviours and risks; and young people's own subjective sense of well-being. Britain came last in the overall ranking and in three of the six categories, including the children's own sense of well-being, precipitating a public outcry and demonstrating variance between economic prosperity and well-being.

Understanding Quality and Success in Early Years Settings: Practitioners' Perspectives (2009)

Elise Alexander, supported by the ESRC
Published as RES-061-23-0012
A study of 18 early years settings that established that early years practitioners align quality with success, and that their views on good quality coincided with their observed practice. It found that relationships, networks and mentoring were fundamental to the sharing of good practice, and that status issues around graduate leadership were divisive.

The Cambridge Primary Review (CPR) (2009 onwards)

Robin Alexander, supported by the Esmée Fairbairn Foundation
An independent enquiry (2006–09) into the condition and future of primary education in England that published 31 interim reports and addressed ten key themes:

- purposes and values
- learning and teaching
- curriculum and assessment
- quality and standards
- diversity and inclusion
- settings and professionals
- parenting, caring and educating
- beyond the school
- structures and phases
- funding and governance.

Overall the report believed primary schools to be doing a good job but called for radical rethinking of purposes, standardisation, curriculum, assessment, staff training and deployment. It called for greater cohesion between stages and moves to narrow the achievement gap of children from different social strata. It also recommended that schooling start at six.

In October 2010 the Cambridge Primary Network was established under Alison Peacock to continue research and professional development in nine regional centres (on 12 university sites) in partnership with the Pearson Group.

Practitioner Use of Research Review (PURR) (2010)

Miranda Bell, Philippa Cordingley, C. Isham and R. Davis
Sponsored by CUREE, GTCE, LSIS and NTRP

A systematic review of how practitioners engage with research to inform and develop their practice. Carried out in Coventry and published by Curee (n.d.).

National Survey of Practitioners with Early Years' Professional Status (2010)

Mark Hadfield, Michael Jopling, Karl Royle and Tim Waller

A three-year longitudinal study commissioned by the Children's Workforce Development Council (CWDC) to identify the achievements and impact on settings of the first practitioners to gain EYPS (Hadfield et al. 2011, 2012).

Improving Quality in the Early Years (2011-2012)

Sandra Mathers and Arjette Karemaker

A 14-month study carried out by Sandra Mathers and Arjette Karemaker of the University of Oxford, with Daycare (now Family and Childcare) Trust and A+ Education Ltd, and funded by the Nuffield Foundation.

This compared the grades awarded by Ofsted for 1,000 nurseries assessed using the Environment Rating Scales (ECERS and ITERS) and focus groups with parents. It found that Ofsted does not necessarily capture all elements of quality and sometimes this inflates grades (Mathers et al., 2012).

The Good Childhood Report (2012)

Gwyther Rees, Haridhan Goswami, Larissa Pople of The Children's Society; Jonathan Bradshaw, Antonia Keung, Gill Main

A 2005 survey of more than 30,000 young people aged 8–15 that found that around nine per cent were unhappy with their lives. The inquiry found that good relationships, a positive self-image, a balanced use of time, a facilitative local environment, having possessions similar to those of their peers, and seeing opportunities for a viable future were vitally important to children's well-being (Rees et al. 2012; see also, Layard and Dunn, 2009). It inspired a Good Childhood Index with ten core indices: family; home; money and possessions; friendships; school; health; appearance; time use; choice and autonomy; the future.

Starting Well: Benchmarking Early Education Across the World (2012)

An Economic Intelligence Unit (EIU) report that ranked national educational provision for young children (across 45 countries) according to social context, availability, affordability and quality. It placed Scandinavia at the top of the Index with the UK in fourth position. Available at www. lienfoundation.org/pdf/publications/sw_report.pdf.

OECD Reports, *Starting Strong: Early Childhood Education and Care, I,II, III*

These reports published comparative policy information for over 20 countries for 1997-1998, 2004 and 2011. Summaries available at www.edac.eu/policies_desc.cfm?v_id=62.

National Foundation for Education research (NFER)

This organisation carries out high quality, independent research and evaluation in education.
Further details at www.nfer.ac.uk/.

Bernard Van Leer Foundation, OMEP, and UNICEF offer useful resources (see websites).

Fictional accounts of childhoods

An historical overview

In *Introducing Children's Literature* Deborah Thacker and Jean Webb (2002) set out to demonstrate the importance of children's fiction to mainstream literary analysis but in doing this they also demonstrate how children's literature reflects the cultural context in which it is written. Children's literature occupies a space that is place and time specific so it changes as culture changes. As Thacker claims in her Introduction to the book, it mirrors 'Western culture's changing definition of childhood and the world events which shape individual experience'.

The oral history tradition

By the eighteenth century the print culture was overlaying the oral tradition of verse, capturing on paper a wealth of traditional nursery rhymes and lullabies, nonsense and playground rhymes (Styles, 1998). Iona and Peter Opie (Opie Project, 2012), who made exhaustive collections of these rhymes using both printed and live sources, explain that rhymes were rarely written for children. Often they were corruptions of ballads, folk songs, plays, poems and sayings used in the local community. These were passed down from generation to generation, and spread spatially by troubadours and travellers passing from community to community. Some nursery rhymes can be attributed to specific authors, usually women. Styles (1998) credits *Old Mother Hubbard* to Sarah Martin (1805), *Twinkle, Twinkle Little Star* to Jane Taylor (1806), *The Spider and the Fly* to Mary Howitt (1834), and *Mary Had a Little Lamb* to Sarah Hale (c.1830).

As a couple, the Opies were passionate anthologists and folklorists. For over 40 years they carried out extensive research into children's culture and, from 1944 onwards, amassed a vast collection of artefacts. Most of their books and ephemeral publications are now housed in Oxford's Bodleian library but Iona Opie kept their extensive collection of toys and games (Opie Project, 2012).

The Opies, together and separately, wrote a significant number of books and articles. The most comprehensive overviews are presented in:

The Oxford Dictionary of Nursery Rhymes (1951)
The Lore and Language of Schoolchildren (1959)
Children's Games in Street and Playground (1969)
The Classic Fairy Tales (1974).

As the style of children's written literature reflects the changing cultural context it makes sense to discuss trends within a broadly historical framework as do key texts in this area (Thacker and Webb, 2002; Gavin, 2012).

The Romantic tradition

Early printed literature for children was highly didactic (Styles, 1998) tending to moralise and evangelise, reflecting the strictly religious ethos of Puritan society. By the eighteenth century, revolutionary uprisings were unsettling long-held traditions (Thacker and Webb, 2002). At a philosophical level, adults faced with political unrest and early industrialisation began to question the relationship between the individual and society, and the alignment of both with views of God. At a more pragmatic level, they queried the role of education in enabling a moral society. Children were seen to need nurturing rather than controlling, to need their imaginations inspired through fairy tale and fantasy rather than dulled by evangelising tales of morality and work. In the Romantic tradition, authors sought to capture the 'unsullied freshness of childhood' during a period of turmoil (ibid: 13).

In England, the poets Coleridge, Wordsworth and Blake created idealised visions of childhood innocence. Indeed, the fluidity of poetic verse can be seen to free childhood from the rule-based (masculine) system of language previously dominant (Kristeva, cited in Thacker and Webb, 2002). The relationship between childhood and culture is clearly visible in Blake's *Songs of Innocence* published in 1789 at the start of the French Revolution and his *Songs of Experience,* considerably more bitter in tone, engraved in 1794 during its aftermath (Willmott, 1990). The ironical contrast between paired poems suggests that Blake is aware of the fragility of both childhood innocence and political reform. The very titles convey this contrast: compare *Infant Joy* to *Infant Sorrow, The Schoolboy* to *The Little Vagabond, The Blossom* to *The Sick Rose.* The imagery and language underline it: contrast the 'clothing of delight' of the Lamb with the 'fearful symmetry' of the Tiger. The content and style reinforce the comparison. In *Songs of Innocence,* the poem *Holy Thursday* describes 'innocent faces clean'. In the poem of the same name in *Songs of Experience* we read of 'Babes reduced to misery, Fed with cold and usurous hand'. Wordsworth, too, was aware of the irony of linking childhood and nostalgia for a lost past and his ballad *The Idiot Boy* (1798) reveals the limitations of Romanticism (McGillis, 2012) while his *Ode: Intimations of Immortality* (1807) challenged the Enlightenment view of the child as an embryonic adult to be moulded rather than actively involved in creating his/her own life (Carpenter, 1985).

Blake's poems, and later Romantic poetry – that of Coleridge, Wordsworth, Clare, Byron, Shelley – is often considered appropriate for children because it tends to describe childhood and/or the natural world, or in the case of ballads like Coleridge's *The Rime of the Ancient Mariner* (1798), it has a strong narrative tone. However, it was not generally written for this audience. Keats, exceptionally, wrote some poems to entertain his younger sister Fanny, *Meg Merrilees,* for example (Styles, 1998).

In America, the 'new' nation aspired to new beginnings, challenging the limitations of the old world. In the early nineteenth century, transcendentalism became a powerful nonconformist philosophy, a movement associated with writers Ralph Waldo Emerson and Amos Alcott. Transcendentalists believed it important to strive for better things, and this sense of agency is noticeable in the work of many authors. It is exemplified in the stories of Alcott's daughter Louisa. Her *Little Women* (1868) are self-reliant and agentive characters.

Victorian times

Victoria's reign saw a return to piety and a proliferation of children's books in the second half of the nineteenth century heralded a 'Golden Age' in children's literature. Dickens' Little Nell (*The Old Curiosity Shop,* 1841) is typical of this genre. Nell's very innocence encourages her grandfather to change his ways, drawing attention to the 'redemptive qualities of the angelic infant' (Thacker and Webb, 2002: 41). Thus children's literature maintains its moral voice but as an undertone. Writers like Charles Kingsley and Lewis Carroll (*Alice's Adventures in Wonderland,* 1865; *Through the Looking Glass,* 1871) wrote fiction that focused on imagined rather than real childhoods, using a narrative voice that appeared to talk directly to children but also appealed to the adult reader seeking 'solace' in a return to childhood innocence. Kingsley's *The Water-Babies* (1863) contained elements of both the earlier moral tone and the fantastic as it shifted between Tom as chimney sweep and the cleansing, imaginary underwater world. This focus on innocence may reflect a concern to preserve the notion of childhood. The harsh realities of working-class childhood during the industrial revolution are well-documented by adult novelists of the period, such as Charlotte Bronte (*Jane Eyre*, 1847) and Dickens (*Oliver Twist*, 1838; *Nicholas Nickleby*, 1839; *David Copperfield*, 1850; *Hard Times*, 1854). As a child, Dickens had experienced extreme poverty, going to work in a shoe-blacking factory at 12 when his father was imprisoned for insolvency. His novels, in particular *Bleak House*, 1853, offer a wide-ranging commentary on the social ills pervading English society, recording how the legal, political and educational systems failed to protect children and adults (Diniejkow, 2012).

Adult literature was also directly influenced by the growing interest in science, evolution and child development. Several adult books start with descriptions of their characters' childhoods as a means of explaining the adults they became. In addition to *Jane Eyre* this occurs in Emily Bronte's *Wuthering Heights* (1847); George Eliot's *The Mill on the Floss* (1860); and Dickens' *Great Expectations* (1861) (Thacker and Webb, 2002: 51). In Mark Twain's work, such hints of realism extend to recognition that innocence is no match for prejudice. Through the actions of Tom Sawyer and Huckleberry Finn, Twain explores race and slavery in the American context. These books are early adventure stories for boys, a genre that became very popular in the late Victorian period. Compulsory schooling reinforced gendered and class divisions, relegating girls to a diet of domestic fiction. Schooling further segregated children from adults, causing children's literature to adopt styles that distinguished it from adult fiction.

The end of the century

In the transition to the 'modern' period, the turn of the century was a period of disruption and conflict between high and popular culture (Thacker and Webb, 2002). It was marked by an ambivalence towards childhood, a perception that was darker and more uncertain, perhaps more pessimistic. Many books reveal ambivalence towards adulthood. A.A. Milnes', Christopher Robin (the *Winnie-the-Pooh* tales) and J.M. Barrie's *Peter [Pan] and Wendy* (1911) opt out of adult society. Kenneth Grahame's Toad (*The Wind in the Willows*, 1908) is irresponsible and breaks the law. Oscar Wilde's *The Happy Prince* (1888) displays a decadent quality and the *Just So Stories* of Kipling invoke harsh lessons. Adult fiction embraced the supernatural: Bram Stoker's *Dracula* (1897); Stevenson's *Dr Jekyll and Mr Hyde* (1886), Wilde's *The Picture of Dorian Gray* (1890) and Wells' *The Time Machine* (1890).

This sense of instability and confusion was further captured in works by Frances Hodgson Burnett (*The Little Princess*, 1905; *The Secret Garden*, 1911), and in Baum's, *The Wonderful Wizard of Oz* (1900). However, Socialist, Edith Nesbitt (for example *The WouldbeGoods*, 1901) re-engaged with the realities of life in urban England, occasionally alleviated by magic carpets and amulets.

The twentieth century and beyond

Probably the most notable change in recent times is in the variety and affordability of books for children. At the start of the century, children mainly accessed books through libraries in schools and the local community but increasingly children could own their own collections. The advent of low-cost colour printing in the 1970s made picture books available to pre-school children. Cheaper production methods enabled greater diversity, both in the types of story published and a broadening of content. The genre expanded. School stories became popular in the 1920s (Richmal Crompton's *Just William* series, Elinor M. Brent-Dyer's *Chalet School* books). Independent children's worlds appeared in the 1930s (Arthur Ransome's *Swallows and Amazons*, Enid Blyton's, *Famous Five* and *Secret Seven*, Laura Ingalls Wilder's stories of the colonisation of the American Wild West). A wealth of imaginative fiction was published after the Second World War: C.S. Lewis's *The Lion, the Witch and the Wardrobe* (1950), Mary Norton's *The Borrowers* (1952); Lucy Boston's *The Children of Green Knowe* (1954). In the 1950s both E.B. White (*Charlotte's Web*, 1952) and Philippa Pearce (*Tom's Midnight Garden*, 1958) introduced the notion of death into children's literature (Thacker and Webb, 2002).

More recently, the advent of author/illustrators in children's books represent a postmodern break with dominant narratives, experimenting with form. John Burningham plays with narrative structure (*Grandpa*, 1984); Raymond Briggs challenges the boundaries between realism and fantasy (*The Snowman*, 1978); Jon Scieszka deconstructs a traditional tale (*The True Story of the Three Little Pigs*, 1989). Some contemporary fiction, J.K. Rowling's *Harry Potter* stories and Phillip Pullman's *Dark Materials* trilogy, blurs the distinction between children and adult fiction, demonstrating that good literature, imaginatively written, can still transcend traditional boundaries (Thacker and Webb, 2002).

Of necessity this overview mentions only a few key authors. However, there are many books that offer insights into the different manifestations of childhood and these are written for a wide range of audiences, from the very young through to adult. Reading stories is a 'fun' way to learn and a format that enables teacher and taught to share a common experience. With this in mind, I have compiled a more comprehensive listing of adults and children's books that depict realistic childhoods. These include both actual and fictionalised accounts and cater for different age groups. If you would like more active support for learning you may like to consult *Exploring Children's Literature* (Gamble and Yates, 2008). Here I simply offer titles that make interesting reading and reading interesting.

Books about childhood

Written for adults

Autobiographical

Foley, Winifred – *A Child of the Forest* (1974) now renamed *Full Hearts and Empty Bellies*; recalls growing up in the Forest of Dean, Gloucestershire in the 1920s.

Frank, Anne – *The Diary of a Young Girl* (1995, edited by Otto Frank and Mirjam Pressler); the real journal of a Jewish teenager living in hiding in Amsterdam during the Second World War.

Johnson, Alan – *This Boy* (2013); UK Home Secretary's account of growing up poor and parentless in post-war London.

Latham, Joyce – *Where I Belong* (1993); *Whistling In The Dark* (1994); growing up in the Forest of Dean, Gloucestershire in the 1930s and 1940s.

Lee, Laurie – *Cider with Rosie* (1959); childhood in a remote Cotswold village in the 1920s.

Marshall, Alan – *I Can Jump Puddles* (2004); 1900s childhood in Australian outback on crutches from six after contracting Polio.

Tan, Amy – *The Joy Luck Club* (1989); *The Kitchen God's Wife* (1991); *The Bonesetters Daughter* (2001); explores mother–daughter relationships and offers fascinating insights into Chinese beliefs and culture.

Thomas, Dylan – *Portrait of the Author as a Young Dog* (1940); short stories capturing the transition from childhood to youth.

Thompson, Flora – *Lark Rise to Candleford* (trilogy, 1939–43); based on author's life in an Oxfordshire hamlet, village and town in the 1880s.

Twain, Mark – *Tom Sawyer* (1876); story based on own childhood in Southern States. *Huckleberry Finn* (1885); uses story to explore effects of upbringing, morality, slavery and racism.

Yen Mah, Adeline – *Falling Leaves* (1997); life as an unwanted Chinese daughter.

Imagined

Dickens, Charles – *Oliver Twist* (1838); life as a London pickpocket. *Nicholas Nickleby* (1839); a child coping alone in a school setting. *David Copperfield* (1849); child as a factory worker. *Great Expectations (1861);* the orphan Pip befriended by Miss Havisham.

Doyle, Roddy – *Paddy Clarke Ha Ha Ha* (1993); boyhood in Ireland through the voice of a ten-year-old.

Eliot, George – *Mill on the Floss* (1860); two mill children growing up in Lincolnshire in the 1820s.

Hill, Susan – *I'm the King of the Castle* (1970); challenges the innocence of childhood as two boys thrown together by circumstances bully and fight each other without their parents noticing what is going on.

Ivey, Eowyn – *The Snow Child* (2012); balances realism and fantasy as it charts life in Alaska in the 1920s and the appearance of a strange child to a childless couple.

Jones, Lloyd – *Mister Pip* (2006); a post-colonial story of brutal war on a Pacific island focused on Matilda, a young teenager.

Lee, Harper – *To Kill a Mocking Bird* (1961); account of a black-on-white rape trial and racism in the American deep south in 1930s; told through the eyes of two children whose lawyer father is involved in the case.

Llewellyn, Richard – *How Green Was My Valley* (1939); childhood in the Welsh, Methodist, mining valleys of Pembrokeshire.

Roberts, Yvonne – *A History of Insects* (2001); a nine-year-old girl's life in colonial Pakistan in the 1950s.

Short reads

Cavendish, Lucy – *Jack and Jill* (2011); children are sent away to live with family to protect them from matters that they are too young to understand.

Thomas, Dylan – *A Child's Christmas in Wales* (1954/5); the poet's reminiscences on his own childhood.

Thomas Ellis, Alice – *A Welsh Childhood* (2000); growing up in mountainous North Wales.

White, Antonia – *Frost in May* (1933); life in a convent school told through a schoolchild's voice.

(Continued)

(Continued)

Written for children

Classic

Alcott, Louisa M. – *An Old Fashioned Girl* (1869); *Little Women* (1870); *Eight Cousins* (1875); family life in eastern America in the late nineteenth century. Morally correct but emancipatory in tone as Alcott's heroines manage their own lives.

Boston, Lucy M. – *The Children of Green Knowe* (1954); a story of childhood with earlier stories embedded.

Coolidge, Susan – *What Katie Did* (1872); childhood in a small American mid-Western town for a young tomboy who becomes an invalid.

Dodge, Mary Mapes – *Hans Brinker, or the Silver Skates* (1860); portrays Dutch life in the early nineteenth century.

Enright, Elizabeth – *The Melendy Quartet – The Saturdays* (1941); *The Four-Storey Mistake* (1942); *Then There Were Five* (1945); *Spiderweb for Two* (1951); four children find entertainment in 1940s rural New York and the city.

Garnett, Eve – *The Family from One End Street* (1937); about a large, happy, working-class family in Sussex in the early twentieth century.

Hodgson Burnett, Frances – *Little Lord Fauntleroy* (1886); Cedric moves from genteel poverty in America to aristocrat in England. *A Little Princess* (1905); a riches to rags to riches story centring on a London boarding school. *The Secret Garden* (1911); captures childhood in the English country house of the nineteenth century and the tendency to overprotect the invalid.

Ingalls Wilder, Laura – *Little House in the Big Woods* (1932); *Little House on the Prairie* (1935); rural life on a farm in Wisconsin and then in Indian territory on the Kansas prairie in the 1870s and 1880s. Crafted from Laura's memories (age five onwards).

Montgomery, L.M. – *Anne of Green Gables* (1908); childhood in a close-knit farming community in Nova Scotia, Canada.

Nesbitt, E.S. – *The Story of the Treasure Seekers* (1899); The *WouldbeGoods* (1901); *The Railway Children* (1906); stories of Victorian childhood, children from 'good' families who try to bolster the family fortunes in times of adversity.

Spyri, Johanna – *Heidi* (1880); the daily life of a young orphan girl, brought up in the Swiss mountains by an elderly grandfather.

Streatfield, Noel – *Ballet Shoes* (1936), *White Boots* (1951); and many others; children from genteel English families who pursue a talent.

Contemporary

Bawden, Nina – *Carrie's War* (1973); being evacuated in England in the Second World War.

Blackman, Malorie (ed.) – *Unheard Voices* (2007); anthology of poetry and texts commemorating the abolition of slavery.

Dahl, Roald – *Boy* (1984); vignettes from a childhood in Wales with parents of Norwegian descent.

Desai, Anita – *The Village by the Sea* (1982); children with adult responsibilities in rural India.

Doherty, Bernie – *Street Child* (2009); the story of Jim Jones, the orphan who inspired Barnardo to open children's homes.

Edwards, Dorothy – *My Naughty Little Sister* (1952) and associated titles.

Gavin, Jamila – *Coram Boy* (2004); the horror and hardships of life in the eighteenth century, when children survived to tell the tale.

Hendry, Frances Mary – *Chains* (2004); a girl pretends to be her brother and discovers that her father's business is slavery.

Holm, Anne – *I am David* (1963); a young boy escapes a concentration camp and travels to Denmark.

Kerr, Judith – *When Hitler Stole Pink Rabbit* (1971); semi-autobiographical account of a Jewish family escaping from Nazi Germany.

Magorian, Michelle – *Goodnight Mr Tom* (1981); an evacuee, abused in London, who is nurtured in his country billet.

Mason, Simon – *The Quigleys* (2003 onwards); humorous stories of a contemporary family.

Morpurgo, Michael – *Waiting for Anya* (1990); transportation of Jewish children in the Second World War. *Friend or Foe* (1977); Second World War relationships; and a range of titles with specific foci.

(Continued)

(Continued)

Naidoo, Beverley – *No Turning Back* (1998); 12-year-old Sipho survives on the streets of Johannesburg. *The Other Side of Truth* (2000); two children embroiled in political terrorism. *Burn My Heart* (2007); children caught up in apartheid in Kenya.

Serraillier, Ian – *The Silver* Sword (1956); four Jewish children escape from Warsaw.

Singer, Isaac Bashevis – *A Day of Pleasure* (1963); recollected stories of a boy growing up in Warsaw in the early twentieth century.

Syal, Meera – *Anita and Me* (1996); semi-autobiographical account of an Indian immigrant family in a Midlands coal mining town.

Taylor, Mildred D. – *Roll of Thunder, Hear My Cry* (1976); a black American family struggles to survive during the Great Depression of the 1930s.

Whelan, Gloria – *Angel on the Square* (2001); a privileged childhood in Tsarist Russia and during the revolution.

Wilson, Jaqueline – *The Diamond Girls; Double Act; The Lottie Project; The Bed and Breakfast Star; Secrets; Cookie; Candy Floss; Lizzie Zipmouth; The Mum-minder; The Story of Tracy Beaker;* and many more titles that deal with difficult childhoods in a humorous but realist fashion.

Yen Mah, Adeline – *Chinese Cinderella* (1999); autobiography; later books are fictionalised.

Zephaniah, Benjamin – *Refugee Boy* (2001); a 14-year-old Ethiopian boy is turned out by his father so that he can find a better life.

Short reads

Batterley, Gertrude – *My Life in a Cottage Home* (2012); memoirs of a child who, following father's eviction from a tied cottage, was sent to a workhouse in the 1920s; published posthumously by her family.

Benjamin, Floella – *Coming to England* (1995); from childhood in Trinidad to childhood in England.

Doherty, Berlie – *Abela* (2007); the story of African Abela and English Rosa and how they become adopted sisters.

Gavin, Jamila – *Out of India: An Anglo-Indian Childhood* (2002); describes childhood as India struggles for independence and Britain experiences the Blitz.

Market, Michelle and Sweet, Melissa – *Brave Girl: Clara and the Shirtwaist Makers' Strike of 1909* (2013); describes life as a child garment worker in New York and explains why they went on strike.

Marshall, James Vance – *Walkabout* (1959); two children survive an aircrash in the Australian desert and are befriended by an Aboriginal boy.

Naidoo, Beverley – *Journey to Jo'Burg* (1985); divided families in South Africa and how two children try to care for a sibling.

Perkins, Mitali – *Rickshaw Girl* (2008); life of a Bangladeshi schoolgirl.

Picture books

Altes, Marta – *I am an Artist*; a child explores different art experiences.

Anholt, Catherine and Laurence – *Harry's Home;* contrasts city life with a visit to the countryside. *Going to Nursery; Billy and the Big New School.*

Ashley, Bernard and Brazell, Derek – *Cleversticks;* a Chinese boy adjusts to pre-school in multicultural America.

Barber, Antonia and Bayley, Nicola – *The Mousehole Cat;* vividly portrays life in a Cornish village.

Bemelmans, Ludwig – *Madeline* stories, set in a French convent but covering many topics.

Butterworth, Nick – *My Mum is Fantastic; My Dad is Brilliant; My Grandma is Wonderful; My Grandpa is Amazing;* and with Inkpen, Mick – *The Sports Day; The School Trip;* stories with universal appeal.

Child, Lauren – *Charlie and Lola;* stories on many childhood topics.

Cooke, Trish and Oxenbury, Helen – *So Much; Full, Full, Full of Love;* portrayals of Afro-Caribbean home life.

Dickinson, Mary and Firmin, Charlotte – *Alex and the Baby; Alex's Bed; Alex's Outing;* single mum and son relationship.

Dupasquier, Philippe – *Dear Daddy; My Dad; A Sunday with Grandpa; I Can't Sleep; Our House on the Hill; No More Television* – family stories. *My Busy Day; Busy Places;* series that observe events in places where people come together.

Edwards, Becky and Flintoft, Anthony – *My First Day at Nursery School;* introduces a new experience.

(Continued)

(Continued)

Garland, Sarah – *Going to Playschool, Doing the Garden, Going Swimming, Coming to Tea, Doing the Shopping, Doing Christmas, Having a Picnic; Doing the Washing; Eddie's Garden; Eddie's Kitchen; Billy and Belle;* busy, noisy, friendly family life.

Gliori, Debi – *The Tobermory Cat;* evokes life on the island of Mull.

Gray, Nigel and Dupasquier, Philippe – *A Country Far Away;* compares children's activities in England and Africa.

Hedderwick, Mairie – *Katie Morag;* series of books set on the Isle of Struay, Scotland.

Heist, Amy – *Charley's First Night;* Henry introduces a small puppy to his home.

Hughes, Shirley – *Lucy and Tom* stories; *Alfie and Annie Rose* stories: *Tales of Trotter Street; Moving Molly; Dogger; The Trouble with Jack; Enchantment in the Garden; The Big Concrete Lorry;* illustrate and recall everyday life for children. *The Lion and the Unicorn* describes life as an evacuee. *A Brush with the Past;* pictures English life from 1900–50.

Hutchins, Pat – The *Titch* stories; *Don't Forget the Bacon; There's Only One of Me; Happy Birthday, Sam; The Doorbell Rang;* English childhood with humour.

Inkpen, Mick – *Baggy Brown and the Royal Baby; We are Wearing Out the Naughty Step; Jojo's Revenge;* from a child's perspective.

James, Simon – *Leon and Bob;* life in an English town with an imaginary friend.

Mayhew, James – *Katie in London; Katie in Scotland;* exploring the city with a fantasy animal as guide.

McClure, Gillian – *We're Going to Build a Dam;* playing on the beach.

Nichols, Grace and Taylor, Eleanor – *No Baby No;* baby explores his household.

Nicholson, Mike and Keay, Claire – *Thistle Street;* daily life and dialect in Scotland.

Ormerod, Jan – *Dad and Me; Messy Baby; Mum and Dad and Me; Sleeping Dad; Reading: Who's Who in Our Street;* for the very young.

Oxenbury, Helen – *The Dancing Class; Eating Out; The Birthday Party; One Day with Mum; Tom and Pippo;* and a range of board books.

Patterson, Rebecca – *My Big Shouting Day; My Busy Being Bella Day; Not on a School Day;* contemporary childhood.

Rubbino, Salvatore – *A Walk in London; A Walk in New York;* children explore the cities with a parent.

Smith, Lane – *Grandpa Green;* an autobiography told through topiary.

Sutcliffe, Mandy – *Belle and Boo, and the Birthday Surprise; Goodnight Kiss; Yummy Scrummy Day;* everyday life vividly portrayed.

Ungerer, Toni – *Fog Island;* captures traditional Irish childhood activities.

Childhoods around the world

Aardema, Verna and Vidal, Beatriz – *Bringing the Rain to Kapiti Plain* (Kenya).

Benjamin, Floella and Chamberlain, Margaret – *My Two Grannies* (compares Trinidad and Yorkshire).

Brown, Monica and Parra, John – *Waiting for the Biblioburro* (Colombia).

Browne, Eileen – *Handa's Surprise; Handa's Hen* (Kenya).

Chamberlain, Mary and Richard and Cairns, Julia – *Mama Panya's Pancakes: A Village Tale from Kenya* (Kenya).

Cunane, Kelly and Juan, Ana – *For You Are a Kenyan Child* (Kenya).

Gower, Catherine and Zhihong, He – *Long-Long's New Year* (China).

Griffiths, Neil and Collins, Peggy – *Fatou, Fetch the Water* (Nigeria).

Hoffman, Mary and Littlewood, Karin – *The Colour of Home* (Somalia).

Jahanforuz, Rita and Mintzi, Vali – *The Girl with a Brave Heart* (Tehran).

Javaherbin, Mina and Ford, A.G. – *Goal* (South Africa).

(Continued)

(Continued)

Krebs, Laurie and Cairns, Julia – *We All Went on Safari: A Counting Journey Through Tanzania* (Tanzania).

Kroll, Virginia and Carpenter, Nancy – *Masai and I* (East Africa).

Ormerod, Jan – *Lizzie Nonsense* (Australia last century).

Sylvere, Antoine – *Toinou: Le cri d'un enfant auvergnat, pays d'Ambert* (1980); a rural childhood in nineteenth century France (the Auvergne), not translated into English.

Summary

This chapter serves as a resource for further reading, both research-based and imaginary. The factual section identified key research projects that impinge on constructions of childhood through their investigation of practice and formulation of further expectations of settings. The fictional section offered a brief historical overview of the literature on childhood common to the English-speaking world, starting with a brief discussion of the oral tradition of rhymes and games documented, in particular, by Peter and Iona Opie. It then provided a bibliography of adult and children's fiction, ranging from full texts to picture books, that offers a realist description of childhood. This included both 'true' accounts and 'fabricated' ones, as sometimes the generalised narrative is a better representation of reality than the individualised account that is subject to personalised variation. Thus, rather than closing down the account of childhood, this final chapter opens up the story by drawing attention to the wealth of material still to be read if you want to know more about childhood. Happy reading!

Points for reflection

- Recall the books you read as a child. What kinds of childhood did they portray? Were they convincing?
- Download and read (at least part of) one of the research studies*. How does it support your understanding of children and their needs?
- What about *your* childhood? Was it easy/hard, happy/sad, fun/serious, sociable/lonely? To what extent was it typical for the time and place in which you grew up?

* Key research studies can be found at:

  SPEEL http://dera.ioe.ac.uk/4591/1/RR363.pdf
  EPPE http://eprints.ioe.ac.uk/5309/1/sylva2004EPPEfinal.pdf
  REPEY http://dera.ioe.ac.uk/4650/1/RR356.pdf
  EYPS www.gov.uk/government/uploads/system/uploads/attachment_
  data/file/183418/DfE-RR239c_report.pdf

Further reading

Factual

Boyden, J. and Boudillon, M. (2012) *Childhood Poverty: Multidisciplinary Approaches.* Basingstoke: Palgrave Macmillan.
Report from an Oxford-based, Young Lives project, that plans to follow two cohorts of children growing up in each of four countries – Ethiopia, India, Peru and Vietnam – in order to inform new policy development for well-being.

Power, A., Willmot, H. and Davidson, R. (2011) *Family and Futures: Childhood and Poverty in Urban Neighbourhoods.* Bristol: The Policy Press.
A ten-year study of urban deprivation in the north of England and London.

Fictional

Pompei (Sue Reid), *Mill Girl* (Sue Reid), *The Great Plague* (Pamela Oldfield), *To Kill a Queen* (Valerie Wilding), *Blitz* (Vince Cross), *The Hunger* (Carol Drinkwater), *Workhouse* (Pamela Oldfield), *Princess of Egypt* (Vince Cross), *Dodger* (Jim Eldridge), *The Sweeps Boy* (Jim Eldridge), *Desert Danger* (Jim Eldridge).
Some of the fictionalised historical accounts, written from a child's perspective, in the Scholastic 'My Story' series.

Bronte, C. – *Jane Eyre* (1847)
Blackmore, R.D. – *Lorna Doone* (1869)
Two good examples of adult classics that start with childhood accounts.

(Continued)

(Continued)

Moss, D. (2011) *Children and Social Change: Memories of Diverse Childhoods*. London: Bloomsbury Academic.
Presents a set of retrospective biographical accounts that provide insights into childhood in troubled contexts, illuminating areas normally difficult to explore.

Watson, V. (2001) *The Cambridge Guide to Children's Books in English*. Cambridge: Cambridge University Press.
Comprehensively lists children's books and writers.

Gamble and Yates (2008); Gavin (2012); Maybin and Watson (2009); Montgomery and Watson (2009); Thacker and Webb (2002).
Offer broad accounts of children's literature – see References for full details.

Websites

www.bernardvanleer.org
Bernard Van Leer Foundation publishes Early Childhood Matters, *twice-yearly.*

http://developingchild.harvard.edu
Centre on the Developing Child offers working papers and articles.

www.oecd-ilibrary.org
OECD offers research, policy and statistical overviews.

www.omepuk.org.uk
World Organisation for Early Childhood Education (OMEP) publishes regular research and policy papers.

www.unicef/org/sowc
UNICEF's annual themed survey, State of the World's Children.

www.childlitassn.org
Children's Literature Association provides information on journals and awards.

Many of the resources on these sites are available for free download.

To gain *free* access to selected SAGE journal articles related to key topics in this chapter, visit: www.sagepub.co.uk/hazelrwright.

REFERENCES

Abbott, L. and Pugh, G. (1998) *Training to Work in the Early Years*. Buckingham: Open University Press.

Action for Children (2011, 2012 and 2013) *The Red Book*. London: Action for Children.

Adams, R. (2013) '"Tough and rigorous" new national curriculum published', *The Guardian*, 8 July [online]. Available at http://www.theguardian.com/education/2013/jul/08/new-national-curriculum-published (accessed June 2014).

Agarwal, V. (2006) 'Awakening latent spirituality: nurturing children in the Hindu tradition', in K.M. Yust, A.N. Johnson, S.E. Sasso and E.C. Roehlkepartain (eds), *Nurturing Child and Adolescent Spirituality*. Lanham, MD: Rowman and Littlefield.

Agger, B. (1991) 'Critical theory, poststructuralism, postmodernism', *Annual Review of Sociology,* 17: 105–131.

Aicken, C., Arai, L. and Roberts, H. (2008) *Schemes to Promote Healthy Weight Among Obese and Overweight Children in England. Report*. London: I-Centre, SSRU, Institute of Education.

Aiginger, K. and Guger, A. (2005) 'The European social model', *Progressive Politics,* 4(3): 4–11.

Ainsworth, M.D.S. and Bell, S.M. (1970) 'Attachment, exploration, and separation', *Child Development,* 41: 49–67.

Al-Azhar University (2005) *Children in Islam*. Unicef. Available at http://www.unicef.org/egypt/Egy-homepage-Childreninislamengsum(1).pdf (accessed June 2014).

Aldrich, R. (1994) 'John Locke', *Prospects,* 24(1/2): 61–79.

Alexander, Elise (2009) *Understanding Quality and Success in Early Years Settings, Practitioners' Perspectives: Full Research Report*. RES-061–23–0012. Swindon: ESRC.

Alexander, R. (2009a) *Children, Their World, Their Education*. Abingdon: Routledge.

Alexander, R. (2009b) *Towards a New Primary Curriculum: A Report from the Cambridge Primary Review. Part 2: The Future*. Cambridge: University of Cambridge Faculty of Education.

Alexander, R. and Flutter, J. (2009) *Towards a New Primary Curriculum: A Report from the Cambridge Primary Review. Part 1: Past and Present*. Cambridge: University of Cambridge Faculty of Education.

Allen, G. (2011a) *Early Interventions: Smart Investment, Massive Savings* (July). London: Cabinet Office.

Allen, G. (2011b) *Early Interventions: The Next Steps* (January). London: Cabinet Office.

Anderson, B. (1991) *Imagined Communities*, 2nd edn. London: Verso.

Andreu-Cabrera, E., Cepero, M., Rojas, F.J. and Chinchilla-Mira, J.J. (2010) 'Play and childhood in ancient Greece', *Journal of Human Sport and Exercise*, 5(3): 339–47.

Apter, T. (1997) *Secret Paths*. London: W.W. Norton.

Archard, D. (2004) *Children: Rights and Childhood*, 2nd edn. Abingdon: Routledge.

Archer, R.L. (1928) *Rousseau on Education*, London: Edward Arnold.

Ariès, P. (1962) *Centuries of Childhood*. Harmondsworth: Penguin.

Armley Mills (2012) Records on display at the Armley Mills Industrial Museum. Details available at www.leeds.gov.uk/museumsandgalleries/Pages/armleymills/History-of-Armley-Mills.aspx.

Arnot, M., David, M. and Weiner, G. (1999) *Closing the Gender Gap*. Cambridge: Polity Press.

Associated Press (2011) '"El Brad Pitt" arrested in Mexico drug swoop', *The Guardian*, 17 June [online]. Available at www.theguardian.com/world/2011/jun/17/el-brad-pitt-arrested-mexico (accessed June 2014).

Audit Commission (1996a) *Counting to Five*. London: HMSO.

Audit Commission (1996b) *Under Fives Count*. London: HMSO.

Aviezer, O., Van IJzendoorn, M.H., Sagi, A. and Shuengel, C. (1994) '"Children of the dream" revisited: 70 years of collective early child care in Israeli kibbutzim', *Psychological Bulletin*, 116(1): 99–116.

Bain, A. (1859) *The Emotions and the Will*. London: John W. Parker [online]. Available at https://archive.org/details/emotionsandwill00baingoog (accessed June 2014).

Bak, M. and Von Brömssen, K. (2010) 'Interrogating childhood and diaspora through the voices of children in Sweden', *Childhood*, 17(1): 113–128.

Baldock, P., Fitzgerald, D. and Kay, J. (2013) *Understanding Early Years Policy*, 3rd edn. London: Sage.

Ball, C. (1994) *Start Right*. London: Royal Society of Arts.

Ball, S. (2008) *The Education Debate*. Bristol: Policy Press.

Bandura, A. (1965) '"Influence of models" reinforcement contingencies on the acquisition of imitative response', *Journal of Personality and Social Psychology*, 1: 589–95.

Bandura, A., Ross, D. and Ross, S.A. (1961) 'Transmission of aggression through imitation of aggressive models', *Journal of Abnormal and Social Psychology*, 63: 575–82.

Barnard, H.C. (1961) *A History of English Education from 1760*. London: University of London Press.

Barnardo's (2012) *What We Do* [online]. Available at www.barnardos.org.uk/what_we_do/who_we_are/history.htm (accessed May 2014)

Barry, R.A., Kochanska, G. and Philibert, R.A. (2008) 'G x E interaction in the organization of attachment', *Journal of Child Psychology and Psychiatry*, 49(12): 1313–20.

Barton, L. (1986) 'The politics of special educational needs', *Disability, Handicap and Society*, 1(3): 273–90.

Baumgarten, E. (2009) 'Judaism', in D.S. Browning and M.J. Bunge (eds), *Children and Childhood in World Religions*. New Brunswick, NJ: Rutgers University Press.

Baxter, J.E. (2005) 'Introduction: the archaeology of childhood in context', *Archaeological Papers of the American Anthropological Association,* (15): 1–9.

Bayliss, J. and Sly, F. (2009) *Children and Young People Around the UK.* London: Office for National Statistics.

BBC1 (2014) *Child of Our Time* [online]. Available at www.bbc.co.uk/programmes/b0072bk8 (accessed May 2014).

BBC News (1999) *UK Politics: Uncovering 'Britain's Most Shameful Secret',* 19 May [online]. Available at http://news.bbc.co.uk/1/hi/uk_politics/348001.stm (accessed September 2014).

BBC News (2000) *Human Rights: The European Convention,* 29 September [online]. Available at http://news.bbc.co.uk/1/hi/uk/948143.stm (accessed May 2014).

BBC News (2010) *Gordon Brown Apologises to Child Migrants Sent Abroad,* 24 February [online]. Available at http://news.bbc.co.uk/1.hi/8531664.stm (accessed August 2014).

BBHS (British Banking History Society) (2010) *A History of English Clearing Banks* [online]. Available at www.banking-history.co.uk/history.html (accessed May 2014).

Bean, P. and Melville, J. (1989) *Lost Children of the Empire.* London: Unwin Hyman.

Beck, U. and Beck-Gernsheim, E. (1995) *The Normal Chaos of Love.* Cambridge: Polity Press.

Bee, H. and Boyd, D. (2012) *The Developing Child,* 13th edn. New York: Allyn and Bacon.

Belkin, L. (2003) 'The opt-out revolution', *The New York Times,* 26 October.

Benavente, J. and Gains, S. (2008) *Families of Choice* [online]. Available at www.ext.colostate.edu/pubs/Columncc/cc050111.html (accessed May 2013).

Best, J. (1998) 'Too much fun: toys as social problems and the interpretation of culture', *Symbolic Interaction,* 21(2): 197–212.

Beveridge, Sir W. (1942) *Social Insurance and Allied Services,* Cmd 6404. London: HMSO.

Big Lottery Fund (2005) *New Opportunities Fund Details of Grants Made for the Financial Year Ended 31 March 2005.* London: Stationery Office.

Biggeri, M., Ballet, J. and Comim, F. (2011) *Children and the Capability Approach.* Basingstoke: Palgrave Macmillan.

Bilton, T., Bonnett, K., Jones, P., Lawson, T., Skinner, D., Stanworth, M. and Webster, A. (2002) *Introductory Sociology,* 4th edn. Basingstoke: Macmillan.

Birch, A. (1997) *Developmental Psychology.* Basingstoke: Palgrave.

BIS (Department for Business, Innovation and Skills) (2010) *Securing a Sustainable Future for Higher Education (The Browne Report)* [online]. Available at www.gov.uk/government/uploads/system/uploads/attachment_data/file/31999/10-1208-securing-sustainable-higher-education-browne-report.pdf (accessed May 2014).

Black, J. (2012) *A History of the British Isles,* 3rd edn. Basingstoke: Palgrave Macmillan.

Blakemore, S-J. and Frith, U. (2005) *The Learning Brain: Lessons for Education.* Oxford: Blackwell.

Bochel, C. and Bochel, H.M. (2004) *The UK Social Policy Process.* Basingstoke: Palgrave Macmillan.

Borgerhoff Mulder, M. (2000) 'Optimizing offspring: the quantity-quality tradeoff in agropastoral Kipsigis', *Evolution and Human Behavior,* 21: 391–410.

Borke, H. (1975) 'Piaget's mountains revisited', *Developmental Psychology,* 11: 240–43.

Bourdieu, P. (1986) 'The forms of capital' (trans. R. Nice), in A.H. Halsey, H. Lauder, P. Brown and A. Stuart Wells (eds) (1997) *Education*. Oxford: Oxford University Press.

Bourdillon, M.F.C. (1994) 'Street children in Harare', *Africa: Journal of the International African Institute*, 64(4): 516–32.

Bowlby, J. (1982 [1969]) *Attachment and Loss, 1,* 2nd edn. New York: Basic Books.

Brehony, K. (2000) 'English revisionist Froebelians and the schooling of the poor', in M. Hilton and P. Hirsch (eds), *Practical Visionaries*. Harlow: Pearson.

Breuilly, E., O'Brien, J. and Palmer, M. (1997) *Religions of the World*. Hove: Wayland Publishers.

Bristow, W. (2010) *Enlightenment, Stanford Encyclopedia of Philosophy* [online]. Available at http://plato.stanford.edu/entries/enlightenment/ (accessed October 2013).

Bronfenbrenner, U. (1977) 'Toward an experimental ecology of human development', *American Psychologist,* 32: 513–531.

Bronfenbrenner, U. (1994) 'Ecological models of human development', in *International Encyclopedia of Education*, 3, 2nd edn. Oxford: Elsevier.

Brosterman, N. (1997) *Inventing Kindergarten*. New York: Harry N. Abrams.

Browne, K.D. and Hamilton-Giachritsis, C. (2005) 'The influence of violent media on children and adolescents', *Lancet,* 365(9460): 702.

Bruner, J.S. (1966) *Towards a Theory of Instruction*. Harvard: Harvard University Press.

Bruner, J.S. (1977 [1960]) *The Process of Education*. Harvard: Harvard University Press.

Bryant, P. (1974) *Perception and Understanding in Young Children*. London: Methuen.

Buckingham, D. (2005) 'Constructing the media competent child', *MedienPädagogik*. Paper delivered at the 'Beyond the Competent Child' conference, Royal Danish School of Educational Studies, Copenhagen, November 2004, www.medienpaed.com.

Buckingham, D. (2007) 'Selling childhood?', *Journal of Children and Media,* 1(1): 15–24.

Buckingham, D. (2009) 'Children's changing cultural environment in the age of digital technology', in M-J. Kehily (ed.), *An Introduction to Childhood Studies,* 2nd edn. Maidenhead: McGraw Hill.

Buckingham, D. (2011) *The Material Child: Growing up in Consumer Culture*. Cambridge: Polity.

Bunge, M.J. (2006) 'The dignity and complexity of children: constructing Christian theologies of childhood', in K.M. Yust, A.N. Johnson, S.E. Sasso and E.C. Roehlkepartain (eds), *Nurturing Child and Adolescent Spirituality*. Lanham, MD: Rowman and Littlefield.

Bunge, M.J. and Browning, D.S. (2009) 'Introduction', in D.S. Browning and M.J. Bunge, *Children and Childhood in World Religions* (eds). New Brunswick, NJ: Rutgers University Press.

Bunge, M.J. and Wall, J. (2009) 'Christianity', in D.S. Browning and M.J. Bunge, *Children and Childhood in World Religions* (eds). New Brunswick, NJ: Rutgers University Press.

Burman, E. (1994) *Deconstructing Developmental Psychology*. London: Routledge.

Butler, J. (1990) *Gender Trouble*. London: Routledge: Chapman and Hall.

Byford, A. (2012) *Russian Child Science, Report 1* [online]. Available at www.dur.ac.uk/resources/russianchildscience/Report1Nov12.pdf (accessed April 2013).

Cabinet Office (2002) *Inter-Departmental Childcare Review: Delivering for Children and Families*. London: Stationery Office.

CACE (Central Advisory Council for Education) (1959) *15 to 18 (The Crowther Report)*. London: HMSO.

CACE (Central Advisory Council for Education) (1963) *Half Our Future (The Newsom Report)*. London: HMSO.

CACE (Central Advisory Council for Education) (1967) *Children and their Primary Schools (The Plowden Report)*. London: HMSO.

Carpenter, H. (1985) *Secret Gardens*. London: Allen and Unwin. Reprinted in J. Maybin and N.J. Watson (2009) *Children's Literature*. Palgrave Macmillan/Open University.

Carr, M. (2001) *Assessment in Early Childhood Settings*. London: PCP.

Cassidy, S. (1999) 'Primary schools ready for changes; Curriculum 2000'. *TES*, 10 September [online]. Available at www.tes.co.uk/article.aspx?storycode=308411.

CEOP (Child Exploitation and Online Protection Centre) (2011) *Scoping Report on Missing and Abducted Children*. London: CEOP.

Child Migrants Trust (2012) *Child Migrant History* [online]. Available at www.child migrantstrust.com/our-work/child-migration-history (accessed January 2014).

Childs, S. (2006) 'Political parties and party systems', in P. Dunleavy, R. Heffernan, P. Cowley and C. Hay, *Developments in British Politics*. Basingstoke: Palgrave Macmillan.

Chitty, C. (2004) *Education Policy in Britain*. Basingstoke: Palgrave Macmillan.

CIA (Central Intelligence Agency) (2013) *The World Factbook 2013–2014*. Washington DC: CIA.

Clark, A. and Moss, P. (2001) *Listening to Young Children: The Mosaic Approach*. London: National Children's Bureau.

CoE (Council of Europe) (2013) *Council of Europe* [online]. Available at www.coe.int/aboutCoe/index.asp (accessed March 2014).

Cole, A. (2009) 'Buddhism', in D.S. Browning and M.J. Bunge, *Children and Childhood in World Religions* (eds). New Brunswick, NJ: Rutgers University Press.

Colton, M., Sanders, R. and Williams, M. (2001) *Working with Children*. Basingstoke: Palgrave Macmillan.

Colvert, E., Rutter, M., Beckett, C., Castle, J., Groothues, C., Hawkins, A., Kreppner, J., O'Connor, T.G., Stevens, S., and Sonuga-Barke, E.J.S. (2008) 'Emotional difficulties in early adolescence following severe early deprivation'. *Development and Psychopathology*, 20: 547–67.

Comenius, J.A. (1896 [1631]) *The Great Didactic* (trans. M.W. Keatinge). New York: Russell and Russell [online]. Available at https://archive.org/stream/greatdidacticjo00keatgoog (accessed June 2014).

Committee on Higher Education (1963) *Higher Education (The Robbins Report)*. London: HMSO.

Corby, B. (2006) *Child Abuse*. Maidenhead: Open University Press.

Cornwall, A. and Nyamu-Musembi, C. (2004) 'Putting the "Rights-Based Approach" to development into perspective', *Third World Quarterly*, 25(8): 1415–37.

Corsaro, W. (2006) *The Sociology of Childhood*, 3rd edn. Thousand Oaks, CA: Sage.

Corston, W. (2014 [1840]) A brief sketch of the life of Joseph Lancaster, in J. Lancaster and W. Corston, *Improvements in Education*. Cambridge: Cambridge University Press.

Crawford, S. (1999) *Childhood in Anglo-Saxon England*. Stroud: Sutton Publishing.

Crawford, S. (2009) 'The archaeology of play things', *Childhood in the Past*, 2: 56–71.

Crenshaw, K. (1989) 'Demarginalizing the intersection of race and sex', *University of Chicago Legal Forum*, 140: 139–67.

Cribb, J., Joyce, R. and Phillips, D. (2012) *Living Standards, Poverty and Inequality in the UK: 2012*, C124. London: Institute for Fiscal Studies.

Cunningham, F. (2005) 'Market economies and market societies', *Journal of Social Philosophy*, 36(2): 129–42.

Cunningham, H. (2005) *Children and Childhood in Western Society Since 1500*, 2nd edn. Harlow: Pearson Education.

Cunningham, H. (2006) *The Invention of Childhood*. London: BBC Books.

Cunningham, P. (2000) 'The Montessori phenomenon', in M. Hilton and P. Hirsch (eds) *Practical Visionaries*. Harlow: Pearson.

Curee (n.d.) *Report of Professional Practitioner Use of Research Review* [online]. Available at www.curee.co.uk/publication/practitioner-use-research-review-full-technical-report (accessed June 2014).

Curtis, A. (1986) *A Curriculum for the Pre-school Child*. London: Routledge.

Curtis, A. and Hills, S. (1979) *My World*. Abingdon: NFER/Routledge.

Dahlberg, G., Moss, P. and Pence, A. (1999, 2nd edn 2007) *Beyond Quality in Early Childhood Education and Care*. London: Falmer Press.

Daniels, H. (2001) *Vygotsky and Pedagogy*. London: RoutledgeFalmer.

Darien, J.C. (1998) 'Parent-child decision making in children's clothing stores', *International Journal of Retail and Distribution Management*, 26(11): 421–28.

De Landsheere, G. (1988) 'History of educational research', in M. Hammersley (ed.) (1993) *Educational Research, 1*. London: Paul Chapman.

Dearing, R. (1996) *Review of Qualifications for 16–19 Year Olds*, Middlesex: SCAA.

Derrida, J. (1974 [1967 in French]) *Of Grammatology* (trans. G. Spivak). Baltimore: The Johns Hopkins University Press.

DES (Department of Education and Science) (1979) *Aspects of Secondary Education in England*, London: HMSO. PART III: Chapter 12: Point 13, p.262 [online] Available at www.educationengland.org.uk/documents/hmi-secondary/hmi-secondary.html.

DES (Department of Education and Science) (1981) *The School Curriculum*. London: DES.

DES (Department of Education and Science) (1982) *Education 5 to 9*. London: HMSO. Chapter 4: Points 4.5, 4.7, 4.8, 4.9, 4.10, pp.56–58 [online] Available at www.educationengland.org.uk/documents/hmi-5to9/hmi-5to9.html#04.

DES (Department of Education and Science) (1983) *9–13 Middle schools*. London: HMSO. Chapter 8: Points, 8.3, 8.8, 8.10, 8.12, 8.20, 8.21, 8.22, pp.121–131 [online]. Available at www.educationengland.org.uk/documents/hmi-9to13/hmi-9to13.html#08.

DES (Department of Education and Science) (1985) *Education 8 to 12 in Combined and Middle Schools*. London: HMSO. Chapter 8: Points 8.4, 8.6, 8.11, 8.16, 8.18, pp.74–81 [online]. Available at www.educationengland.org.uk/documents/hmi-8to12/hmi-8to12.html#08.

DES (Department of Education and Science) (1990) *Starting with Quality (The Rumbold Report)* London: DES.

DES (Department of Education and Science) (2002) *14–19: Extending Opportunities, Raising Standards*, CM 5342. London: HMSO.

Desforges, C. and Abouchaar, A. (2003) *The Impact of Parental Involvement, Parental Support and Family Education on Pupil Achievement and Adjustment: A Literature Review*, RR433. London: DfES.

Dewaraja, L.S. (1994) *The Position of Women in Buddhism* [online]. Available at www.hinduwebsite.com/buddhism/essays/position_of_women.asp (accessed November 2012).

Dewey, J. (1899, revised 1915) *The School and Society*. Chicago: University of Chicago Press.

Dewey, J. (1910) *How We Think*. Boston, MA: D.C. Heath and Co.

Dewey, J. (1916) *Democracy and Education*. New York: Macmillan.

Dewey, J. (1938) *Experience and Education*. USA: Kappa Delta Pi.

DfE (Department for Education) (2011a) *Support and Aspiration: A New Approach to Special Educational Needs and Disability, A Consultation*, CM 8027. London: TSO.

DfE (Department for Education) (2011b) *Supporting Families in the Foundation Years*. London: DfE.

DfE (Department for Education) (2011c) *The Munro Review of Child Protection: Final Report: A Child-Centred System*, CM 8062. London: HMSO.

DfE (Department for Education) (2013a) *More Great Childcare*. London: DfE.

DfE (Department for Education) (2013b) *Sure Start Children's Centres Statutory Guidance* [online]. Available at www.education.gov.uk.

DfE (Department for Education) (2014a) *Special Educational Needs and Disability Code of Practice: 0 to 25 Years: Statutory Guidance*. London: DfE.

DfE (Department for Education) (2014b) *Statistical First release: Provision for Children Under Five Years of Age in England: January 2013*. SFR 20/2014. London: DfE.

DfES (Department for Education and Skills) (2002) *Birth to Three Matters*. London: DfES.

DfES (Department for Education and Skills) (2003a) *14–19: Opportunity and Excellence*. Nottingham: DfES.

DfES (Department for Education and Skills) (2003b) *Every Child Matters*, CM 5860. London: The Stationery Office.

DfES (Department for Education and Skills) (2003c) *The Future of Higher Education*. London: DfES.

Diniejkow, A. (2012) *Charles Dickens as Social Commentator and Critic* [online]. Available at www.victorianweb.org/authors/dickens/diniejko.html (accessed August 2013).

Downer, L.J. (1972) *Leges Henrici Primi*. Oxford: Clarendon Press.

Drummond, M.J. (2000) 'Susan Isaacs', in M. Hilton and P. Hirsch (eds) *Practical Visionaries*. Harlow: Pearson.

DT (Department for Transport) (2010) *Reported Road Casualties in Great Britain: 2010 Annual Report*. London: DT.

Dunleavy, P. (2006) 'The Westminster model and the distinctiveness of British politics', in P. Dunleavy, R. Heffernan, P. Cowley and C. Hay (eds), *Developments in British Politics*. Basingstoke: Palgrave Macmillan.

Dunn, J. (1998) *The Beginnings of Social Understanding*. Oxford: Blackwell.

Durkheim, E. (1951 [1897]) *Suicide, a study in Sociology* (trans. J.A. Spaulding and G. Simpson). Glencoe, IL: The Free Press [online]. Available at https://archive.org/details/suicidestudyinso00durk.

Durkheim, E. (1984 [1893]) *The Division of Labor in Society* (trans. W.D. Halls). New York: The Free Press, 1984.

Durkheim, E. (1995 [1912, 1915 in English]) *The Elementary Forms of the Religious Life* (trans. K. Fields). New York: Free Press [online]. Available at https://archive.org/details/elementaryformso00durkrich.

Duvall, S-S. (2010) 'Perfect little feminists?', *Journal of Children and Media*, 4(4): 402–17.

DWP (Department for Work and Pensions) (2005), *Family Resources Survey: United Kingdom 2004–05*, London: Department for Work and Pensions, ONS, available at http://webarchive.nationalarchives.gov.uk/+/http://www.dwp.gov.uk/asd/frs/2004_05/pdfonly/frs_2004_05_report.pdf.

Dwyer, P. (2004) 'Creeping conditionality in the UK', *Canadian Journal of Sociology*, 29(2): 265–87.

Early Education (2014) *Early Education* [online]. Available at www.early-education.org.uk/ (accessed May 2014).

Eaton, G. (2013) 'Inequality before and after Thatcher', *New Statesman*, 9 April.

Ecclestone, K. and Hayes, D. (2009) *The Dangerous Rise of Therapeutic Education*. Abingdon: Routledge.

Edgington, M. (2007) 'Early years in crisis? Reflecting on the past ten years, hoping for the future', *Early Years Educator*, 9(4): 22–24.

Education in England at www.educationengland.org.uk/.

Elliott, J. (2009) 'Where "choice feminism" has got us', *Across the Pond: A Feminist Blog*, 25 April [online]. Available at http://femsacrossthepond.wordpress.com/2009/04/25/where-choice-feminism-has-got-us/ (accessed June 2014).

Engels, R. (1993 [1845]) *The Condition of the Working Class in England* (ed. D. McLellan). Oxford: Oxford University Press.

Erikson, E.H. (1963) *Childhood and Society*, 2nd edn. New York: Norton.

Esping-Anderson, G. (1990) *The Three Worlds of Welfare Capitalism*. Cambridge: Polity Press.

ETTAD (Enabling teachers and trainers to improve the accessibility of adult education) (2007) *Understanding Disability* [online]. Available at http://uk.ettad.eu/Understanding%20Disability%20-%20guide%20to%20good%20practice.pdf (accessed June 2014).

EU (European Union) (2013) *European Union* [online]. Available at http://europa.eu/index_en.htm (accessed October 2013).

European Commission (EC) (2011) *Demography Report 2010*. Luxembourg: Publications Office of the European Union.

Eurostat (2014) *Europe in Figures - Eurostat Yearbook* [online]. Available at http://epp.eurostat.ec.europa.eu/statistics_explained/index.php/Europe_in_figures_-_Eurostat_yearbook (accessed June 2014).

Evangelou, M., Sylva, K., Edwards, A. and Smith, T. (2008) *Early Learning Partnership Project (ELPP)*, RR039. London: DCSF.

Factor, J. (2004) 'Tree stumps, manhole covers and rubbish tins: the invisible playlines of a primary school playground', *Childhood*, 11(2): 142–54.

Fantz, R.L. (1963) 'Pattern vision in newborn infants', *Science*, 140: 296–97.

Farmer, C. (2005) *Home Office Citizenship Survey: Top Level Findings from the Children and Young People's Survey*. London: Home Office and Department for Education and Skills.

FCCCS (Families, Children and Child Care Study) (2014) *The Families, Children and Child Care Study* [online]. Available at www.familieschildrenchildcare.org/fccc_frames_home.html (accessed May 2014).

Feeney, P. (2010) *A 1960s Childhood*. Stroud: The History Press.

Fenton, N. (2006) 'Daily Telegraph campaign to halt "death of childhood"', *The Telegraph*, 13 September [online]. Available at www.telegraph.co.uk/news/yourview/1528718/Daily-Telegraph-campaign-to-halt-death-of-childhood.html (accessed June 2014).

Field, F. (2010) *The Foundation Years: Preventing Poor Children Becoming Poor Adults*. London: Cabinet Office.

Fieldhouse, R. and associates (1996) *A History of Modern British Adult Education*, Leicester: NIACE.

Flanagan, C. (1996) *Applying Psychology to Early Child Development*. London: Hodder and Stoughton.

Foods Ethics Council (n.d.) *Backgrounder on Children's Diets* [online]. Available at www.foodethicscouncil.org/node/224 (accessed July 2013).

Foucault, M. (1970 [1966]) *The Order of Things..* London: Tavistock Publications.

Foucault, M. (1972 [1969]) *Archaeology of Knowledge*. London: Tavistock Publications.

Foucault, M. (1977) *Discipline and Punish*. New York: Vintage.

Foucault, M. (1978, 1985, 1986) *The History of Sexuality* (3 vols). New York: Random House.

Freud, A. (1937 [1936]) *The Ego and the Mechanisms of Defense*. London: The Hogarth Press.

Freud, S. (1913 [1899]) *The Interpretation of Dreams*. London: George Allen and Co.

Friedman-Rudovsky, J. (2010) 'Hope for the children of Juarez', *Young Children in Cities, Early Childhood Matters*, 115: 32–37. The Hague: Bernard van Leer Foundation.

Fulcher, J. and Scott, J. (2011) *Sociology*, 4th edn. Oxford: Oxford University Press.

Furedi, F. (2004) *Therapy Culture*. London: Routledge.

Furedi, F. (2008) *Paranoid Parenting*, 2nd edn. London: Continuum.

Galton, F. (1875) 'Statistics by Intercomparison, with Remarks on the Law of Frequency of Error'. *Philosophical Magazine*, 49(322): 33–46 [online]. Available at http://galton.org/essays/1870–1879/galton-1875-intercomparison.pdf (accessed June 2014).

Gamble, N. and Yates, S. (2008) *Exploring Children's Literature*, 2nd edn. London: Sage.

Gardner, H. (1998) 'Foreword: complementary perspectives on Reggio Emilia', in C. Edwards, L. Gandini and G. Forman (eds), *The Hundred Languages of Children*. Greenwich, CT: Ablex Publishing.

Garfinkel, H. (1984 [1967]) *Studies in Ethnomethodology*. Cambridge: Polity Press.

Garforth, F.W. (1964) *Locke's Thought Concerning Education*. London: Heinemann.

Gavin, A.E. (2012) *The Child In British Literature*. Basingstoke: Palgrave Macmillan.

Gerheart, B.R. (1972) *Education of the Exceptional Child*. Lanham, MD: University Press of America.

Giddens, A. (1984) *The Constitution of Society*. Berkeley, CA: University of California Press.

Giddens, A. (1991) *Modernity and Self-Identity*. Stanford, CA: Stanford University Press.

Giddens, A. (1998) *The Third Way*. Cambridge: Polity.

Giddens, A. (2006) *Sociology*, 5th edn. Cambridge: Polity Press.

Giladi, A. (2009) 'Islam', in D.S. Browning and M.J. Bunge (eds), *Children and Childhood in World Religions*. New Brunswick, NJ: Rutgers University Press.

Gillard, D. (2006) *The Hadow Reports* [online]. Available at www.education england.org.uk/articles/24hadow.html (accessed May 2014).

Gillard, D. (2011) *Education in England: A Brief History* [online]. Available at www.educationengland.org.uk/history/ (accessed June 2014).

Gittins, D. (1998) *The Child in Question,* Basingstoke: Macmillan.

Goffman, E. (1971[1959]) *The Presentation of Self in Everyday Life*. London: Penguin.

Golden, M. (1990) *Children and Childhood in Classical Athens*. Baltimore, MD: John Hopkins Press.

Gordon, E.C. (1991) 'Accidents among medieval children as seen from the miracles of six English saints and martyrs', *Medical History,* 35: 145–63.

Goswami, U. (2004) 'Annual review: neuroscience and education', *British Journal of Educational Psychology,* 74: 1–14.

Goswami, U. (2006) 'Neuroscience and education: from research to practice?', *Nature Reviews: Neuroscience,* 7(5): 406–11.

Gray, C. (2012) 'Ethical research with children and vulnerable groups', in I. Palaiologou, *Ethical Practice in Early Childhood*. London: Sage.

Greer, G. (1970) *The Female Eunuch*. London: MacGibbon and Kee.

Hadfield, M. and Jopling, M. (2012) *Second National Survey of Practitioners with Early Years Professional Status*, DFE-RR239a. London: DfE.

Hadfield, M., Jopling, M., Royle, K. and Waller, T. (2011) *First National Survey of Practitioners with Early Years' Professional Status*. Leeds: CWDC.

Habermas, J. (1987 [1984]) *Theory of Communicative Action*. Boston, MA: Beacon Press.

Hakim, C. (2004) *Key Issues in Women's Work*. London: Glasshouse Press.

Hakim, C. (2011) *Honey Money*. London: Allen Lane.

Halcrow, S.E. and Tayles, N. (2008) 'The bioarchaeological investigation of child-hood and social age', *Journal of Archaeological Method and Theory,* 15: 190–215.

Hammersley, M. and Atkinson, P. (1983 [1995]) *Ethnography,* 2nd edn. London: Routledge.

Hampshire, K. (2002) 'Fulani on the move', *Journal of Development Studies.* 38(5): 1025–37.

Hanawalt, B. (1977) 'Childrearing among the lower classes of late medieval England', *The Journal of Interdisciplinary History,* 8(1): 1–22.

Hanawalt, B. (1993) *Growing Up in Medieval London*. Oxford: Oxford University Press.

Hanson, M. (2012) Excerpts from 'What the grown-ups were doing: An Odyssey through 1950s suburbia'. London: Simon and Schuster. In 'The magic of fifties suburbia', *Mail Online,* 22 February.

Harden, J. (2000) 'There's no place like home', *Childhood,* 7(43): 43–59.

Harkness, S. and Super, C.M. (1985) 'The cultural context of gender segregation in children's peer groups', *Child Development,* 56(1): 219–24.

Harkness, S. and Super, C.M. (2001) 'The ties that bind: social networks of men and women in a Kipsigis community of Kenya', *Ethos*, 29(3): 357–70.

Hartley, T.R. (1934) 'The public school of Sparta', *Greece and Rome*, 3(9): 129–39.

Harvey, D. (1990) *The Condition of Postmodern Identity*. Oxford: Blackwell.

Heiland, H. (1993) 'Friedrich Froebel', *Prospects*, 23(3/4): 473–91.

Henderson, A. (ed.) (2011) *Insights from the Playgroup Movement*. Stoke-on-Trent: Trentham Books.

Hendrick, H. (1997) *Children, Childhood and English Society 1880–1990*. Cambridge: Cambridge University Press.

Hendrick, H. (1997 [1990]) 'Constructions and reconstructions of British childhood', in A. James and A. Prout (eds) *Constructing and Reconstructing Childhood*, 2nd edn. London: RoutledgeFalmer.

Hendrick, H. (2003) *Child Welfare*. Bristol: The Policy Press.

Hendrick, H. (2011 [1994]) *Child Welfare, England, 1872–1989*. London: Routledge.

Herm, A. (2008) 'Recent migration trends', *Eurostat: Statistics in Focus: 98/2008* [online]. Available at http://epp.eurostat.ec.europa.eu/cache/ITY_OFFPUB/KS-SF-08-098/EN/KS-SF-08-098-EN.PDF (accessed June 2014).

Heywood, C. (2001) *A History of Childhood*. Cambridge: Polity Press.

High/Scope Educational Research Foundation (1991) *Supporting Young Learners*. Ypsilanti, MA: High/Scope Press.

Hill, M. and Tisdall, K. (1997) *Children and Society*. Harlow: Prentice Hall.

Hillman, M., Adams, J., and Whitelegg, J. (1990) *One False Move*. London: Policy Studies Institute [online summary]. Available on Policy Studies Institute website at http://www.psi.org.uk/site/publication_detail/904 (accessed June 2014).

HM Government (2013) *'Staying Put': DfE, DWP and HMRC Guidance* [online]. Available at http://dera.ioe.ac.uk/17711/1/Staying_Put_Guidance.pdf (accessed June 2014).

HM Treasury (2004) *Choice for Parents, the Best Start for Children: Ten year Strategy for Childcare*. Nottingham: DfES.

HMSO (1908) School Attendance of Children Below the Age of Five: The Acland Report, Cd.4259 [online]. Available at http://www.educationengland.org.uk/documents/acland1908/acland08.html (accessed June 2014).

HMSO (2011) *Start Active, Stay Active*. London: Her Majesty's Stationery Office.

HoC (House of Commons) (1942, 30 June) *Hansard House of Commons Parliamentary Debates, 5th Series, Report of The Supply Committee*, 385 (cols.115, 116). Available at http://hansard.millbanksystems.com/commons/1942/jun/30/ministry-of-health.

HoC (House of Commons) (2003) *The Victoria Climbié Inquiry (Laming Report)* CM 5730. London: HMSO.

HoC (House of Commons) (2009a) *Looked-After children, Third Report of Session 2008–09, Vol. I*. HC 111-I. London: HoC.

HoC (House of Commons) (2009b) *National Curriculum*, HC 344-1. London: HMSO.

Hochschild, A. (2005) *Bury the Chains*. Boston: Houghton Mifflin.

Hopkins, J.R. (1995) 'Erik Homburger Erikson (1902–1994)', *American Psychologist*, 50(9): 796–97.

Howard, R. (2013, 15 April) *Cross-party Support Confirmed for Launch of Early Intervention Foundation* [online]. Available at www.daynurseries.co.uk/news/article.cfm/id/1559714 (accessed March 2014).

HSCIC (The Health and Social Care Information Centre) (2013) *Statistics on Obesity, Physical Activity and Diet: England, 2013*. London: NHS.

HSCIC (The Health and Social Care Information Centre) (2014) *Statistics on Obesity, Phsical Activity and Diet: England, 2014*. Available at www.hsclc.gov.uk/catalogue/PUB10364/obes-phys-acti-diet-eng-2014-rep.pdf (accessed August 2014).

Humphreys, M. (1994) *Empty Cradles*. London: Doubleday (reprinted 2011 as *Oranges and Sunshine*, London: Corgi).

Humphries, J. (2010) *Childhood and Child Labour in the British Industrial Revolution*. Cambridge: Cambridge University Press.

Humphries, S., Mack, J. and Perks, R. (1988) *A Century of Childhood*. London: Sidgwick and Jackson/Channel Four TV.

Huntsinger, C.S. (2007) 'Child study movement', in R.S. New and M. Cochran (eds), *Early Childhood Education: an International Encyclopedia, 1*. Westport, CT: Praeger: 132–33.

International Humanist and Ethical Union (2009) *BBC Religions: Humanism* [online]. Available at www.bbc.co.uk/religion/religions/atheism/types/humanism.shtml (accessed February 2013).

IoE (Institute of Education) (2014) *Centre for Longitudinal Studies* [online]. Available at http://www.cls.ioe.ac.uk (accessed May 2014).

Isaacs, S. (1930) *Intellectual Growth in Children*. London: Routledge.

Isaacs, S. (1933) *Social Development in Young Children*. London: Routledge.

Isaacs, S. (1963 [1932]) *The Children We Teach*. London: University of London Press.

Ivic, I. (1994) 'Lev S. Vygotsky (1896–1934)', *Prospects*, XXIV(3/4): 471–85.

Jackson, S. (2008) 'Families, domesticity and intimacy', in D. Richardson and V. Robinson (eds), *Gender and Women's Studies*, 3rd edn. Basingstoke: Palgrave Macmillan.

James, A. and James, A. (2008) *Key Concepts in Childhood Studies*. London: Sage.

James, A. and Prout, A. (1997 [1990]) *Constructing and Reconstructing Childhood*, 2nd edn. London: RoutledgeFalmer.

James, A., Jenks, C. and Prout, A. (1998) *Theorizing Childhood*. Cambridge: Polity Press.

Jayaram, V. (2012a) *Buddha Dhamma: The Philosophy of Buddhism* [online]. Available at www.hinduwebsite.com/buddhism/buddhist_philosophy.asp (accessed November 2012).

Jayaram, V. (2012b) *Hinduism and Children* [online]. Available at www.hinduwebsite.com/hinduism/h_children.asp (accessed November 2012).

Jenks, C. (1982) *The Sociology of Childhood*. London: Batsford.

Jenks, C. (2005 [1996]) *Childhood,* 2nd edn. London: Routledge.

Jirtle, R.L. and Weidman, J. (2007) 'Imprinted and more equal', *American Scientist*, 95(2): 143–49.

Jolibert, B. (1993) 'Sigmund Freud (1856–1939)', *Prospects*, XXIII(3/4): 459–72.

Jones, B.D. (ed.) (2012) *Women Who Opt Out*. New York: New York University Press.

Jones, E. (1961) *The Life and Work of Sigmund Freud* (eds L. Trilling and S. Marcus). New York: Basic Books.

Kamp, K.A. (2001) 'Where have all the children gone?', *Journal of Archaeological Method and Theory*, 8(1): 1–34.

Kamp, K.A., Timmerman, N., Lind, G., Graybill, J. and Natowsky, I. (1999) 'Discovering childhood', *American Antiquity,* 64(2): 309–15.

Kearney, H. (2012) *The British Isles,* 2nd edn. Cambridge: Cambridge University Press.

Kelly, T. (1992) *A History of Adult Education in Great Britain,* 3rd edn. Liverpool: Liverpool University Press.

Kershaw, R. and Sacks, J. (2008) *New Lives for Old.* Richmond: National Archives.

Kilpatrick, W.H. (1951) 'Introduction', in *The Education of Man: Aphorisms by Heinrich Pestalozzi.* New York: Philosophical Library.

Klein, M. (1932) *The Psychoanalysis of Children.* London: The Hogarth Press.

Knight, S. (2009) *Forest Schools and Outdoor Learning in the Early Years.* London: Sage.

Kwon, Y-I. (2002) 'Changing Curriculum for Early Childhood Education in England'. *ECRP (Early Childhood Research and Practice),* 4 (2) [online]. Available at http://ecrp.uiuc.edu/v4n2/kwon.html.

Laurence, R. (2005) 'Childhood in the Roman Empire', *History Today,* 55(10).

Layard, R. and Dunn, J. (2009) *A Good Childhood.* London: Penguin (for the Children's Society).

Lazenby, F.D. (1949) 'Greek and Roman household pets parts 1 and 2, *The Classical Journal,* 44(4): 245–52; 44(5): 299–307.

Lerner, R.M. (2005) Foreword to U. Bronfenbrenner (ed) (2005) *Making Human Beings Human.* Thousand Oaks, CA: Sage.

Levy-Shiff, R. (1983) 'Adaptation and competence in early childhood: communally raised kibbutz children versus family raised children in the city', *Child Development,* 54(6): 1606–14.

Lewin-Jones, J. and Mitra, B. (2009) 'Gender roles in television commercials and primary school children in the UK', *Journal of Children and Media,* 3(1): 35–50.

Lillehammer, G. (1989) 'A child is born: the child's world in an archaeological perspective', *Norwegian Archaeological Review,* 22(2): 89–105.

Linebarger, D.L. and Walker, D. (2005) 'Infants' and toddlers' television viewing and language outcomes', *American Behavioral Scientist,* 48: 624–45.

Ling, R. (2007) 'Children, youth, and mobile communication', *Journal of Children and Media,* 1(1): 60–7.

Linné, O. and Jones, M. (2000) 'The coverage of lone-parents in British newspapers', *Nordicom Review,* 1(1): 59–70.

Livingstone, S. (2007) 'Do the media harm children?', *Journal of Children and Media,* 1(1): 5–14.

Lloyd, E. (2012) 'The marketization of early years education and childcare in England', in L. Miller and D. Hevey (eds), *Policy Issues in the Early Years.* London: Sage.

Lokja, B., Banout, J., Banoutova, L., Verner, V. and Van Damme, P. (2011) 'Diversity of shifting cultivation cycles among small-scale farmers in Peruvian Amazon', *Agricultural Sciences,* 2(2): 68–77.

Lord Privy Seal's Office (1939) *Evacuation: Why and How? Public Information Leaflet (3)* [online]. Available at www.homefrontthirsk.org.uk/details.php?search_all=37 (accessed June 2014).

Louv, R. (2005) *Last Child in the Woods.* Chapel Hill, NC: Algonquin Books.

Lowe, R. (2009) 'Childhood through the ages', in T. Maynard and N. Thomas (eds), *An Introduction to Early Childhood Studies,* 2nd edn. London: Sage.

LTCW (2011) 'Local approaches to tackle multiple disadvantage', *Learning Together Chester and Warrington – Newsletter*, 1 March [online]. Available at http://www.learning-together.co.uk/newsletter-view.asp?ID=41 (accessed June 2014).

Lucas, P. (1991) 'Exploration of North America', in E. Foner and J.A. Garraty (eds), *The Reader's Companion to American History.* Boston, MA: Houghton Mifflin Harcourt.

Lukàcs, G. (1971 [1920]) *History and Class Consciousness.* Cambridge, MA: MIT Press.

Lyotard, J-F. (1984 [1979]) *The Postmodern Condition: A Report on Knowledge.* Manchester: Manchester University Press.

Macintyre, S. (2009) *A Concise History of Australia.* Cambridge: Cambridge University Press.

MacNaughton, G. (2005) *Doing Foucault in Early Childhood Studies.* London: Routledge.

Magadi, M. (2010) 'Risk factors of severe child poverty in the UK', *Journal of Social Policy,* 39(2): 297–316.

Main, M. and Solomon, J. (1986) 'Discovery of a new, insecure-disorganized/ disoriented attachment pattern', in T.B. Brazelton and M. Yogman (eds), *Affective Development in* Infancy. Norwood, NJ: Ablex.

Maisey, R. Speight, S. and Marsh, V. with Philo, D. (2013) *The Early Education Pilot for Two Year Old Children: Age Five Follow Up.* RR225. London: DfE.

Majors, K.A. (2013) 'Children's perceptions of their imaginary companions and the purposes they serve', *Childhood,* 20(4): 555–65.

Mand, K. (2010) 'I've got two houses. One in Bangladesh and one in London … everybody has', *Childhood,* 17(2): 273–87.

Margaret Thatcher Foundation (1972) 'Written statement launching Education White Paper' [online]. Available at www.margaretthatcher.org/document/102233 (accessed June 2014).

Martens, L., Southerton, D. and Scott, S. (2004) 'Bringing children (and parents) into the sociology of consumption', *Journal of Consumer Culture,* 4(2): 155–82.

Marx, K. (1887 [1867]) *Capital, A Critique of Political Economy 1: The Process of Production of Capital* (edited by F. Engels) [online]. Available at https://libcom.org/files/Capital-Volume-I.pdf.

Marx, K. (1907 [1885]) *Capital, A Critique of Political Economy 2: The Process of Circulation of Capital* (edited by F. Engels) [online]. Available at https://libcom.org/files/Capital-Volume-II.pdf.

Marx, K. (1909 [1894]) *Capital, A Critique of Political Economy 3: The process of capitalist production as a whole* (completed and edited by F. Engels) [online]. Available at https://libcom.org/files/Capital-Volume-III.pdf.

Maybin, J. and Watson, N.J. (2009) *Children's Literature: Approaches and Territories.* London: Palgrave Macmillan/Open University.

Mayhew, H. (1861) *London Labour and the London Poor, 1.* London: Griffin, Bohn and Co., 1861–1862 [online in Tufts digital library]. Permanent URL at http://hdl.handle.net/10427/53837. Section on child street sellers available at http://dl.tufts.edu/catalog/tei/tufts:MS004.002.052.001.00001/chapter/c17s1 (accessed June 2014).

McCulloch, G. (2002) 'Secondary education', in R. Aldrich *A Century of Education* (ed.). London: RoutledgeFalmer.

McDowall Clark, R. (2010) *Childhood in Society for Early Childhood Studies.* Exeter: LearningMatters.

McGarrigle, J. and Donaldson, M. (1974) 'Conservation accidents', *Cognition*, 3: 341–50.

McGillis, R. (2012) 'Irony and performance', in A.E. Gavin, *The Child in British Literature*. Basingstoke: Palgrave Macmillan.

McIntosh, M. (1996) 'Social anxieties about lone motherhood and ideologies of the family', in E. Bortolaia Silva (ed.) *Good Enough Mothering?* London: Routledge.

McKenzie, J. (2001) *Changing Education*. Harlow: Pearson Education.

Mead, G.H. (1967 [1934]) *Mind, Self, and Society*. Chicago: University of Chicago Press.

Mills, J. and Mills, R.W. (2000) *Childhood Studies*. London: Routledge.

Mills, R. (2000) 'Perspectives of childhood', in J. Mills and R. Mills (eds) *Childhood Studies*. London: Routledge.

Mizen, P. and Ofosu-Kusi, Y. (2010) 'Asking, giving, receiving: friendship as survival strategy among Accra's street children', *Childhood*, 17(4): 441–54.

Montessori, M. (1965 [1912]) *The Montessori Method*. Cambridge, MA: Robert Bentley.

Montessori, M. (1988 [1949]) *The Absorbent Mind*. Oxford: Clio Press.

Montgomery, H. and Watson, N.J. (2009) *Children's Literature: Classic Texts and Contemporary Trends*. London: Palgrave Macmillan/Open University.

Moore, R.C. (1986) *Childhood's Domain: Play and Place in Child Development*. London: Croom Helm.

Moran, G.F. and Vinovskis, M.A. (1985) 'The great care of godly parents: early childhood in Puritan New England', *Monographs of the Society for Research in Child Development*, 50(4/5): 24–37.

Morgan, D.H.J. (1996) *Family Connections*. Cambridge: Polity Press.

Morgan, K.O. (2010) *The Oxford History of Britain*. Oxford: Oxford University Press.

Morrow, V. (2011) *Understanding Children and Childhood*, 2nd edn. Lismore: Centre for Children and Young People, Southern Cross University.

Moss, D. (2011) *Children and Social Change: Memories of Diverse Childhoods*. London: Bloomsbury Academic.

Moss, S. (2012) *Natural Childhood*. Swindon: National Trust.

Moyles, J., Adams, S. Musgrove, A. (2002) *SPEEL: Study of Pedagogical Effectiveness in Early Learning*, RR 363. London: DfES.

Munari, A. (1994) 'Jean Piaget (1896–1980)', *Prospects*, XXIV(1/2): 311–27.

Nakagawa, Y. (2006) 'The child as compassionate Bodhisattva and as human sufferer/spiritual seeker: intertwined Buddhist images', in K.M. Yust, A.N. Johnson, S.E. Sasso and E.C. Roehlkepartain (eds), *Nurturing Child and Adolescent Spirituality*. Lanham, MD: Rowman and Littlefield.

Naterer, A. and Godina, V.V. (2011) 'Bomzhi and their subculture: an anthropological study of the street children subculture in Makeevka, eastern Ukraine', *Childhood*, 18(1): 20–3.

National Commission on Education (1993) *Learning to Succeed*. London: Heinemann for Paul Hamlyn Foundation.

NATO (North Atlantic Treaty Organization) (2013) *What is NATO?* [online]. Available at www.nato.int/nato-welcome/index.html (accessed October 2013).

Nayar, L. (2011) 'A Tough School'. *Outlook*. Available at http://www.outlookindia.com/article/A-Tough-School/271591 (accessed June 2014).

Neill, A.S. (1998 [1960]) *Summerhill School*. London: St Martin's Press.

Neuman, S. (1991) 'Occupational sex segregation in the Kibbutz', *Kyklos*, 44(2): 203–91.

New Lanark Trust for Education (2001) *Information Notes for Teachers* [online]. Available at www.newlanark.org/edu-teachersnotes.pdf (accessed January 2014).

New Zealand Ministry of Education (1996) *Te Whāriki: Early Childhood Curriculum*, Wellington NZ: Learning Media Ltd. Also available online at www.minedu.govt.nz (accessed January 2014).

Nicholson, L. (1997) 'The myth of the traditional family', in H.L. Nelson (ed.) *Feminism and Families*. London: Routledge.

NOO (National Obesity Observatory) (2013) *National Child Measurement Programme* [online]. Available at www.noo.org.uk (accessed May 2014).

NSPCC (National Society for the Prevention of Cruelty to Children) (2012) *A Pocket History of the NSPCC* [online]. Available at http://www.nspcc.org.uk/what-we-do/about-the-nspcc/history-of-NSPCC/history-of-nspcc-booklet_wdf75414.pdf (accessed June 2014).

NSPCC (National Society for the Prevention of Cruelty to Children) (2014a) *An Introduction to Looked After Children* [online]. Available at http://www.nspcc.org.uk/Inform/resourcesforprofessionals/lookedafterchildren/introduction_wda88884.html (accessed June 2014).

NSPCC (National Society for the Prevention of Cruelty to Children) (2014b) *Statistics on Looked After Children (March)* [online]. Available at http://www.nspcc.org.uk/Inform/resourcesforprofessionals/lookedafterchildren/statistics_wda88009.html (accessed June 2014).

Nuffield Foundation (2014) *English and Romanian Adoptee Study* [online]. Available at www.nuffieldfoundation.org/english-and-romanian-adoptee-study (accessed April 2013).

Nutbrown, C. (2012) *Foundations for Quality: The Independent Review of Early Education and Childcare Qualifications: Final Report*. London: DfE.

Nutbrown, C. (2013) *Shaking the Foundations of Quality? Why 'Childcare' Policy Must not Lead to Poor-Quality Early Education*. Sheffield: University of Sheffield.

OECD (Organisation for Economic Co-operation and Development) (2013) *About the OECD* [online]. Available at www.oecd.org/about/ (accessed October 2013).

OECD (Organisation for Economic Co-operation and Development) iLibrary (2013) *OECD iLibrary* [online]. Available at www.oecd-ilibrary.org/ (accessed October 2013).

Ofcom (Office of Communication) (2014) Childhood Obesity – Food Advertising in Context. Available at http://stakeholders.ofcom.org.uk/binaries/research/tv-research/report2.pdf (accessed June 2013).

Ofqual (Office of Qualifications and Examinations Regulation) (2013) *A Level Reform* [online]. Available at http://ofqual.gov.uk (accessed June 2013).

Ofsted (Office for Standards in Education, Children's Services and Skills) (2013) *Press Release: NR2013–24*, 12 April [online]. Available at www.ofsted.gov.uk/news/single-inspection-framework-for-childrens-services (accessed May 2013).

Ofsted (Office for Standards in Education, Children's Services and Skills) (2014a) *Press Release: NR2014–14*, 21 March [online]. Available at www.ofsted.gov.uk/news/ofsted-chief-unveils-new-blueprint-for-inspecting-good-and-outstanding-schools?news=22441(accessed June 2014).

Ofsted (Office for Standards in Education, Children's Services and Skills) (2014b) *Press Release: Integrated inspection consultation* 23 June [online]. Available at www.ofsted.gov.uk/news/integrated-inspections-assess-contribution-of-all-profes-sionals-help-care-and-protection-of-children-0?news=23376 (accessed June 2014).

ONS (Office for National Statistics) (2011) 'Households and families' (ed. J. Beaumont). *Social Trends 41*.

ONS (Office for National Statistics) (2013) 'Civil partnerships in the UK, 2012', in *Statistical Bulletin* [online], 8 October [online]. Available at www.ons.gov.uk/ons/dcp171778_329457.pdf (accessed June 2014).

Opie, I. and Opie, P. (1951) *The Oxford Dictionary of Nursery Rhymes*. Oxford: Oxford University Press.

Opie, I. and Opie, P. (1959) *The Lore and Language of Schoolchildren*. Oxford: Oxford University Press.

Opie, I. and Opie, P. (1969) *Children's Games in Street and Playground*. Oxford: Oxford University Press.

Opie, I. and Opie, P. (1974) *The Classic Fairy Tales*. Oxford: Oxford University Press.

Opie Project (2012) *Childhoods and Play* [online]. Available at www.opieproject.group.shef.ac.uk/opies-biography.html (accessed August 2013).

Orme, N. (2001a) 'Child's play in medieval England', *History Today*, 51(10): 49.

Orme, N. (2001b) *Medieval Children*. New Haven: Yale University Press.

Palmer, S. (2006) *Toxic Childhood*. London: Orion.

Panter-Brick, C. (2002) 'Street children, human rights, and public health', *Review of Anthropology*, 31: 147–71.

Parliament.UK (2014) *Reforming Society in the 19th Century* [online]. Available at www.parliament.uk/about/living-heritage/transformingsociety/livinglearning/19thcentury/ (accessed June 2014).

Parr, J. (1980) *Labouring Children*. London: Croom Helm.

Pascal, C. and Bertram, T. (2000) *Effective Early Learning*. London: Sage.

Patton, L.L. (2009) 'Hinduism', in D.S. Browning and M.J. Bunge (eds) *Children and Childhood in World Religions*. New Brunswick, NJ: Rutgers University Press.

Pavlov, I. (1904) *Physiology of Digestion,* Nobel lecture, December 12 [online]. Available at www.nobelprize.org/nobel_prizes/medicine/laureates/1904/pavlov-lecture.html (accessed January 2014).

Payler, J. (2007) 'Opening and closing interactive spaces: shaping four-year-old children's participation in two English settings', *Early Years,* 27(3): 237–54.

Peacock, L, (2013) 'Parents "to run after-school clubs" under proposals to lengthen school day', *The Telegraph*, 14 June [online]. Available at www.telegraph.co.uk/women/mother-tongue/10119442/Liz-Truss-Parents-to-run-after-school-clubs-under-government-proposals-to-lengthen-school-day.html (accessed June 2014).

Peristiany, J.G. (1939) *The Social Institutions of the Kipsigis*. London: Routledge.

Perry, B.D. (2002) 'Childhood experience and the expression of genetic potential', *Brain and Mind,* 3: 79–100.

Playgroup Movement (2014) *Playgroup Movement* [online]. Available at www.playgroupmovement.org.uk (accessed January 2014).

Pollock, L. (1983) *Forgotten Children: Parent–Child Relations from 1500 to 1900*. Cambridge: Cambridge University Press.

Porter, B. (2012) 'Cutting the British Empire down to size', *History Today*, 62(10): 22–29.

Postman, N. (1994) *The Disappearance of Childhood,* 2nd edn. New York: Vintage Books.

Pre-School Learning Alliance (2014) 'Our history' [online]. Available at www.pre-school.org.uk/about-us/history (accessed June 2014).

Primary National Strategy (2005) KEEP: *Key Elements of Effective Practice.* London: DfES.

PSI (n.d.) *Children's Independent Mobility* (Briefing) [online]. Available at www.psi.org.uk/images/uploads/Briefing-Childrens_Independent_Mobility_v4_3.pdf.

Pryor, F. (2011) *The Making of the British Landscape.* London: Penguin.

Putnam, R. (2000) *Bowling Alone.* New York: Simon and Schuster.

QCA (Qualifications and Curriculum Authority) (2000) *Curriculum Guidance for the Foundation Stage.* London: DfEE.

Rasmussen, K. (2004) 'Places for children – children's places', *Childhood,* 11(2): 155–73.

Rawson, B. (2003) *Children and Childhood in Roman Italy.* Oxford: Oxford University Press.

Read, B. (2014) 'SEN funding changes: personalized budgets don't add up', *Guardian – Professional Teacher Network* [online blog]. Available at www.theguardian.com/teacher-network/teacher-blog/2014/apr/10/special-educational-needs-cuts-primary-school (accessed June 2014).

Reay, D. (2000) 'A useful extension of Bourdieu's conceptual framework?', *The Sociological Review,* 48: 568–85.

Rees, G., Goswami, H., Pople, L., Bradshaw, J., Keung, A. and Main, G. (2012) *The Good Childhood Report.* London: The Children's Society.

Rees, R., Caird, J., Woodman, J. and Thomas, J. (2011) *Understanding the Social Aspects of Obesity in Childhood* (poster). London: EPPI-Centre, SSRU, Institute of Education.

Reeves, C. (2007) 'Why attachment? Whither attachment?', *Beyond the Couch: The Online Journal of the American Association for Psychoanalysis in Clinical Social Work,* (2) December [online]. Available at www.beyondthecouch.org/1207/reeves.htm (accessed June 2014).

Ribbens McCarthy, J. and Edwards, R. (2011) *Key Concepts in Family Studies.* London: Sage.

Roberts, R. (1971) *The Classic Slum: Salford Life in the First Quarter of the Century.* London: Penguin.

Rogers, C. (1994 [1969]) *Freedom to Learn for the 80s,* 3rd edn. Columbus, OH: Merrill.

Rogoff, B. (1995) 'Observing sociocultural activity on three planes', in K. Hall and P. Murphy (2008) (eds) *Pedagogy and Practice.* London: Sage.

Röhrs, H. (1994) 'Maria Montessori', *Prospects,* 24(1/2): 169–83.

Romberg, T.A. (1992) *Mathematics Assessment and Evaluation.* Albany, NY: State University of New York.

Rose, J. (2006) *Independent Review of the Teaching of Early Reading.* Nottingham: DfES Publications.

Rose, J. (2009) *Independent Review of the Primary Curriculum.* Nottingham: DCSF.

Rosewarne, S., Hard, L., White, E.J. and Wright, L. (2010) 'Exploring transition through collective biographical memory work', *Australasian Journal of Early Childhood,* 35(3): 24–32.

Rousseau. J-J. (1889 [1762]) *Émile; or, Concerning Education* (Extracts, trans. E. Worthington). Boston: D.C. Heath [online]. Available at http://brittlebooks.library.illinois.edu/brittlebooks_open/Books2009-08/rousje0001emile/rousje0001emile.pdf (accessed June 2014).

Russell, R. and Tyler. M. (2002) 'Thank heaven for little girls', *Sociology,* 36(3): 619–37.

Rutter, M. (1981 [1972]) *Maternal Deprivation Reassessed*, 2nd edn. Harmondsworth: Penguin.

Rutter, M., Andersen-Wood, L., Beckett, C., Bredenkamp, D., Castle, J., Groothues, C., Kreppner, J., Keaveney, L., Lord, C., O'Connor, T.G., and the ERA Study Team (1999) 'Quasi-autistic patterns following severe early global privation', *Journal of Child Psychology and Psychiatry,* 40 (4): 537–49.

Salmon-Mack, T. (n.d.) 'Childhood: Jewish childhood', *The Yivo Encyclopedia of Jews in Eastern Europe* [online]. Available at www.akadem.org/medias/documents/1_childhood_EN.pdf (accessed January 2013).

Santrock, J.W. (2011) *Child Development*, 13th edn. New York: McGraw-Hill.

Saxton, M. (1994) 'Bearing the burden? Puritan wives', *History Today*, 44(10): 28.

SCAA (1996) *Desirable Outcomes for Children's Learning on Entering Compulsory Education*. London: Schools Curriculum Authority.

Scanlon, T., Tomkins, A., Lynch, M.A. and Scanlon, F. (1998) 'Street children in Latin America', *BMJ*, 316 (7144): 1596–1600.

Schaffer, H.R. (1996) *Social Development*. Oxford: Blackwell.

Schaffer, H.R. and Emerson, P.E. (1964) 'The development of social attachments in infancy', *Monographs of the Society for Research in Child Development*, 29: 94.

Schermerhorn, C. (2009) 'Left behind but getting ahead', in G. Campbell, S. Miers and J.C. Miller (eds) *Children in Slavery Through the Ages*. Athens, OH: Ohio University Press.

Schultz, A. (1967 [1932]) *The Phenomenology of the Social World*. Evanston, IL: Northwestern University Press.

Schwarz, H and Ray, S. (2005) (eds) *Companion to Postcolonial Studies: An Historical Introduction*, 2nd edn. Oxford: Blackwell.

Segal, J. (2004) *Melanie Klein,* 2nd edn. London: Sage.

Seligman, S. (2005) 'Dynamic systems theories as a metaframework for psychoanalysis', *Psychoanalytic Dialogues*, 15: 285–319.

Sen, A. (1987) *The Standard of Living* (ed. G. Hawthorn). Cambridge: Cambridge University Press.

Sen, A. (1999) *Development as Freedom*. Oxford: Oxford University Press.

SENmagazine (2014) 'Gearing up for the new SEN system'. *SENmagazine* [online]. Available at www.senmagazine.co.uk/news/sennews/sennews/gearing-up-for-the-new-sen-system.

Shahar, S. (1990) *Childhood in the Middle Ages*. London: Routledge.

Shakespeare, T. and Watson, N. (2002) 'The social model of disability', *Research in Social Science and Disability,* 2: 9–28.

Shapira, A. and Madsen, M.C. (1969) 'Cooperative and competitive behavior of kibbutz and urban children in Israel', *Child Development,* 40(2): 609–17.

Shaw, B. Watson, B., Frauendienst, B., Redecker. A., Jones, T. with Hillman, M. (2013) *Children's Independent Mobility* (Report). London: Policy Studies Institute [online]. Available at www.psi.org.uk/images/uploads/CIM_Final_report_v9_3_FINAL.PDF.

Shepher, J. (1969) 'Familism and social structure: the case of the kibbutz', *Journal of Marriage and Family,* 31(3): 567–73.

Shire, M. (2006) Learning to Be Righteous: A Jewish Theology of Childhood. In K.M. Yust, A.N. Johnson, S.E. Sasso and E.C. Roehlkepartain, *Nurturing Child and Adolescent Spirituality*. Lanham, MD: Rowman & Littlefield.

Singh, J.P. (2007) 'Culture or Commerce?', *International Studies Perspectives*, 8: 36–53.

Siraj-Blatchford, I. and Manni, L. (2007) *Effective Leadership in the Early Years Sector: The ELEYS Study*. London: Institute of Education.

Siraj-Blatchford, I., Mayo, A., Melhuish, E., Taggart, B. and Sylva, K. (2011) *Performing Against the Odds: Developmental Trajectories of Children in the EPPSE 3-16 Studies*. London: DfE.

Siraj-Blatchford, I., Sylva, K., Muttock, S., Gilden, R., Bell, D. (2002) *Researching Effective Pedagogy in the Early Years (REPEY)*, RR356. London: DfES.

Skinner Foundation (2012) *Skinner Foundation* [online]. Available at http://bfskinner. org/about-b-f-skinner-2 (accessed January 2014).

Smith, A. (1994) 'The origins of nations', in J. Hutchinson and A. Smith (eds), *Nationalism*. Oxford: Oxford University Press.

Smith, L. (2000) *A Brief Biography of Jean Piaget*, archives of the Jean Piaget Society [online]. Available at www.piaget.org/aboutPiaget.html (accessed January 2014).

Smith, P.K., Cowie, H. and Blades, M. (2003) *Understanding Children's Development*, 4th edn. Oxford: Blackwell.

Soëtard, M. (1994a) 'Jean-Jacques Rousseau', *Prospects*, 24(3/4): 423–38.

Soëtard, M. (1994b) 'Johann Heinrich Pestalozzi', *Prospects*, 24(1/2): 297–310.

Sørensen, A. (1992) 'Women's organisations among the Kipsigis', *Africa: Journal of the International African Institute*, 62(4): 547–66.

Sorin, R. (2005) 'Changing images of childhood', *International Journal of Transitions in Childhood*, 1: 12–21.

SOWC (State of the World's Children) (2012) *Children in an Urban World*. New York: UNICEF.

Spierling, K.E. (2008) 'Protestant reformation', *Encyclopedia of Children and Childhood in History and Society* [online]. Available at www.faqs.org/childhood/ (accessed November 2012).

Starns, P. (2012) *Blitz Families: The Children who Stayed Behind*. Stroud: The History Press.

Steedman, C. (2004) 'McMillan, Margaret (1860–1931)', *Oxford Dictionary of National Biography*. Oxford: Oxford University Press. Also available online at www. oxforddnb.com/view/printable/34801 (accessed June 2014).

Stronach, I. and Maclure, M. (1997) *Educational Research Undone*. Buckingham: Open University Press.

Styles, M. (1998) *From the Garden to the Street*. London: Continuum. Reprinted in J. Maybin and N.J. Watson (2009) *Children's Literature*. London: Palgrave Macmillan/Open University.

Super, C.M. and Harkness, S. (1982) 'The development of affect in infancy and early childhood', in M. Woodhead, D. Faulkner and K. Littleton (eds) (1998) *Cultural Worlds of Early Childhood*. London: Routledge.

Swain, J. and French, S. (2000) 'Towards an affirmation model', *Disability and Society*, 15(4): 569–82.

Sykes, B. (2001) *The Seven Daughters of Eve*. London: Corgi.

Sylva, K., Melhuish, E., Sammons, P., Siraj-Blatchford, I. and Taggart, B. (2004) *The Effective Provision of Pre-school Education (EPPE): Final Report*. London: DfES.

Sylva, K., Melhuish, E., Sammons, P. Siraj-Blatchford, I. and Taggart, B. (2008). *Final Report from the Primary Phase: Pre-school, School and Family Influences on Children's Development during Key Stage 2 (7-11)*, RR061. London: DCSF.

Sylva, K., Melhuish, E., Sammons, P., Siraj-Blatchford, I. and Taggart, B. (2012) *Effective Pre-school, Primary and Secondary Education 3-14 Project (EPPSE 3-14). Final Report from the Key Stage 3 Phase,* RR202. London: DfE.

Tait, D. (2011) *A 1970s Childhood.* Stroud: The History Press.

Tan, A. (2003) *The Opposite of Fate.* London: Flamingo.

Thacker, D.C. and Webb, J. (2002) *Introducing Children's Literature.* London: Routledge.

The Children's Society (2012) 'Written evidence to the Commons Select Committee on Foundation Stage: Children's Centres', December 2012 [online]. Available at www.publications.parliament.uk/pa/cm201213/cmselect/cmeduc/writev/surestart/m15.htm (accessed May 2013).

Thomas de Benitez, S. (2011) *State of the World's Street Children: Research.* London: Consortium for Street Children.

Thompson, T. (1981) *Edwardian Childhoods.* London: Routledge and Kegan Paul.

Thorndike, E.L. (1911) *Animal Intelligence* (Chapter 5) [online]. Available at http://psychclassics.yorku.ca/Thorndike/Animal/chap5.htm (accessed June 2014).

Tickell, C. (2011) *The Early Years: Foundations for Life, Health and Learning.* London: HMSO.

Trowler, P. (2003) *Education Policy,* 2nd edn. London: Routledge.

Tuchman, B.W. (1978) *A Distant Mirror.* New York: Alfred A. Knopf.

Turmel, A. (2008) *A Historical Sociology of Childhood.* Cambridge: Cambridge University Press.

Tutaev, B. (1961) 'Do-it-yourself nurseries', Letter to *The Guardian* [reproduced online]. Available at www.pre-school.org.uk/media/press-releases/283/belle-tutaev-founder-of-pre-school-learning-alliance-awarded-obe (accessed June 2014).

UCL (University College London) (2013) *Who was Jeremy Bentham?,* 26 February [online]. Available at www.ucl.ac.uk/Bentham-Project/who (accessed May 2013).

Uhrmacher, P.B. (1995) 'Uncommon schooling', *Curriculum Inquiry,* 25(4): 381–406.

Ullrich, H. (1994) 'Rudolf Steiner', *Prospects,* 24(3/4): 555–72.

UN (United Nations) (1948) *Universal Declaration of Human Rights,* 60th anniversary edn. UN Department of Public Information [online]. Available at www.ohchr.org/EN/UDHR/Documents/60UDHR/bookleten.pdf (accessed June 2014).

UN (United Nations) (1997) *Renewing the United Nations: Programme for Reform* [online]. Available at www.undg.org/docs/1400/Renewing_the_UN_A_Programme_for_Reform_A51_950.pdf (accessed June 2014).

UN (United Nations) (2013) *United Nations* [online]. Available at www.un.org/en/aboutun/index.shtml (accessed October 2013).

UNCRC (United Nations Convention on the Rights of the Child) (1989) *United Nations Convention on the Rights of the Child* [online]. Available at www.unicef.org.uk/UNICEFs-Work/Our-mission/UN-Convention/ (accessed June 2014).

UNDP (United Nations Development Programme) (2013) *Human Development Index* [online]. Available at http://hdr.undp.org/en/statistics/hdi (accessed May 2013).

UNFPA (United Nations Population Fund) (2008) *Human Rights: The Human Rights-Based Approach* [online]. Available at www.unfpa.org/rights/approaches.htm (accessed May 2013).

UNICEF (United Nations Children's Fund) (2003) 'Annex B. Human rights-based approach: statement of common understanding', in *The State of the World's Children, 2004* [online]. Available at www.unicef.org/sowc04/sowc04_contents.html (accessed June 2014).

UNICEF (United Nations Children's Fund) (2007) *Child Poverty in Perspective,* Report Card 7. Florence: Innocenti Research Centre.

UNICEF (United Nations Children's Fund) (2013) *UNICEF* [online]. Available at www.unicef.org/about/who/index_history.html (accessed October 2013).

US Geological Survey (2013) *Historical Perspective* [online]. Available at http://pubs.usgs.gov/gip/dynamic/historical.html (accessed May 2014).

Vallier, I. (1962) 'Structural differentiation, production imperatives and communal norms: the kibbutz in crisis', *Social Forces,* 40(3): 233–42.

Van Emden, R. (2011) Excerpts from 'The quick and the dead'. London: Bloomsbury. In 'Remembrance Day', *The Guardian,* 12 November. Available at www.guardian.co.uk/lifeandstyle/2011/nov/12/first-world-war-surviving-children (accessed June 2014).

Vandenberghe, F. (1999) *Globalisation and Individualisation in Late Modernity* [online]. Available at www.academia.edu/859728/Globalisation_and_Individualisation_in_Late_Modernity._A_Theoretical_Introduction_to_the_Sociology_of_Youth (accessed April 2013).

Vandewater, E.A., Park, S-E., Huang, X. and Wartella, E.A. (2005) 'No – you can't watch that', *American Behavioral Scientist,* 48: 608–23.

Vargas-Silva, C. (2012) *EU Migrants in Other EU Countries,* briefing from The Migration Observatory [online]. Available at www.migrationobservatory.ox.ac.uk (accessed May 2014).

Veash, N. (2000) 'Violent death claims survivors of Brazil's child massacres', *The Independent,* 9 September [online]. Available at www.independent.co.uk/news/world/americas/violent-death-claims-survivors-of-brazils-child-massacres-699359.html (accessed June 2014).

Victorian Web (2014) *Biographies in Science Section* [online]. Available at www.victorianweb.org (accessed January 2014).

Vlachou, A.D. (1997) *Struggles for Inclusive Education.* Maidenhead: Open University Press.

Von Bulow, D. (1992) 'Bigger than men? Gender relations and their changing meaning in Kipsigis society, Kenya', *Africa: Journal of the International African Institute,* 62(4): 523–46.

Vulliamy, E. (2011) 'Ciudad Juarez is all our futures', *The Guardian,* 20 June [online]. Available at www.theguardian.com/commentisfree/2011/jun/20/war-capitalism-mexico-drug-cartels (accessed June 2014).

Vygotsky, L.S. (1962 [1934]). *Thought and language* (trans. E. Hanfmann & G. Vakar) Cambridge, MA: MIT Press.

Vygotsky, L.S. (1978) *Mind and Society.* Cambridge, MA: Harvard University Press.

Wagner, P. (2008) *Modernity as Experience and Interpretations.* Cambridge: Polity Press.

Walby, S. (1990) *Theorizing Patriarchy.* Oxford: Basil Blackwell.

Wallace-Hadrill, A. (2011) *Roman Empire: The Paradox of Power* [online]. Available at www.bbc.co.uk/history/ancient/romans/empire_01.shtml (accessed May 2014).

Waller, T. (2007) 'The trampoline tree and the swamp monster with 18 heads', *Education,* 3–13, 35(4): 393–407.

Walsh, M., Stephens, P. and Moore, S. (2000) *Social Policy and Welfare,* Cheltenham: Nelson Thornes.

Walvin, J. (2007) *A Short History of Slavery.* London: Penguin.

Warnock, M. (1978) *Special Educational Needs: Report of the Committee of Enquiry into the Education of Handicapped Children and Young People*. London: HMSO.

Warnock, M. (2005) Summary of pamphlet published by the Philosophy of Education Society of Great Britain, from Douglas Silas Solicitors [online]. Available at www.specialeducationalneeds.co.uk (accessed May 2013).

Wells, J.C.K. (2010) 'Maternal capital and the metabolic ghetto', *American Journal of Human Biology*, 22: 1–17.

Westbrook, R.B. (1993) 'John Dewey', *Prospects*, 23(1/2): 277–91.

Whitbread, N. (1972) *The Evolution of the Nursery-Infant School*. London: Routledge and Kegan Paul.

White, J. (2006) *The Aims of School Education*. London: Institute for Public Policy Research (IoE e-print).

Whiteman, P. and De Gioia, K. (2012) 'Perspectives', in P. Whiteman and K. De Gioia, K. (eds) *Children and Childhoods 1*. Newcastle: Cambridge Scholars Publishing.

WHO (World Health Organization) (2013) *World Health Organization* [online]. Available at www.who.int/about/en (accessed October 2013).

Wilkes, S. (2011) *The Children History Forgot*. London: Robert Hale.

Wilkinson, R. and Pickett, K. (2009) *The Spirit Level*. London: Allen Lane.

Williams, R. (2010) 'Primary curriculum and academic diplomas to be axed', *The Guardian*, 7 June [online]. Available at www.theguardian.com/politics/2010/jun/07/primary-curriculum-academic-diplomas-axed (accessed June 2014).

Willmott, R. (1990) *William Blake: Songs of Innocence and of Experience*. Oxford: Oxford University Press.

Wilson, S. (n.d.) *Poststructuralism and Contemporary Art, Past, Present, Future* [online]. Available at www.courtauld.ac.uk/people/wilson-sarah/poststructuralism.pdf (accessed May 2014).

Winnicott, D.W. (1953) 'Transitional objects and transitional phenomena', *International Journal of Psycho-Analysis*, 34: 89–97.

Winnicott, D.W. (1971) *Playing and Reality*. London: Tavistock Publications.

Winter, K. and Connolly, P. (1996) '"Keeping it in the Family": Thatcherism and the Children Act 1989', in J. Pilcher and S. Wragg (eds) *Thatcher's Children?* London: Falmer Press.

Wolfe, P. (2010) *Brain Matters*, 2nd edn. Alexandria, VA: Association for Supervision and Curriculum Development (ASCD).

Wood, D.J. (1998) *How Children Think and Learn*, 2nd edn. Oxford: Blackwell.

Wood, J. and Wood, M. (1995) '*An example of Life in England during the 1920s and 1930s: Victor Holmes 1925-1937*' [online]. Available at www.worldthroughthelens.com/victor.php (accessed June 2014).

Woods, P., Ashley, M. and Woods, G. (2005) *Steiner Schools in England*, RR645. London: DfES.

Wright, H.R. (2011) *Women Studying Childcare*. Stoke-on-Trent: Trentham Books.

Wright Mills, C. (2000 [1959]) *The Sociological Imagination*. New York: Oxford University Press.

Wyness, M. (2000) *Contesting Childhood*. London: Falmer.

Wyse, D. and Styles, M. (2007) 'Synthetic phonics and the teaching of reading', *Literacy*, 41(1): 35–42.

Yildirim, Y. (2006) 'Filling the heart with the love of God: Islamic perspectives on spirituality in childhood and adolescence', in K.M. Yust, A.N. Johnson, S.E. Sasso and E.C. Roehlkepartain (eds), *Nurturing Child and Adolescent Spirituality*. Lanham, MD: Rowman and Littlefield

Yuval-Davis, N. (2006) 'Intersectionality and feminist politics', *European Journal of Women's Studies*, 13(3): 193–209.

Zal, H.M. (1992) *The Sandwich Generation*. Boston, MA: Da Capo Press.

INDEX